MW00719710

BigSky Politics

Campaigns and Elections in Modern Montana

Big Sky Politics

Campaigns and Elections in Modern Montana

Jon Bennion

With forewords by
Pat Williams and Tim Babcock

FIVE VALLEYS PUBLISHING
An Imprint of Champions Publishing, Inc.

Cover and text design by:
Michael Dougherty
Type & Graphics, Bozeman, MT

Publisher's Cataloging in Publication
(Provided by Quality Books, Inc.)

Bennion, Jon.
   Big Sky politics: campaigns and elections in modern
   Montana / Jon Bennion ; forewords by Pat Williams, Tim
   Babcock.
      p. cm.
   Includes bibliographical references and index.
   ISBN 1-888550-13-9

   1. Elections--Montana--History.   2. Montana--Politics
   and government.   I. Title.

   JK7392.B46 2004   324.9786'033
                                QBI04-200068

Published by: Five Valleys Publishing
                   1000 Longstaff St. #2
                   Missoula, Montana 59801

An imprint of: Champions Publishing, Inc.
                   301 Evergreen, Suite 201D
                   Bozeman, Montana 59715
                   (406) 585-0237

Printed in Canada

"To me, Montana is a symphony...The history of Montana is the song of a people who, repeatedly shattered, have held together, persevered, and, at last, taken enduring root...Modern transitions notwithstanding, something remains in the state that is durably unique and uniquely durable. It is to be found in the character of the people."
—Mike Mansfield, August 24, 1967

Very special thanks to these organizations and individuals whose financial contributions made this first printing possible:

Susan Muralt

Colonel Sam and Kathleen Roberts

Montana Chamber of Commerce

Teamsters Local 190

Montana Federation of Republican Women

Forward Montana

Montana Democratic Party

Montana Republican Party

Local Government Center, MSU - Bozeman

The Burton K. Wheeler Center

Joe Reber

Kathy Ogren

*The League of Women Voters
of the Bozeman Area Education Fund*

Montana AFL-CIO

The Montana League of Women Voters Education Fund

Montana Newspaper Association

Table Of Contents

Foreword

by Pat Williams
Montana Congressman 1979-1997
Senior Fellow
Center for the Rocky Mountain West
of the University of Montana

Since our beginnings, the vivid hues of Montana's politics, left and right, have colored our state's history, given it vibrancy, engaged our citizens and made our politics not only interesting, but also important.

The politicians of our past–from William Fisk Sanders and Hugo Aronson to Burton K. Wheeler and Mike Mansfield–are the stuff of legends and lore. We Montanans enjoy telling and retelling the stories, and that includes me as well as the co-introducer to this book, my friend, Governor Tim Babcock. Like others, Tim and I revel in the tales about this state's amazing politicians and events. However, any state with the political color of Montana lends itself easily, perhaps too easily, to myth and lore. And although the political tales are fun and occasionally instructive, it is facts which anchor our understanding and give our history significance.

All Montanans have taken pride in those times

when our state government and those of our communities boldly became civic laboratories for the generation of progressive public policy change. We have also sadly witnessed those few years when Montana became a place of obstinate refusal to grasp its tomorrows. Montanans have consistently had among the highest election day voter turnouts of any state, but there have been those times when we have seemed inattentive to the point of political somnolence. Our preferences have been very different east to west with eastern Montanans usually voting for moderate to conservative candidates and with westerners more than reversing that trend in support of moderate to liberal candidates.

The vibrant and often schizophrenic politics in Montana demand both attention and understanding. In this book, *Big Sky Politics*, Jon Bennion has put down the facts, thus answering many questions about Montana's contemporary politics just as did his predecessor, Ellis Waldron, in his 1958 *Atlas of Montana Politics Since 1864*. Following but improving Waldron's style, Bennion's update is a thorough compilation of Montana's election day facts since 1946. This is a needed and long-awaited book.

Foreword

by Tim Babcock
Montana Governor 1962-1969

As each of us in our lives move forward, it is always beneficial to stop and consider where we have been, where we would like to be now and where we would like to go from here on into the future. To see what has worked in our lives, we should stop and take a good look and discard or correct those policies which have failed.

It seems evident that some of our environmental laws need to be reevaluated. Some of the permitting process needs to be reconsidered, as Montana has always been known as the Treasure State. We need to restore the mining, lumber and agricultural industries, a means of development, so those industries can become active and vibrant, improve our economy and bring back good paying jobs for our Montana citizens.

In 1972 our new constitution brought tremendous change to our state, some good and some not so good. Government is more open and accessible to the people. Sometimes the "Right to Know" and the "Right to Privacy" collide, and we get carried away with the initiative and referendum policies. Better to have clear and complete debates about the issues by the representatives we elect to the legislature and leave the interpretation of the law to the judges.

The diverse history of Montana will lead down many roads. Montana is the 4th largest state and has 145,552 square miles of land area, 1,490 square miles of water area and is 630 miles across. The 2001 population estimate is only 904,443 people. Montana has extreme weather conditions, changing quickly from hot to cold, which has a tremendous affect on our infrastructure.

We live in the best state in the Union. What we need most of all is an active participation in the process of government by all of our citizens. We are very grateful to Jon Bennion for gathering all the good material that will make it easier for us to look at the politics of the past so we can better evaluate and improve the politics of the future. Let's go forward with the very best ideas for our Treasure State.

Congratulations and many thanks to Jon Bennion on a job well done.

Preface

Montanans have always been active participants in their government and elections. Although the state is sparse in population, modern Treasure State politics is rich with fascinating stories and distinct patterns. The history surrounding our state's politics not only provides a glimpse of the past, but also a window into elections to come.

There are few comprehensive studies on Montana politics available. In 1958, Ellis Waldron, professor of political science at the University of Montana, compiled certified election statistics going back to the first elections in the Montana territory in a guide entitled *An Atlas of Montana Politics Since 1864*. The atlas was purely a reference guide containing simple maps and raw numbers of election results.

Twenty years later, Waldron teamed up with associate professor of geography, Paul Wilson, and issued a more comprehensive guide of Montana politics. The revised guide, entitled *Atlas of Montana Elections: 1889-1976*, included commentary on each general election and computerized maps detailing election results.

Perhaps the most prominent post-war analysis of trends and political cycles was done by historian, Michael P. Malone. In his revised edition of *Montana: A History of Two Centuries*, Malone describes developments in modern Montana politics right up to the start of the recent conservative tide of the last decade and a half.

For almost thirty years, Montanans have not had an up-to-date account of state elections and campaigns. Despite recent advances in the internet and other information sources, election results are still difficult to find. Even when these statistics are available, they rarely have a range of more than ten years and do not contain helpful commentary on important issues of the time.

In this book, I've tried to take the best of both worlds by compiling statistics of major state elections in the postwar era, adding commentary on the issues and candidates, and including an analysis of the political trends of the last half-century. My hope is that this study will be a valuable asset to journalists, public officials, students, teachers and politicos.

There were many people who helped contribute information for this book. Pat Williams and Tim Babcock were both invaluable sources. They never hesitated to take time out of their schedules to discuss their experiences in politics and contribute to the work. Their interviews, forewords and efforts to see the book published are greatly appreciated.

Chuck Johnson of the Lee Newspaper State Bureau also provided many helpful suggestions concerning the structure and content of the book. I feel lucky to have him involved.

I started this book without any idea of how the publishing world works. Two people helped coach me through the process. Jeffrey Greene of the University of Montana Political Science Department introduced me to this sometimes complex world. Michael Dougherty of Ultimate Press taught me the technicalities of publishing and I look forward to working with him in the future.

Thanks to Keith Baer, Dorothy Eck, William "The

Duke" Crowley, Pete Peterson, Thelma Baker, Law Firm 1, and the Mike Mansfield Archive Department for their efforts.

I am grateful to my family, especially my parents, John and Margaret, who have supported me in all of my pursuits. Most of all, I am also indebted to my wife, Jessi, who encouraged me throughout the research process and gave insightful ideas during the editing of Big Sky Politics.

Political Overviews and History

Brief Political History: 1864-1945

During territorial days and in the years prior to World War II, Montana clearly preferred candidates on the Democratic ticket. Twelve out of fourteen elections for territorial delegate to Congress went to the Democratic candidate. When Montana finally became a state in 1889, it could vote in presidential elections and select its own governor. From 1889 to 1946, Montana voted for eight Democrats and six Republicans in presidential races. In that same period, the Treasure State voted for eleven Democrats and three Republicans for governor. This preference stemmed largely from the origins of migrants into the state.

It has long been said that the left wing of the army of General Price, a prominent Confederate leader, never surrendered. Instead, it retreated to Montana. It is only a saying, but it correctly illustrates a picture of early settlers in the area that would become Montana. Congress established the Montana territory in 1864 while the Civil War raged in the east. Early settlers came to the western portion of the territory in search of gold. Many of these prospectors came from Missouri and Arkansas—states with large secessionist populations. One of the first cities founded within the borders was named Varina, the name of Jefferson Davis' wife. Analyst N. P. Langford, estimated that eighty percent of these early residents were Southern sympathizers. This Confederate majority was completely loyal to the Democratic Party and this fierce loyalty undoubtedly delayed Montana's admission into the Union.

As Montana's mining business expanded and the need for workers increased, other groups migrated to the state. The largest group was Irish immigrants who also tended to vote Democratic. Time after time, they voted in one block and delivered decisive blows to Republican candidates in unionized areas of the state. Marcus Daly and William Clark, the major industrial leaders of Montana, actively encouraged their workers to vote Democratic and were usually the largest financial contributors to the party.

Just after Montana became a state, Populism spread through the agrarian southern and western states. Credit-poor farmers of rural Montana and silver miners of urban Montana embraced the Populist message. When William Jennings Bryan ran for president under the Democrat-Populist ticket in 1896, the Treasure State gave him 80%—the largest majority any presidential candidate has received from the Montana electorate. In that same year, candidates calling for Populist policies carried every major state office.

After the turn of the century, Montana followed the lead of many other states in reforming government and electing progressive candidates. In 1904, voters supported a ban on child labor by 88%. A few years later, Montanans voted in favor of adopting the referendum and initiative process, giving them a direct role in the shaping of laws. In 1912, ballots in favor of direct election of U.S. Senators and presidential primaries passed with 78%.

Montana was also ahead of the curve on other progressive measures. Women were given the right to vote in Montana years before that right was guaranteed by the U.S. Constitution. In 1916, Montana sent Jeanette Rankin to Congress as the first woman to serve in that body. Other Montana leaders like Thomas Walsh, Joseph Dixon and Burton Wheeler served in Washington, DC and worked for progressive, reform-minded measures.

The Hi-Line and central Montana areas helped fuel progressive reforms. Large numbers of Scandinavian and German immigrants settled in northern Montana to work the land and they brought a liberal, even socialistic ideology. These farmers were often at odds with the workers in the cities, but the two factions came together under the New Deal.

While it was not impossible for a Republican candidate to win in the Treasure State, it was more often than not an up-hill battle. When the territory was first created, Republican appointed governors were sent from the East as administrators and were often seen as carpetbaggers. There were a few occasions, however, when a Republican could be elected. Progressive Republicans like Jeanette Rankin and Joseph Dixon won majorities in the early 20th century. A Republican candidate could also exploit the rift that existed between the Copper Kings and squeak into office. By the 1940's, the Wheeler Democrats were helping to elect Republicans like Governor Sam Ford.

Presidential Overview: 1946-2000

In this time period, Montana has voted for the winner of the national contest eleven out of fourteen times. The three times Montana picked incorrectly, it support-

ed Republicans (Nixon in 1960, Ford in 1976, a.
in 1996). When it's wrong, Montana tends to err on .
side of being more conservative than the rest of the
country.

Starting with the election of 1952, Montana has
shown a clear and consistent preference for Republicans in presidential elections. Since the end of World
War II, Montana voters have supported Republicans in
eleven elections and Democrats in three elections.

In the three elections where Montana supported a
Democrat, the Democrat ended up winning the election
at the national level as well (Truman, Johnson, and
Clinton). In each of these elections, the Democrat hap-
pened to be from a southern state (Truman from
Missouri, Johnson from Texas, and Clinton from
Arkansas).

There are obvious regional preferences in
Montana's choices for chief executive. Since the end of
World War II, Montana has never given a majority to a
presidential candidate from a northeastern state. When
given a choice between a candidate from the south and
one from the west, Montanans have usually favored
the candidate from the west. (The one exception hap-
pened in 1964 when Montana gave Lyndon Johnson of
Texas more votes then Barry Goldwater of Arizona.)
When given a choice between a candidate from the
south and the northeast, Montanans will choose the
candidate from the south.

Governor Overview: 1946-2000

Since the end of World War II, Montanans have gener-
ally supported Republicans for governor. Since 1946,
voters have given majorities to Republicans eight times
and Democrats six. Two of these Democrats, John

Bonner and Forrest Anderson, have been regarded as conservative Democrats by most historians. Thus, like their presidential choices, Montanans have favored conservative executives in the governor's seat during the last fifty years.

Where did they come from?

1. Bonner - *Silver Bow County*
2. Aronson - *Glacier County*
3. Nutter - *Richland County*
4. Babcock - *Yellowstone County*
5. Anderson - *Lewis & Clark County*
6. Judge - *Lewis & Clark County*
7. Schwinden - *Roosevelt County*
8. Stephens - *Hill County*
9. Racicot - *Lincoln County*
10. Martz - *Silver Bow County*

What political offices did they hold before?

1. Bonner - *Attorney General*
2. Aronson - *State Legislator*
3. Nutter - *State Legislator*
4. Babcock - *State Legislator, Lieutenant Governor*
5. Anderson - *Montana Supreme Court Justice, Attorney General*
6. Judge - *State Legislator, Lieutenant Governor*
7. Schwinden - *State Legislator, Lieutenant Governor*
8. Stephens - *State Legislator*
9. Racicot - *Attorney General*
10. Martz - *Lieutenant Governor*

Senate Overview: 1946-2002

It's no exaggeration to say that liberal Democrats have dominated U.S. Senate elections in Montana since the beginning of direct election by the voters. Since 1946, Republicans have only won four out of twenty contests. And once a candidate won a senate seat, he usually stayed there awhile. Incumbents have only lost 3 times in the same time period (Wheeler in 1946, Ecton in 1952, and Melcher in 1988).

Where did they come from?

1. Ecton - *Gallatin*
2. Murray - *Silver Bow*
3. Mansfield - *Silver Bow*
4. Metcalf - *Ravalli*
5. Melcher - *Rosebud*
6. Baucus - *Lewis & Clark*
7. Burns - *Yellowstone*

What political offices did they hold before?

1. Ecton - *State Legislator*
2. Murray - *None*
3. Mansfield - *U.S. House*
4. Metcalf - *Montana Supreme Court Justice, U.S. House*
5. Melcher - *State Legislator, US House*
6. Baucus - *State Legislator, US House*
7. Burns - *Yellowstone County Commissioner*

Congressional Overview: 1946-2002

1st District. One of the most predictable elections tended to be in Montana's Western Congressional District. Also called the First District, it supported Democrats 20 times out of 22 elections from 1946 to 1990.

Where did they come from?

1. Mansfield - *Silver Bow*
2. Metcalf - *Ravalli*
3. Olsen - *Silver Bow*
4. Shoup - *Missoula*
5. Baucus - *Lewis & Clark*
6. Williams - *Silver Bow*

2nd District. While it may not have been as consistent as its sister district in the west, Montana's Eastern District usually voted for conservative Republicans. Also referred to as the Second District, it supported Republicans 17 out of 22 general elections from 1946 to 1990.

Where did they come from?

1. D'Ewart - *Park*
2. Fjare - *Big Timber*
3. Anderson - *Pondera*
4. Battin - *Yellowstone*
5. Melcher - *Rosebud*
6. Marlenee - *Daniels*

At-Large District. Created after the 1990 census, which showed Montana had experienced stagnant growth, the Montana at-large congressional district contains more people than any other district in the United

States. After initially supporting a liberal Democrat in two general elections, it has since voted for conservative Republicans in the last four general elections. Since the start of its existence in 1992, the at-large district has supported a Democrat twice and Republicans four times.

Where did they come from?

1. Williams - *Silver Bow*
2. Hill - *Lewis & Clark*
3. Rehberg - *Yellowstone*

State Legislature Overview: 1946-2002

Control of the legislature since World War II could not be more balanced. Republicans have controlled the State House fifteen times while Democrats have been in the majority fourteen times. In the State Senate, Republicans have dominated fourteen times, Democrats have controlled fourteen times and once there was a tie. In the same time period, Republicans simultaneously controlled both houses nine times and Democrats have done similarly eight times.

Changing Dynamic: 1946-1964

After World War II, a new era of electoral competitiveness changed voting patterns and the political landscape in Montana. The Treasure State had been firmly loyal to the Democratic Party during the administration of FDR, but that period of one-party dominance lasted only a decade.

After the president's failure to pack the Supreme Court with like-minded individuals and the United States' entrance into World War II, a noticeable split in the Montana Democratic Party formed. Montana's senior senator, Burton K. Wheeler, became an outspoken critic of FDR and a spokesperson for conservative Democrats in Montana. His followers became swing voters in general elections and would often cross party lines giving the Republican candidate a majority. After World War II and the defeat of Wheeler in the Democratic primary, many of his supporters left the party and changed the political landscape. Their defection ushered in a new era in Montana elections.

When a census was done in 1950, the results showed that Butte was no longer Montana's largest city. After reaching its peak in 1920 due to its mining industry, statistics showed that Butte had lost about a fourth of its population. This decline was caused by the withering of the Anaconda Company. Once the fourth largest company in the world, Anaconda suffered from foreign competition and falling demand. At one time, the company dominated Montana state politics, but its influence was fading fast. In 1959, Anaconda sold its newspaper business—a clear sign that it could not keep up with running a state while trying to run a mining business.

Great Falls replaced Butte at the top of the list with an influx of industry and military personnel. Great Falls Air Force Base had played a role in World War II and even the Berlin Airlift, but its importance to national defense grew even more in the post-war era. For a long time it served as a training ground for bomber pilots. In 1956, after Colonel Einar Malmstrom was killed in a plane crash two years earlier, the base was renamed in his honor. In 1960, Malmstrom Air Force Base became the nation's first operational inter-continental ballistic missile site. Federal money and military employees pouring into the area helped Great Falls become Montana's Cold War metropolis.

Close behind Great Falls was Billings, a town started in 1882 as a railroad center. Billings' growth during the post-war era was aided by the discovery of oil in Eastern Montana. New refineries opened and workers flooded into the city limits from rural areas to find jobs.

When the next census was taken in 1960, results showed a change that would affect elections for decades to come. For the first time in the state's history, urban residents outnumbered rural residents. With a majority of Montanans now living in cities, candidates began changing the issues they ran on and spending more time campaigning in urban areas. This population shift marked a change that continues to the present day.

1946

The world had no time to take a deep breath after World War II, the greatest conflict in the history of mankind. While Europe laid in shambles after an Allied victory over the Axis powers, the globe was becoming increasingly polarized. Tensions in countries such as China and Korea gave many Americans reason to believe that a World War III was not just probable, but inevitable. The Soviet Union, America's temporary ally during the war, was now the United States' competitor in the race for global influence and military superiority. Nations chose sides and lined up behind one of the two new superpowers.

A number of polls taken in the first few months showed that a majority of Montanans believed that an atomic war with the Soviet Union would erupt before the end of the decade. It was this fear that would be the greatest influence in the coming off-year election.

During this time of uncertainty, Senator Burton K. Wheeler, a four-term progressive Senator from Butte, sought an additional six-year term. He faced strong opposition in the Democratic primary from Leif Erickson of Sidney. Wheeler had a distinguished career in the Senate, but by 1946, he lacked support from Democratic loyalists. While he avidly supported FDR's New Deal, Wheeler had been outspoken opponent of the president's "court-packing" plan. He had also come out against a fourth term for the popular president, which angered many liberals within the state.

But most damaging was Senator Wheeler's position on World War II. As an isolationist, Wheeler had protested American intervention in the conflict prior to 1941. When Japan attacked Pearl Harbor, he voted in favor of declaring war, but he continued to scrutinize the president's foreign policy. Veterans, with these comments in mind, largely supported his opponent.

Leif Erickson, a former associate justice of the Montana Supreme Court, was able to win the party's nomination by rallying the traditional Democratic base. New Dealers, farmers and unionized workers largely abandoned Wheeler for the younger, more progressive Erickson. In 1944, Erickson had lost in a bid for governor against incumbent Sam C. Ford, yet he had earned the respect of many state officials, including James E. Murray, Montana's junior Senator. Murray played a key role in Erickson's primary victory over Wheeler.

The election was still hard fought which was apparent in the results: Wheeler, 44,513; Erickson, 49,419. In a statement conceding the election, Wheeler attributed his loss to his unwillingness to "go along blindly with a Democratic administration in the last few years" and "sacrifice principles for party expediency."[1] Later, he blamed Senator Murray's role in the election and the "New York and Hollywood groups" that Murray lined up against him.

If history was any clue in the general election for U.S. Senate, Leif Erickson's triumph in the Democratic primary could have been tantamount to a victory in November. Since the direct election of Senators in 1912, Montana had never sent a Republican to Washington as one of its senators. Zales N. Ecton, a wealthy rancher and state senator of Manhattan, was the Republican nominee facing these odds.

Ecton, a conservative, went on the offensive from the beginning. His slogan, "Had Enough?" was based on a theme used by Republicans all over the country who hoped to capitalize on President Truman's unpopularity.[2] His background as a veteran of World War I sharply contrasted with Erickson's, who had no military experience. He also attacked Erickson's strong support from CIO-PAC, a political committee made up of labor, and accused him of having communist leanings.

The Democratic nominee countered with the slogan, "Action, not Reaction; Construction, not Obstruction," but he remained on the defensive throughout the campaign.[3] The national trend towards the Republican Party was too much for Leif Erickson to overcome, and Zales Ecton rode the conservative tide to victory. (Ecton, 54%; Erickson, 45%)

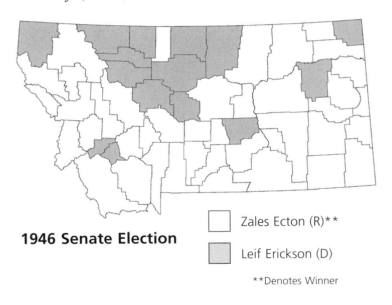

1946 Senate Election

Zales Ecton (R)**

Leif Erickson (D)

**Denotes Winner

Montana's two congressional districts saw no change. Democrat Mike Mansfield, who was first elected to the House in 1942, easily defeated Republican challenger, Walter Rankin, in Montana's Western District. Rankin pledged to investigate "Un-American" persons and criticized Mansfield for blocking such efforts. At this point in his career, Mansfield already had wide respect as a statesman and could hardy be considered a communist. He earned thousands of votes over the years through his success in bringing federal dollars to Montana for projects such as the Hungry Horse Dam, which was completed in 1944. People also respected his straight-talk and his vast amounts of knowledge about domestic and foreign affairs. (Mansfield, 58%; Rankin, 42%)

In the Eastern District, incumbent Republican, Wesley D'Ewart, who had won a special election a year earlier, won re-election over a challenge from State Auditor John J. Holmes, a Democrat. In the 1945 special election, the nation watched as the first election since FDR's death went to a Republican. Many correctly predicted that this signaled a national Republican resurgence in the coming off-year election. D'Ewart urged voters to be "real Americans" and oppose socialism.[4] (D'Ewart, 54%; Holmes, 45%)

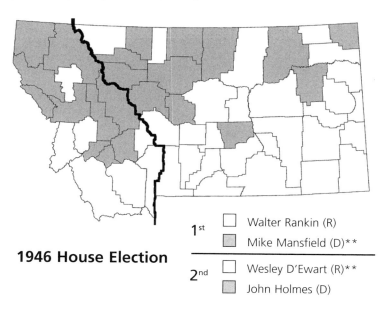

1946 House Election

1st ☐ Walter Rankin (R)
    ■ Mike Mansfield (D)**

2nd ☐ Wesley D'Ewart (R)**
    ■ John Holmes (D)

Nationwide, Republicans took control of both houses of Congress and controlled a slim majority of the governor seats. It marked the strongest showing of the GOP since before the Great Depression. Democrats were so shocked that a few Senators actually called for Truman's resignation. The president said that he would do no such thing, but many viewed him as a lame duck after this resounding defeat for Democrats.

In the State Legislature, Republicans benefited from the national trend towards the GOP. They gained two seats in the State Senate and five seats in the State House. (State Senate: 41 Republicans, 15 Democrats; State House: 58 Republicans, 31 Democrats) 72% of registered voters turned out for the election.

1948

If 1946 was the year of Republicans, than 1948 was clearly the comeback of the Democratic Party. No one predicted such a nationwide resurgence of the party of Jackson after it had suffered a resounding defeat in the previous election. Pundits and pollsters all predicted another GOP landslide. Fortune magazine published a poll on September 9th that gave Thomas Dewey, the Republican governor of New York, a 15% margin over the incumbent president, Harry Truman. The magazine then ceased all polling because it seemed as though nothing could narrow this impossible lead.

The first major issue in the campaign was Truman himself. All over the country, Republicans used him as a punching bag, including Montana's GOP candidates for governor, senator and congressman. They appeared in ads with Truman's opponent with hopes of benefiting from Dewey's coattails.

The other major issue of the campaign was for-

James Murray represented Montana in the U.S. Senate from 1935-1961. Photo from the Mike Mansfield collection of the K. Ross Toole Archives at the Maureen and Mike Mansfield Library.

eign policy. The growing conflict with the "Reds" now had a name: the Cold War. In 1948, Western Berlin was the center of attention because of the Russian blockade. Tensions in China and Korea continued to flare as well. Many in the United States, including Montana, still feared the prospect of atomic world war.

Another headache for Democrats came with the issue of civil rights. A few southern delegations walked out of the party convention and held their own convention, complete with nominations. Montana Democratic delegates to the convention voted against the civil rights platform that was eventually adopted, but did not walk out. By supporting the civil rights platform, Truman could no longer count on the support of the Deep South and many conservative Democrats.

These growing problems seemingly spelled doom

for Truman. The country, including Montana, definitely leaned towards Dewey in the early months of 1948. A week before the election, Dewey was so confident in victory that it was reported that he was "studying possible cabinet appointments." But pollsters and experts overestimated Truman's unpopularity. By the end of September, when he was barnstorming the country and criticizing the Republican Congress as "idiot" and "do-nothing", the incumbent president was closing the gap. His message appealed to everyone from farmers to inner-city residents.

On Election Day, some attribute Truman's upset to Republicans staying home. This was not the case in Montana, however, where voter turnout was the highest in a generation. Harry S. Truman won re-election over Thomas Dewey and carried Democrats all across the country. (Truman, 53%; Dewey, 43%)

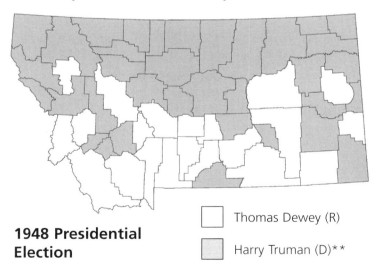

1948 Presidential Election

Thomas Dewey (R)

Harry Truman (D)**

Democrats took back both houses of Congress in one of the most surprising elections in US history. In the race for US Senate, two-term Democratic senator, James E. Murray of Butte, faced a strong challenge from Thomas Jefferson Davis of Butte, the former president of the Rotary Club. Most analysts around the country considered it a toss-up, if not leaning in favor of Davis. Murray, an ardent liberal, ran on his experience in Washington with the slogans, "You Know Where He Stands" and "Don't trade a record for a promise." He advocated in favor of the Missouri Valley Authority and national health care insurance.

Tom Davis campaigned that he was not just from Montana, but "FOR Montana." He had the help of outside groups that painted Murray as a Red sympathizer. Citing an article from the Daily Worker, which mentions Murray as a hero, ads against the Senator popped up in Montana's major newspapers.[5] The public did not take the bait and Murray defeated Davis in the general election. (Murray, 57%; Davis, 43%)

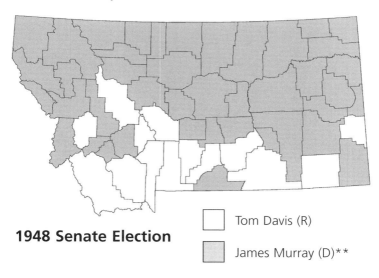

1948 Senate Election

☐ Tom Davis (R)

▨ James Murray (D)**

By 1948, Congressman Mike Mansfield was very well liked by voters in the First Congressional district. He trounced his opponent, Republican Albert Angstman, calling himself "the 'can do' candidate with the 'can did' record." (Mansfield, 68%; Angstman, 32%)

Congressman Wesley D'Ewart barely survived a challenge from Willard Fraser in the Democratic tidal wave. Earlier, D'Ewart echoed overconfident Republicans by predicting a GOP sweep of all major offices in the state.[6] In the end, he barely kept his own job. He was the only state or congressional GOP candidate in Montana to win re-election. (D'Ewart, 51%; Fraser, 49%)

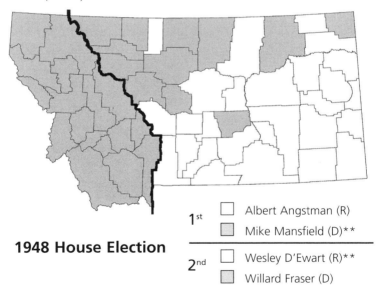

1948 House Election

1ˢᵗ ☐ Albert Angstman (R)
◻ Mike Mansfield (D)**

2ⁿᵈ ☐ Wesley D'Ewart (R)**
◻ Willard Fraser (D)

In the race for Montana's chief executive, Republican Governor Sam C. Ford was seeking a third term. His opponent, John Bonner, was the former attorney general. Bonner's strategy focused on highlighting his personal qualities. He boasted that he was a "native

Montanan," an attribute that no governor in Montana's history could claim. He was also a veteran of World War II. His slogan summed it all up: "Ask the person who knows him."

Bonner communicated his message via radio more than any other state candidate, which no doubt gave him an edge. He used this medium to attack Ford's record on state highways and the state liquor operations. Also, in an era when over thirty states around the country had adopted a sales tax, Bonner aggressively campaigned against such an idea for Montana.

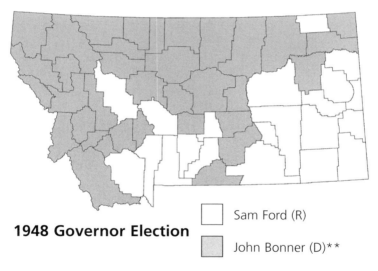

1948 Governor Election

☐ Sam Ford (R)

◼ John Bonner (D)**

Ford shared the overconfidence of most Republicans. He published ads with pictures of himself next to presidential candidate, Thomas Dewey. Many times he campaigned on national issues rather then state policies. He launched criticisms on national public figures such as Truman for his foreign policy and Senator Murray's advocacy of the Missouri Valley authority. He was probably just as shocked at the election results as other Republicans across the country when he was soundly defeated.

(Bonner, 56%; Ford, 44%)

When the dust settled around the state, Democrats had captured all but one of the major state elections in 1948. In the state legislature, Democrats benefited from the national shift by taking the State House and gaining eight seats in the State Senate. (State Senate: 31 Republicans, 23 Democrats; State House: 54 Democrats, 36 Republicans) 82% of registered voters turned out for the election.

1950

In 1950, America was once again gripped in war. This time, world powers and ideological enemies concentrated their efforts on the Korean peninsula. President Truman was so engulfed in the war effort that he made only one campaign appearance, a speech on television, to aid Democratic candidates for Congress. A "whistle-stop" tour he had planned for the West had to be cancelled. Truman had also presented the largest peace-time budget with increased foreign aid to allies and higher taxes at home, which made him, once again, an unpopular figure and a punching bag for the GOP.

Republicans picked up twenty-nine seats in the House and six seats in the Senate, but they did so without ousting Mansfield in the First Congressional District. War and uncertainty had made the electorate in Montana fearful of changing horses in the middle of the race. Congressman Mansfield enjoyed high popularity ratings from his style of communicating, mastery of foreign affairs, and his ability to bring in federal appropriations. In this re-election campaign he pledged to, "Build Montana, Maintain our Security, and Achieve World Peace."

His opponent and fellow university professor,

Ralph Y. McGinnis of Missoula, was a war veteran who called himself the "Fighting Republican."[7] He called for tough action against communists and aggressive internal investigations within the government of alleged communist activities. He criticized Mansfield for "appeasing communists" in China and Korea and blocking funding for the Committee on Un-American activities.

Mansfield stayed silent for much of the campaign, deciding to take the high road instead. In the last few days of the campaign, however, he defended his record and called McGinnis a "liar." (Mansfield, 61%; McGinnis, 39%)

In the east, Democrats again nominated John J. Holmes, the state auditor and former insurance man from Great Falls, to oppose incumbent Wesley D'Ewart. Holmes criticized D'Ewart for being soft on communism, but the Republican warded off the attacks and won a third full term.[8] (D'Ewart, 55%; Holmes, 45%).

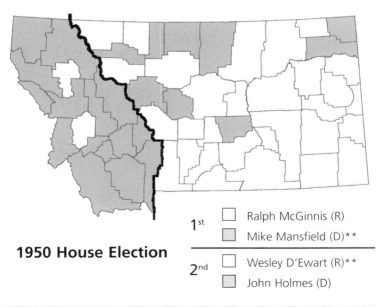

1950 House Election

1st ☐ Ralph McGinnis (R)
     ◼ Mike Mansfield (D)**

2nd ☐ Wesley D'Ewart (R)**
     ◼ John Holmes (D)

Republicans took back the State House with a gain of thirteen seats and maintained a slim majority in the state senate. (Montana House: 49 Republicans, 41 Democrats; Montana Senate: 28 Republicans, 26 Democrats) 77% of registered voters turned out for the election.

1952

It had been twenty years since a Republican had been elected to the White House, but in 1952, the GOP found a man to change that. General Dwight D. Eisenhower, commander of the Allied forces in Europe during World War II, had it all: a military background, a Washington outsider image and a paternal likeness that reminded many Americans of their own grandfather. His sweep-

Western district Congressman and U.S. Senate candidate, Mike Mansfield, President Harry Truman, Senator James Murray, Governor John Bonner, and Eastern district congressional candidate, Willard Fraser campaign together at the Tiber Dam groundbreaking in 1952. Photo from the Mike Mansfield collection of the K. Ross Toole Archives at the Maureen and Mike Mansfield Library.

ing victory over Democrat Adlai Stevenson, a former
governor of Illinois, helped elect a Republican
Congress.

Montana fell in love with Eisenhower like the rest
of the country. While the Treasure State had supported
the New Deal at every opportunity, a fresh face was
desired by many voters. Change, a simple concept used
by FDR to win his first presidential bid, now became
the battle cry of Republicans all across the country.
Eager for change, Montana gave Ike one of the largest
percentages of any presidential candidate in history.
(Eisenhower, 59%; Stevenson, 40%)

**1952 Presidential
Election**

☐ Dwight Eisenhower (R)**

▨ Adlai Stevenson (D)

Senator Zales Ecton, the one-term Republican,
faced a tough re-election bid against the widely popular western district congressman, Mike Mansfield.
Ecton's first term in the Senate was uneventful.
Because he had arguably accomplished little in six
years, he ran his campaign much like he did in 1946.
He pledged to fight against communism and corrup-

tion.[9] But his inability to make an impact on the state was detrimental. Mansfield, on the other hand, had a laundry list of appropriations and federal projects that he had helped secure for Montana.

With McCarthyism at its height around the country, redbaiters made efforts to paint Mansfield as a friend of communists. McCarthy himself backed Ecton and national speakers came to distort Mansfield's record in an all-out smear campaign. The Eisenhower tide probably helped Ecton, but it wasn't enough to defeat the humble, straight-talker from Butte. (Mansfield, 51%; Ecton, 49%).

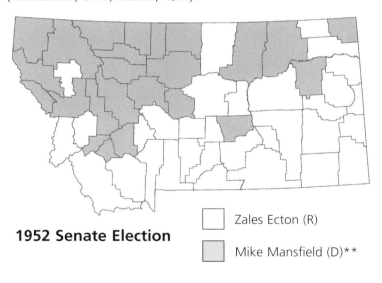

1952 Senate Election

☐ Zales Ecton (R)

▨ Mike Mansfield (D)**

Wellington Rankin, the Republican candidate in the First District, hoped to pick up one for the GOP in the seat vacated by Mike Mansfield. He ran on a platform of smaller government, lower taxes and fighting communism.[10] His opponent was an associate justice of the Montana Supreme Court, Lee Metcalf. As a veteran of World War II, Metcalf had been an army prosecutor and had helped set up democratic elections in Germany. The Democrat boasted that the Nazis and Communists had failed to gain popular support in these American supervised elections. Metcalf's ads said, "Is against all forms of totalitarianism."[11] Metcalf's attempt to neutralize any redbaiting and win in this traditionally Democratic district paid off, but he barely survived the Eisenhower storm. Heavily unionized counties gave him the majorities needed to win. (Metcalf, 50.3%; Rankin, 48.9%)

Incumbent Wesley D'Ewart of the Eastern Congressional district easily won re-election over Democrat Willard Fraser who had opposed him four years earlier. D'Ewart did much better in this big GOP year by carrying every county in the district. (D'Ewart, 62%; Fraser, 38%)

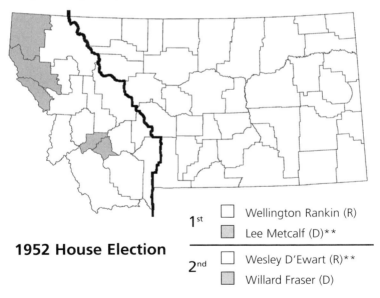

1952 House Election

1st ☐ Wellington Rankin (R)
   ☐ Lee Metcalf (D)**

2nd ☐ Wesley D'Ewart (R)**
   ☐ Willard Fraser (D)

Republicans everywhere benefited from the cry for change, including Montana GOP candidates. Incumbent

Governor John Bonner faced a tough challenge from J. Hugo Aronson, a Glacier county senator. Dubbed the "Galloping Swede" because of his immigrant background and his hard work ethic, Aronson ran as proof that the American Dream was reality. He was a self-made businessman with experience in ranching, oil and banking. His slogan: "Will substitute business for politics in Montana." Bonner ran on many of the same issues he used in his first campaign and tried to paint Aronson as a pawn of big business. The Democrat's strategy wasn't enough to fight off the Republican storm. (Aronson, 51%; Bonner, 49%)

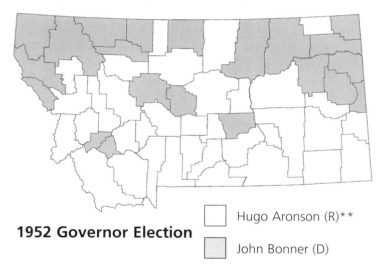

1952 Governor Election

☐ Hugo Aronson (R)**

☐ John Bonner (D)

The Eisenhower landslide also helped Republicans at the local level. A record 86% of registered voters turned out to help the GOP widened their margins in the State House and Senate. (State House: 62 Republicans, 28 Democrats; State Senate: 36 Republicans, 20 Democrats)

1954

History was against the GOP in their bid to strengthen Republican majorities in Congress in 1954. Only once since 1858 had the president's party managed to increase their numbers in an off-year election. The country's economy was in a recession and Democrats capitalized on this issue to take back both houses of Congress on November 2nd.

A bitter fight to unseat Senator James Murray became the center of national attention. Montana's Eastern Congressman, Wesley D'Ewart sought to oust the aging liberal in a heavyweight battle that came down to the wire. Party leaders and players from both sides came to the Big Sky to stump for their party's candidate. Murray had support from Adlai Stevenson, Minority Leader Lyndon Johnson, and Senator Hubert Humphrey of Minnesota. D'Ewart brought administration officials, Vice-President Richard Nixon, and even President Eisenhower.

Despite the fact that McCarthyism's peak was in the past, charges of "coddling communists" where lobbed early on against Murray. Campaign literature, entitled Senator Murray and the Red Web over Congress, was published and distributed all over Montana. It charged the senior senator with authoring articles for communist publications, making favorable comments towards communist nations like the Soviet Union and employing communist-leaning workers on his committee. When Nixon campaigned for D'Ewart, he accused the Democratic Party nationwide of having red roots and heavily criticized Senator Murray's record on fighting the communists.

Montana's former Democratic Senator, Burton Wheeler, openly campaigned against Murray in a letter to state Republican officials and then, in public appearances. Still apparently steaming over his loss in a primary in 1946 that Murray helped engineer, Wheeler said, "I know of no man in the United States Senate today who is less capable of representing out great state than Senator Murray."[12]

Murray avidly contested charges that he was too old for the job. He also published an ad that infuriated the Eisenhower administration where he showed a picture of the president along with a presidential "endorsement" saying that Murray is a "distinguished American."[13] He continued to run the ad despite protests from the Eisenhower administration. This prompted a visit by the president himself where he clarified his true pick for the Senate.

Murray aggressively defended himself of all charges and went on the attack. D'Ewart was criticized for his votes on veteran issues and his support of the administration's farm policies. 1954 was an especially hard year for agriculture and Murray aggressively

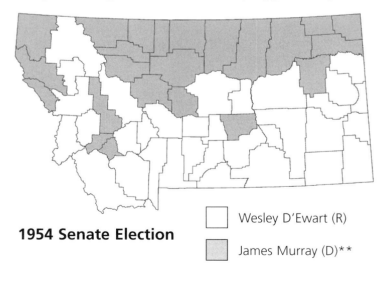

1954 Senate Election

☐ Wesley D'Ewart (R)

▨ James Murray (D)**

sought the support of the farm community.

Murray managed to win with strong, traditional support from Butte and majorities in the agricultural Hi-Line. The plurality was less than 2,000 votes out of around 227,000 cast. (Murray, 50.4%; D'Ewart, 49.6%)

In Montana's Western District, Winfield Page, a Republican legislator and Missoula architect touting his record of support for University projects, fought to retire freshman congressman, Lee Metcalf. Page tried to portray Metcalf as an ineffective legislator who had introduced twenty-six bills that all died in committee. Metcalf countered with endorsements of prominent House Democrats who praised his outspoken nature and hard work. Metcalf won re-election with a much larger margin than his victory two years earlier. (Metcalf, 56%; Page, 44%)

In the seat left open by Wesley D'Ewart, Orvin Fjare, a Republican from Big Timber, barely fended off Democrat LeRoy Anderson, a state senator from

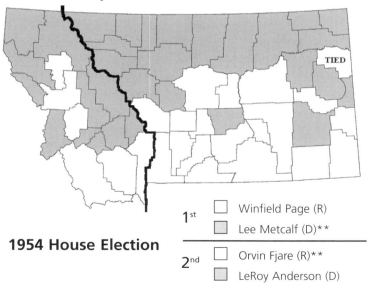

1954 House Election

TIED

1st — Winfield Page (R)
Lee Metcalf (D)**

2nd — Orvin Fjare (R)**
LeRoy Anderson (D)

Conrad. Fjare, a 36-year-old political newcomer, was one of the youngest congressmen ever elected from Montana. Some of his newspaper ads showed a boyish portrait with cartoon designs of cowboys, soldiers and bombers. His achievements included serving as the vice-president of the Junior Chamber of Commerce.[14] In an effort to point his opponent's youth, Anderson proclaimed that he was "*BETTER* Qualified" and said there was "no substitute for ability and experience."[15] The youthful Republican pulled off a squeaker on Election Day. (Fjare, 50.6%; Anderson, 49.4%)

At the local level, Democrats made gains in both houses of the legislature. They picked up a whopping 21 seats in the State House to take control and added three seats in the State Senate. (State House: 49 Democrats, 45 Republicans; State Senate: 33 Republicans, 23 Democrats) 77% of registered voters turned out for the election.

1956

1956 is a perfect example of split ticket voting in Montana. By and large, most Montanans sent Democrats as their representatives in Helena and Washington, yet they re-elected the Republican J. Hugo Aronson as Governor and gave another large plurality to President Eisenhower. Much like the rest of the country, voters of the Treasure State were starting to identify themselves less with a particular political party and instead looking at the personal qualities, experience and record of the candidates themselves.

President Eisenhower coasted to re-election in a rematch against Adlai Stevenson. During Eisenhower's first term, the nation enjoyed relative peace and calm for the first time in more than a decade. This stark contrast from the Roosevelt and Truman years helped propel the Republican to a second term. Eisenhower received a comfortable 57% in Montana—a percentage that paralleled his favorability four years prior. (Eisenhower, 57%; Stevenson, 43%)

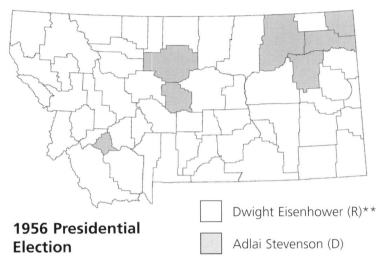

1956 Presidential Election

☐ Dwight Eisenhower (R)**

▨ Adlai Stevenson (D)

The Galloping Swede had tough opposition from the handsome, liberal Attorney General, Arnold Olsen. Aronson's administration was much like the president's because it seemed much quieter than its predecessors. The state enjoyed sustained growth and enjoyed a calmer political atmosphere under Aronson. The Republican boasted that construction of highways were at an all time high, while costs remained low. He launched his campaign for re-election with the slogan, "Montana's on the GO with HUGO." Aronson, who was never one for campaign promises, criticized his opponent of promising everything under the sun.

A number of Democrats were critical of Olsen's style of campaigning, including former Governor John Bonner and Senior State Senator, George Wilson.[16]

Olsen waged a fairly aggressive campaign, accusing Aronson of representing the "philosophy of government by the few, for the few."[17] He attacked Aronson's record including everything from gambling to the prison system.

But the major issue of the campaign centered around oil lease laws for school funding. Aronson supported a twelve and a half percent royalty from companies drilling for oil on state lands. As a member of the State Land Board, Olsen and Democrat State Superintendent of Public Instruction, Mary M. Condon, blocked such efforts, saying that it was a giveaway and businesses should be required to pay more. Aronson countered by accusing the two state officials of losing eleven million dollars for state schools through their opposition. By November, more Montanans believed Aronson and gave him their vote. (Aronson, 51%; Olsen, 49%)

Metcalf received his largest majority to date in a race against Bill, "W.D." McDonald. In his re-election bid, the Democratic representative pointed to his votes for a minimum wage and increases in Social Security. McDonald echoed criticisms of the previous election by saying that Metcalf was "ineffective" because only six of his bills had been passed. Montanans in the west saw no reason to replace Metcalf. (Metcalf, 62%; McDonald, 38%)

In the Eastern Congressional district, Montanans sent a Democrat as their representative for the first time since World War II. In a rematch of two years earlier, Democrat LeRoy Anderson edged Republican incumbent Orvin Fjare in another close battle. The campaign centered around the Eisenhower administration's unpopular farm policies, which Fjare had supported, and the delayed construction of the Yellowtail

Dam. After this election, Montana's entire delegation was Democratic. (Anderson, 50.9%; Fjare, 49.1%)

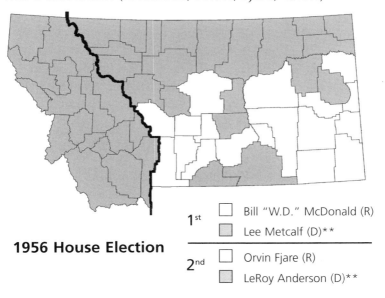

1956 House Election

1st ☐ Bill "W.D." McDonald (R)
    ☐ Lee Metcalf (D)**

2nd ☐ Orvin Fjare (R)
    ☐ LeRoy Anderson (D)**

Eisenhower won with an Electoral College landslide, but he went back to Washington with increased majorities for Democrats in Congress. Democrats also made gains in both houses in Helena. (State House: 59 Democrats, 35 Republicans; State Senate: 31 Democrats, 25 Republicans) 83% of registered voters turned out for the election.

1958

Consistent with history, Democrats chalked up huge victories at the national and state level in the off-year election of 1958. They increased their majorities in both houses of Congress and captured the majority of governorships up for grabs. After the election, Eisenhower had little leverage in his final two years in the White

House and Vice-President Nixon faced an uphill battle in his impending campaign for president in 1960.

Mike Mansfield had one of the most impressive victories in Montana history in his re-election contest against little known Republican Lou Welch. Mansfield won in all 56 counties and had a three to one margin of victory. The junior senator had high favorability ratings for his responsive constituent services, knowledge of foreign affairs and his leadership post in the Senate as majority whip for the Democrats under majority leader Lyndon Johnson. He asked Montanans to "Judge him by his record and his service to Montana and the Nation." (Mansfield, 76%; Welch, 24%)

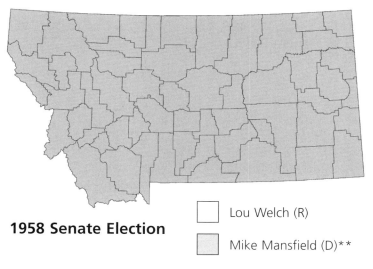

1958 Senate Election

☐ Lou Welch (R)

▨ Mike Mansfield (D)**

Congressman Metcalf also had majorities in every county in the Western district. Metcalf was opposed by Jean Walterskirchen, a 61 year-old grandmother and former school teacher who criticized the incumbent's close ties to labor bosses. She toured the western third of the state with the slogan, "Freedom at stake in '58." Metcalf boasted that of the 422 bills passed by the

House, five were sponsored by himself. As the self-proclaimed "Leader in Results," the liberal Democrat coasted to re-election and a fourth term. (Metcalf, 69%; Walterskirchen, 31%)

In the east, Freshman Democrat LeRoy Anderson trounced his opponent, Ashton Jones in this traditionally Republican district. Anderson repeated his criticisms of the Eisenhower administration's farm policies that won him the seat two years earlier. Jones claimed that Anderson did little to fund the Yellowtail Dam, a promise the Democrat made in the last election, and blasted him for missing a third of the roll call votes. In November, voters gave the incumbent a comfortable plurality over the Republican. (Anderson, 61%; Jones, 39%)

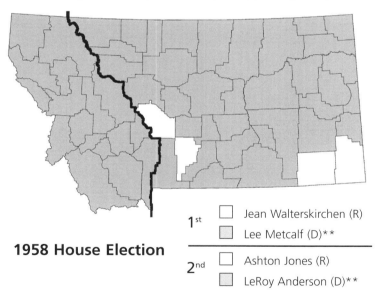

1st ☐ Jean Walterskirchen (R)
▨ Lee Metcalf (D)**

1958 House Election

2nd ☐ Ashton Jones (R)
▨ LeRoy Anderson (D)**

Democratic candidates for legislature benefited from the national tide and gained seats in both houses. They picked up seven seats in the State Senate and two seats in the State House. (State House: 61 Democrats,

31 Republicans; State Senate: 38 Democrats, 17 Republicans) 75% of registered voters turned out for the election.

1960

America was closely divided by 1960. Much of the attention at the national level was again focused heavily on foreign policy. The Soviet Union and the US were competing for the favor of third world countries in an ideological and military contest. The space race was on as well with the two superpowers, with the USSR out in the lead.

For president, the country had a clear choice between the California conservative, Vice-President Richard Nixon, and the magnetic Massachusetts liberal, Senator John F. Kennedy. Television played a key role in the race. Kennedy looked younger and more vibrant in a series of debates against Nixon. The Vice-President seemed cold and distant from the millions of viewers

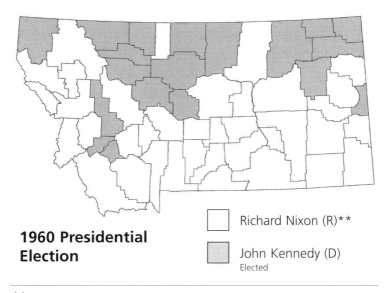

1960 Presidential Election

☐ Richard Nixon (R)**

▨ John Kennedy (D)
Elected

who tuned in. Kennedy's Catholicism was considered a problem, however, because the traditionally Democratic South was ardently Protestant. In the end, this did not affect his candidacy as much as pundits predicted. The race was close, especially in terms of the popular vote, but Kennedy prevailed.

This general election marked the first time since 1900 that Montana gave its electoral votes to the losing candidate. Montana gave Nixon a slim majority, following most other western states, but the results paralleled the closeness of the race nationwide. In the Electoral College, Kennedy pulled off a decisive victory. (Nixon, 51%; Kennedy, 49%)

The battle to replace the outgoing senior senator, James Murray, was also a close battle. Before Congressman Lee Metcalf could face off against former congressman, Orvin Fjare of Big Timber, he had to beat Democratic Congressman from the Eastern District, LeRoy Anderson, and former governor, John Bonner, in the Democratic primary. The debate got personal, but Metcalf, a member of the "M-Squad" with Murray and Mansfield, prevailed.

The choice in the general election seemed fairly clear—Metcalf favored increased government spending, increased health coverage and increased conservation measures while Republican Fjare argued for less spending, lower taxes and fiscal restraint.[18] Metcalf criticized "Republican inflation," which plagued the nation and pledged to expand Social Security. He contrasted himself with his opponent by emphasizing his own experience as a four-term veteran of the House. Fjare had little public service experience aside from one term in the House as the Eastern District's Representative.

Fjare countered by accusing his opponent of being a big spender. He also claimed that Metcalf had missed almost a third of his roll call votes. He campaigned with ads showing endorsement's from Nixon and stuck to his strict support of free enterprise. The contest was close, but Metcalf was elected to replace the aged Murray. (Metcalf, 50.7%; Fjare, 49.3%)

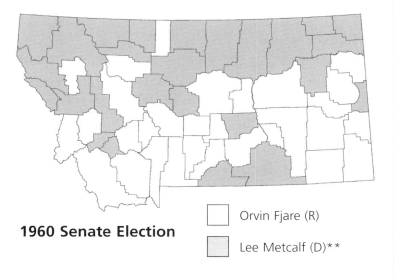

1960 Senate Election

☐ Orvin Fjare (R)

▨ Lee Metcalf (D)**

Metcalf's candidacy for Senate left his Western District seat open for Arnold Olsen, the perpetual Democratic candidate who was a former attorney general and unsuccessful candidate for governor and chief justice. His Republican opponent was George Sarsfield, an attorney and political newcomer from Butte. Olsen won on a pledge to put "Peoples' interests always first."[19] (Olsen, 53%; Sarsfield, 47%)

Republican recaptured the Eastern Congressional district in an open seat election. James "Big Jim" Battin, a lawyer and state legislature, edged Democrat Leo Graybill, a Belt lawyer, in a close contest. Battin ran on a platform of smaller, more efficient federal government. (Battin, 51%; Graybill, 49%)

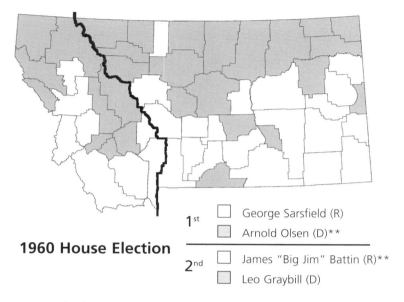

1960 House Election

1st ☐ George Sarsfield (R)
   ▢ Arnold Olsen (D)**

2nd ☐ James "Big Jim" Battin (R)**
    ▢ Leo Graybill (D)

With the popular Galloping Swede vacating the governor's office, both parties were hopeful of winning the seat in November. Donald Nutter, a Sidney attorney and former state senator was the Republican hopeful while Democrats nominated Lieutenant Governor Paul Cannon.

Nutter, 44, ran jointly with Lieutenant Governor candidate Tim Babcock as "the BEST team for a Greater Montana." As a conservative, Nutter called for reduced taxes for businesses and individuals. He also promised to "update and streamline departments" in the state government, or in other words, work for deep spending cuts.[20] A sales tax, Nutter claimed, may be necessary to diversify revenues.

Cannon, 63, sought to distinguish himself from his opponent through his extensive public service record. He published a "six-point program for prosperity" which listed many goals, but few details. The Nutter-Babcock ticket proved to be too strong, however, and

Montana elected a Republican as chief executive once again. (Nutter, 55%; Cannon, 45%)

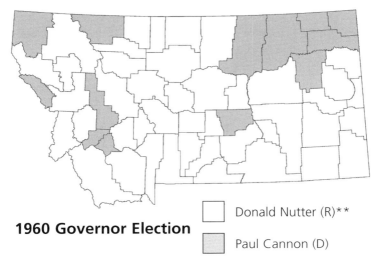

1960 Governor Election

☐ Donald Nutter (R)**

■ Paul Cannon (D)

Democrats held on to their majority in the State Senate, but Republicans earned a whopping 23 seats in the State House, enough to take control. (State Senate: 38 Democrats, 17 Republicans; State House: 54 Republicans, 40 Democrats) 86% of registered voters turned out for the election.

1962

The off-year election of 1962 made few waves in Big Sky Country. By and large, Montanans decided to keep the status quo in this uneventful contest.

In the Western District, Arnold Olsen won on his "Government with a Heart" platform against liberal Republican Wayne Montgomery. The Republican, a rancher from Lima, made his slogan, "Montana is worth fighting for," but the incumbent won re-election.[21] (Olsen, 53%; Montgomery, 47%)

President John Kennedy gets off Air Force One followed by Senators Mike Mansfield and Lee Metcalf at a visit to Great Falls in 1962. Photo from the Mike Mansfield collection of the K. Ross Toole Archives at the Maureen and Mike Mansfield Library.

In the East, James "Big Jim" Battin won re-election in a rematch with Democrat Leo Graybill, a Yale-educated lawyer and professor from Belt. The Democrat got help from the Montana senatorial delegation and tried to label Battin an "obstructionist", but it wasn't enough to topple the incumbent.[22] (Battin, 55%; Graybill, 45%)

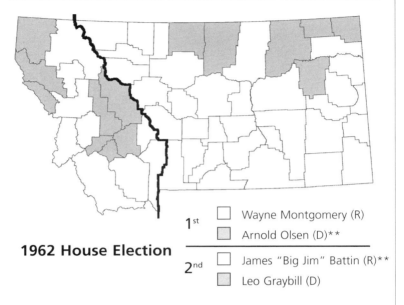

1962 House Election

1st — ☐ Wayne Montgomery (R) / ▨ Arnold Olsen (D)**

2nd — ☐ James "Big Jim" Battin (R)** / ▨ Leo Graybill (D)

Republicans made a few gains in the legislature, but there was no change in control in either house. (State Senate: 35 Democrats, 21 Republicans; State House: 57 Republicans, 37 Democrats) 78% of registered voters turned out for the election.

1964

Both the nation and the state mourned the loss of their two executives as the campaign cycle for 1964 commenced. Governor Donald Nutter was killed in a plane crash in early 1962 as he traveled around the state. This propelled Lieutenant Governor Tim Babcock into the governorship. And then in November of 1963, President John Kennedy was assassinated in a motorcade through Dallas, Texas.

There were many other world events that added to the instability. Communist China went nuclear and tested an atomic bomb for the first time. The Indochinese

From left to right: Congressman Arnold Olsen, Senator Mike Mansfield, President Lyndon Johnson and Governor Tim Babcock at the White House celebrating Montana's 100th territorial anniversary. Photo from the Mike Mansfield collection of the K. Ross Toole Archives at the Maureen and Mike Mansfield Library.

conflict, although relatively small, was a growing concern for many who saw American intervention escalating. Khruschev, leader of the USSR, was ousted in a party coup largely for his bumbling of the Cuban Missile crisis.

On the home front, spending was the highest since World War II as Congress went on a pork barrel binge. President Johnson promoted his Great Society program, a resurrection of the New Deal philosophy of government expansion. And the civil rights era was peaking with such charismatic and inspirational figures as Martin Luther King, Jr.

The nation rallied behind Kennedy's successor, Lyndon Johnson, and rejected the archconservative message of Arizona Senator and Republican presidential nominee, Barry Goldwater. The Democrat successfully portrayed the Goldwater as unfit for the office of chief executive and commander-in-chief. The

Republican alienated himself from independents with his message and shocked many by declaring that "extremism is no vice." Johnson swept most of the nation, save the Deep South, in an electoral and popular vote landslide. Montana threw its support behind the Texas Democrat as well. (Johnson, 59%; Goldwater, 41%)

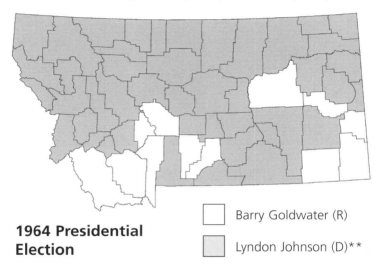

1964 Presidential Election

☐ Barry Goldwater (R)

▨ Lyndon Johnson (D)**

The governor's race was much closer as Republican Babcock battled with Democrat Roland Renne, a former Montana State University president. Babcock's record was much like the staunchly conservative Nutter. He was an early supporter of Barry Goldwater and he continued Nutter's tradition of refusing to declare United Nations Day in the state. On October 27th, Babcock's birthday, ten rallies were held around the state with ten different governors and senators who called for the governor's election.[23]

Renne charged Babcock of using his office to make money on businesses he owned. He urged the governor to release his financial record much like presidential candidates are required. As governor, Renne said that he would increase education funding, lower property taxes and better manage the state's custodial institutions. The race was close but Babcock weathered the national Democratic landslide. (Babcock, 51%; Renne, 49%)

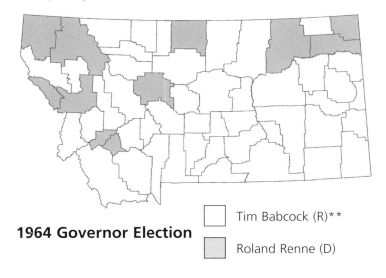

1964 Governor Election

☐ Tim Babcock (R)**

▨ Roland Renne (D)

Mike Mansfield, majority leader of the Senate since Johnson's departure, coasted to re-election. The senior senator used the same laid-back, folksy campaign style with a heavy focus on federal projects he had secured for the state. With little real opposition, Mansfield concentrated his efforts on helping other Democrats in Montana gain election.

His opponent, Alex Blewett, was a Republican legislator from Great Falls. He campaign asked voters to "Choose a Senator for Montana, not just from Montana."[24] In a similar tone, Blewett criticized Mansfield for perfecting "the art of camouflage, never making a firm stand on any issue."[25] Grasping for any issue to give his campaign traction, Blewett also questioned whether Mansfield owned property in Montana or paid property taxes. On election day, voters overwhelmingly supported the majority leader. (Mansfield, 65%; Blewett, 35%)

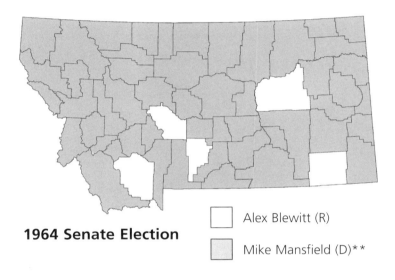

1964 Senate Election

Alex Blewitt (R)

Mike Mansfield (D)**

Both Congressman in the Eastern and Western districts were re-elected. Arnold Olsen fought liberal Republican Wayne Montgomery in a rematch. Olsen called for increases in government spending, especially with health care while Montgomery tried to siphon off labor votes. The Democrat was returned with a comfortable majority. (Olsen, 54%; Montgomery, 46%)

"Big Jim" Battin faced off with Jack Toole, a Shelby rancher and former president of the Montana Cattlemen's Association. With the battle cry "It's Time for Toole," the Democrat criticized Battin's choice of committee assignments on the judiciary and foreign affairs committees.[26] He pledged to serve on the

Agriculture committee if elected. Easterners stuck with the Republican. (Battin, 54%; Toole, 46%)

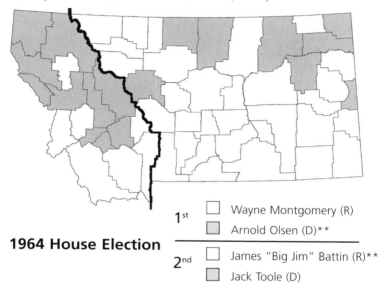

1964 House Election

1st — ☐ Wayne Montgomery (R)
☐ Arnold Olsen (D)**

2nd — ☐ James "Big Jim" Battin (R)**
☐ Jack Toole (D)

The Legislative races were a mixed bag, but Democrats gained control of both houses. Republicans gained three seats in the senate, but lost 19 seats in the State House. (State Senate: 32 Democrats, 24 Republicans; State House: 56 Democrats, 38 Republicans) 86% of registered voters turned out for the election.

Progressivism Returns: 1965-1975

S tarting with legislative reapportionment mandated by the U.S. Supreme Court, Montana entered into an era characterized by sweeping, progressive reforms. In *Baker v. Carr,* and *Reynolds v. Sims* the Court held that state legislatures must draw their districts according to population. Before this decision, each county in Montana had at least one senator and one representative. Opponents of this arrangement dubbed this apportionment as "one cow, one vote" and called for apportionment based on "one person, one vote." Many residents of densely populated counties like Yellowstone, Cascade and Silver Bow were critical of the fact that sparsely populated counties like Petroleum and Treasure had equal representation in the state senate.

The decision handed down from the federal court to reapportion was met with resistance in the state legislature. Different plans were proposed but none of them met the requirements of the court's decision. Eventually, a three-judge federal panel redrew the legislative districts in Montana based on the new standard. This dramatic change marked the end of rural domination in the state legislature.

With new majorities of urban-minded voters, calls for a new constitution increased. Most Montanans agreed that the constitution drafted in the last century was outdated and needed to be replaced with a completely new document—one that could address the concerns and problems of their time. In 1970, 65% of Montana voters supported a call for a constitutional convention. When elections were held for delegates, 58 Democrats, 36 Republicans and six Independents were sent to Helena to draft a more modern document capable of meeting the challenges of 20th century Montana.

The new constitution was one of the most progressive in the nation. In many cases, it went beyond the U.S. Constitution. For example, it included an express right to privacy, a right to a clean and healthful environment, a right to citizen participation and a right to an education. When a final draft was completed in 1972, it was put to a public vote. Needing only a majority of votes, it narrowly passed with 50.55%. The margin was only 2,532 votes. Urban voters widely supported it while almost every rural county voted against it.

During this progressive slant in Montana electoral history, Republicans shot themselves in the foot by calling for a sales tax. For many years the subject of a sales tax had been a hot topic of debate. In the late 60's, Republicans, headed by then Governor Babcock, championed the idea of a sales tax. The proposal did not sit well with voters and Babcock was voted out in 1968. Three years later, when voters were choosing their constitutional convention delegates, Republicans again spearheaded an effort to enact a two-percent sales tax and had it put on the ballot. The response was overwhelmingly against it as 70% of the voters killed the referendum. Many GOP candidates were forever haunted in future elections because of their support for the sales tax.

During this period, Montana's economy was prosperous. The state's gas, oil, and coal industries grew extensively during the 1970's, when the United States was stricken with an energy shortage. Coal production increased dramatically, from less than 3 million to almost 40 million tons per year. The lumber and agriculture industries prospered as well. Tourism also emerged as one of the state's top industries. This prosperity throughout the state brought money into the state coffers, which allowed the state government to expand.

1966

The GOP made a national comeback in the off-year election of 1966, but it wasn't enough to help Tim Babcock take Lee Metcalf's seat in the US Senate. As Vietnam flared and the Great Society created large deficits and inflation, Babcock sought to capitalize on growing public discontent. While a majority of Montanans supported the war, they wanted to see a quick resolution of the conflict.

Babcock criticized Metcalf's vote against extra war appropriations and his vote against bombing Northern Vietnam—something only 14 other senators had voted against. He contended that the Democrat was a "rubber stamp" of the administration's domestic policies, but his votes against war funds were a slap in the face to the soldiers who were fighting in the jungles of Vietnam.[27]

Metcalf downplayed the Vietnam issue in the campaign. Rejecting the "rubber stamp" label, Metcalf didn't hesitate to throw punches at the administration's farm policies, which were very unpopular with the agricultural community.[28] The liberal also had ideological allies such as Senators Hubert Humphrey, George

McGovern and Bobby Kennedy stump for him around the state. And as always, Mansfield made a tour around the state in support of Metcalf.

Metcalf attacked Babcock's support of Goldwater in the last presidential election and emphasized his own work in bringing federal dollars to Big Sky Country.[29] There was also a hint of discontent among voters for a sitting governor seeking another elected office. Continuing their traditional support of liberal Democrats in the Senate, Montanans gave Metcalf a second term. (Metcalf, 53%; Babcock, 47%)

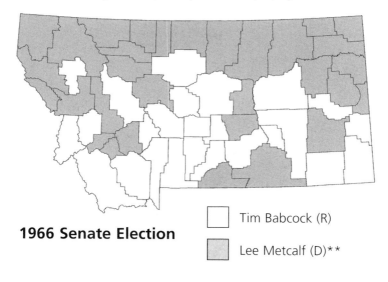

1966 Senate Election

☐ Tim Babcock (R)

■ Lee Metcalf (D)**

Arnold Olsen showed some vulnerability in a challenge from Republican Dick Smiley, a radio station owner and Gallatin county legislator. The Democrat had been a strong supporter of administration spending—something that Smiley blamed for the high inflation plaguing the nation. Smiley did very well in the rural areas, but Olsen's union support helped him edge the Republican. (Olsen, 50.8%; Smiley, 49.2%)

Democrat John Melcher fought to unseat incumbent Battin in the Eastern District. Melcher, a veterinarian from Forsyth, had been a three-term mayor of his hometown and a state legislator. Melcher echoed criticisms of high inflation and rising interest rates, but the case was hard to make since both Congress and the President were Democrats. Battin attacked the administration's farm policies, especially Secretary of Agriculture, Orvile Freeman. The Republican benefited from a nationwide lean towards the GOP and won a fourth term. (Battin, 60%; Melcher, 40%)

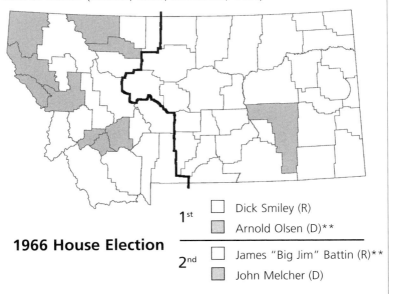

1st ☐ Dick Smiley (R)
    ▨ Arnold Olsen (D)**

1966 House Election

2nd ☐ James "Big Jim" Battin (R)**
    ▨ John Melcher (D)

After only one session of control, the Democrats lost the state house and had their majority in the senate eroded. (State Senate: 30 Democrats; 25 Republicans; State House: 64 Republicans, 40 Democrats) 80% of registered voters turned out for the election.

1968

Going into the election of 1968, the Democrats were divided at the national level. Hawk and Dove factions feuded over Vietnam, the party's convention was marred with rioting and their eventual nominee, Vice-President Humphrey, gained the nomination without entering a single primary election. If that wasn't enough, George Wallace, a former Democratic governor from Alabama, launched an independent run for president supported by many disenfranchised, white Southerners.

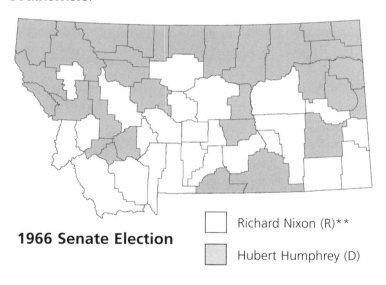

1966 Senate Election

☐ Richard Nixon (R)**

▨ Hubert Humphrey (D)

    The Republicans turned to their 1960 nominee, Richard Nixon. Nixon held the upper-hand throughout the election. As the frontrunner, Nixon refused to debate his opponents, stayed evasive on the topic of Vietnam and promised to restore "law and order" to the country. The labor vote was fractioned as many workers turned to the Republican Party. There were worries that the election would be thrown to the House of Representative due to the strong three-way race, but Nixon prevailed in November. He did so with a majority of Montana voters. (Nixon, 51%; Humphrey, 42%; Wallace 7%)

While Americans were throwing out one administration nationally, Montanans were throwing out another at the state level. Tim Babcock lost a bid for re-election against Attorney General Forrest Anderson, which ended a sixteen-year streak of Republican control of the governor's office. They did this in large part over the issue of a sales tax. As Governor, Babcock advocated a three-percent sales tax proposal in order to pay for the increasing costs of government. Babcock estimated that the state would need at least 60 million dollars more in revenue. The governor tried to tie Anderson's candidacy with that of Humphrey's and called himself "the only honest man with the only positive plan."[30]

Anderson was more optimistic in his estimates for additional revenue. He projected a need of only 20 to 25 million dollars—an amount he said could be made up in better management of state departments.[31] His campaign slogan, one of the most famous in Montana history, downplayed the need of a sales tax: "Pay More? What For!" Toward the end of the campaign, Anderson said that a ten percent increase in the income tax, a more progressive choice, may be needed. Wayne Montgomery, the former Republican turned "New Reformer" also campaigned for governor, but won few votes. The Attorney General won a decisive victory over Babcock in the November election. (Anderson, 54%; Babcock, 42%; Montgomery, 4%)

In a rematch of two years previous, Dick Smiley again tried to retire Democratic incumbent Arnold

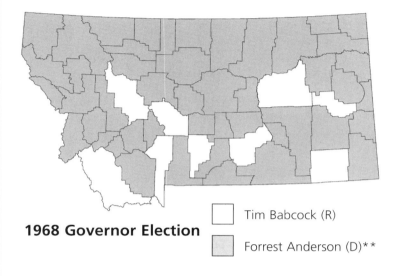

1968 Governor Election

Tim Babcock (R)

Forrest Anderson (D)**

Olsen. The results of the last general election showed that Olsen was vulnerable. The Republican echoed Nixon's theme of "law and order," and criticized Democratic attempts to enact gun control.[32] Polls showed Smiley ahead right up until Election Day. These poll numbers kept Olsen on the attack. The Democrat alluded that Smiley avoided service in the war, supported the sales tax and had violated the Code of Fair Campaign Practices.[33] Election results showed a stronger win for the incumbent the second time around. (Olsen 54%; Smiley, 46%)

In the Eastern District, Representative Battin crushed his liberal Democrat opponent, Robert Kelleher. Kelleher, a Billings attorney, campaigned on a variety of farm issues.[34] Battin, a member of the powerful House Ways and Means Committee, kept his criticism focused on the outgoing administration's farm policy and gun control stance. Battin easily won a fifth-term (Battin, 68%; Kelleher, 32%)

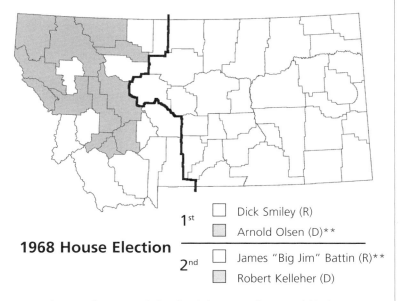

1968 House Election

1st ☐ Dick Smiley (R)
☐ Arnold Olsen (D)**

2nd ☐ James "Big Jim" Battin (R)**
☐ Robert Kelleher (D)

The make-up of the legislature changed little. Republicans lost six seats but maintained control. The Senate remained unchanged. (State House: 58 Republicans, 46 Democrats; State Senate: 30 Democrats, 25 Republicans) 86% of registered voters turned out for the election.

1970

1970 was one of the most unconventional elections in Montana history. For the first time in 30 years, a Republican won in the traditionally Democratic Western district while a Democrat won in the normally Republican Eastern District.

Former Republican Missoula mayor, Dick Shoup, challenged veteran politician, Arnold Olsen, in the West. Flanked by "Shoup's Troops," the Republican's female campaign team, Shoup traveled the state criticizing Olsen's record on gun control, crime and the

John Melcher represented Montana's eastern district in the U.S. Congress from 1969-1977. He was later elected to the U.S. Senate where he served from 1977-1989. Photo from the Mike Mansfield collection of the K. Ross Toole Archives at the Maureen and Mike Mansfield Library.

environment.[35] Olsen had not voted for gun control, but he avoided the touchy issue throughout the election. Shoup was also critical of Olsen's assignments to the insignificant Postal and Civil Service Committees. In the end, the rural voters rallied behind Shoup on his pledge to curb gun control laws in Washington and sent Olsen back to Montana. (Shoup, 50.5%; Olsen, 49.5%)

John Melcher made a comeback and captured the Eastern district in a special election in 1969. "Big Jim" Battin had vacated the seat and accepted an appointment as a U.S. District Judge. Jack Rehberg, a state senator from Yellowstone county, made an attempt to oust the newly elected Democrat in a normal general election. Rehberg spent much of his time in the urban areas and banked largely on support from his hometown of Billings. He criticized Melcher's vote against the Conference Committee report of an organized crime bill and pledged to work with the Republican administration. His slogan was, "Jack will do in Washington what he says in Montana!"

Melcher, "A Man on the Move for Eastern Montana," was a decorated World War II veteran who concentrated his efforts on rural areas and Great Falls. Although national figures such as Barry Goldwater, Vice-President Spiro Agnew and US Attorney General John Mitchell campaign against him, Melcher stuck to agriculture issues and won his first general election contest as an incumbent. His decisive victory proved that he was a rising star in Montana Democratic circles. (Melcher, 64%; Rehberg, 36%)

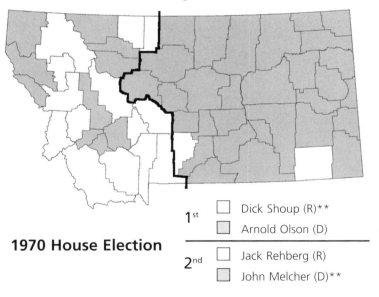

1970 House Election

1ˢᵗ ☐ Dick Shoup (R)**
☐ Arnold Olson (D)

2ⁿᵈ ☐ Jack Rehberg (R)
☐ John Melcher (D)**

Facing his last election for public office, Mike Mansfield drew Republican Harold "Bud" Wallace of Missoula as his opponent. The GOP candidate, a former swimming coach at the University of Montana, had an uphill battle. He attacked early and many considered his candidacy overly negative. He criticized everything from Mansfield's "inconsistent voting record" to his alleged abuse of the Congressional franking privilege.[36] He even dared to label Mansfield "soft on communism."[37]

Republican senators across the nation disassociated themselves with Wallace's campaign. Even President Nixon came out and endorsed Mansfield. The Democrat probably would have had his largest plurality ever had it not been for his vote for gun control two years earlier. Wallace won six rural counties and ran close to Mansfield in other rural areas to finish closer than anyone expected him to. (Mansfield, 61%; Wallace, 39%)

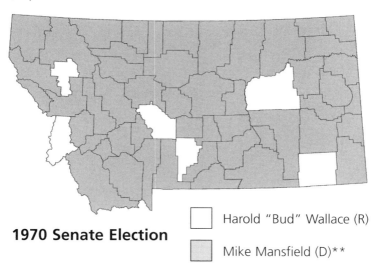

1970 Senate Election

☐ Harold "Bud" Wallace (R)

☐ Mike Mansfield (D)**

In Legislative races, the State Senate again remained unchanged while Republicans lost three seats in the Montana House. (State House: 55 Republicans, 49 Democrats; State Senate: 30 Democrats, 25 Republicans)

Voters also largely supported a ballot to call a constitutional convention. The original constitution, first enacted in 1889, was seen as outdated, especially in urban areas. In the vote, western and Hi-line counties gave the largest majorities. All but five counties, all rural, failed to approve the measure. (Call for a Constitutional Convention: Yes, 65%; No, 35%) 78% of registered voters turned out for the election.

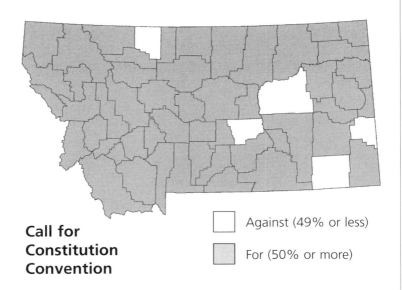

Call for Constitution Convention

☐ Against (49% or less)

▨ For (50% or more)

1972

By 1972, America was desperately looking for a way out of Vietnam. Liberal Democrat George McGovern of South Dakota promised to do it immediately at any cost if elected. Nixon said that he preferred a more honorable exit from the war that had killed so many young Americans. Although the Watergate scandal broke late in the campaign, no clear tie had been made to the

Oval Office by Election Day.

McGovern's candidacy left much to be desired. When picking a running mate, The South Dakotan first selected Senator Eagleton of Missouri, who had a history of depression treated with shock therapy. Embarrassed in front of the nation, Eagleton withdrew himself from the running. McGovern effectively rallied the younger voters behind him, but the rest of the nation had trouble seeing him as chief executive. On Election Day, Nixon crushed McGovern in an Electoral College landslide. In Montana, McGovern only picked up the Democratic strongholds of Silver Bow and Deer Lodge counties. (Nixon, 58%; McGovern, 38%)

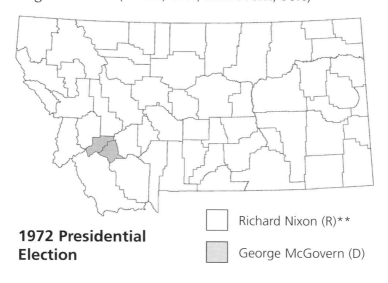

1972 Presidential Election

☐ Richard Nixon (R)**

▨ George McGovern (D)

In the governor's race, Forrest Anderson decided not to run again because of health reasons. Democrats nominated Lieutenant Governor, Tom Judge to run in Anderson's place. "Big Ed" Smith, a maverick Republican from Dagmar, edged other contenders in

the GOP primary. Smith was one of the few
Republicans untainted by support of the sales tax. His
split from the Republicans on many controversial votes
in the legislature made him a luke-warm candidate
with his political base.

Judge profited from a growing economy and a
youthful, yet experienced image, which he embodied in
his theme, "Ability you can trust."[38] The Republican
Party was still licking its wounds from the sales tax
battle, which gave the Democrat the ability to launch a
positive campaign based on job growth, lower taxes
and the environment. Judge came out on top in
November. (Judge, 54%; Smith, 46%)

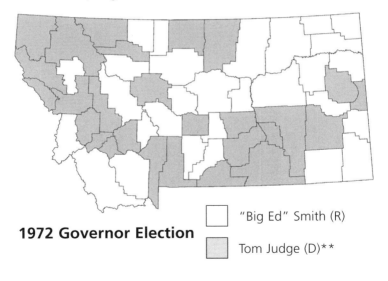

1972 Governor Election

☐ "Big Ed" Smith (R)

▨ Tom Judge (D)**

In a final bid for election to the US Senate, the
aging liberal, Lee Metcalf, confronted a tough challenge
from the well-financed, well-staffed campaign of
Republican Henry Hibbard, a rancher-legislator from
Helena. Hibbard attacked Metcalf's statements in favor
of gun registration, his vote for amnesty for draft

dodgers and his "wholehearted" support of presidential candidate, George McGovern.[39] Metcalf was unapologetic for his support of McGovern and blasted the administration's domestic policies.[40] Hibbard came close, but not close enough in his bid to unseat Metcalf. (Metcalf, 52%; Hibbard, 48%)

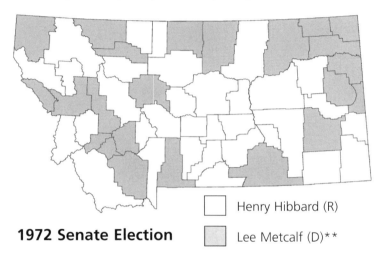

1972 Senate Election

Henry Hibbard (R)

Lee Metcalf (D)**

Arnold Olsen tried to retake his seat in the West from Republican Dick Shoup, but he was largely seen as a has-been. He ran ads showing him teaching a youngster how to shoot a gun—an attempt to erase his anti-Second Amendment image. The damage was done, however, and gun control wasn't the hot issue it was two years earlier. Olsen's hometown newspaper, the Montana Standard, endorsed Shoup and the Republican won a decisive victory. (Shoup, 54%; Olsen, 46%)

In the East, Democrat John Melcher once again crushed his opponent to show that he owned Montana's Second Congressional District. The Republicans nominated another Billings legislator, Dick Forester to take on the Democrat. Forester tried to link Melcher with McGovern's candidacy, but it was completely ineffective. Melcher had gained recognition for spearheading the investigation of wheat sales to the Soviet Union. Montanans agreed with his slogan, "A good man to keep on the job," and sent him back to Washington.[41] (Melcher, 76%; Forester, 24%)

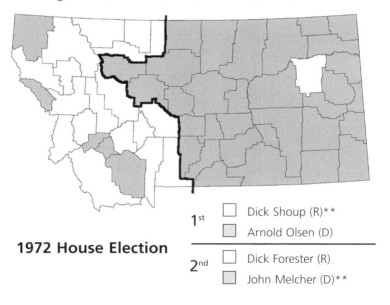

1st   ☐ Dick Shoup (R)**
      ◻ Arnold Olsen (D)

1972 House Election

2nd   ☐ Dick Forester (R)
      ◻ John Melcher (D)**

A constitutional convention convened in January and by 1972, a new constitution was drafted. Urban areas and progressive voters largely supported the proposal while rural areas and conservative voters rallied against it. The new constitution passed, but the margin of victory was slim: 2,532 votes.

The Democrats gained control of the state House with a nine seat pick-up and minimized their losses in the state senate to three. (State Senate: 27 Democrats, 23 Republicans; State House: 54 Democrats, 46 Republicans)

85% of registered voters turned out for the election.

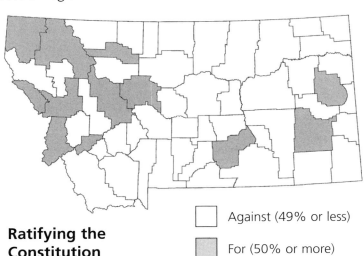

**Ratifying the
Constitution**

☐ Against (49% or less)

■ For (50% or more)

1974

1974 was not a good year to run as a Republican.
Nixon resigned earlier in the year as the reality of
impeachment neared and newly appointed Vice President, Gerald Ford, pardoned him right before the off-
year congressional elections. Nationwide, Democrats
rode to victory on the public's disgust of the administration and dirty politics.

Montana was no exception. Young Democratic
legislator, Max Baucus, beat two-term Republican Dick
Shoup in the Western District. Baucus, 32, earned the
nomination over other Democratic contenders through
his walking tour of the district. His trek went from
Gardiner in the south to Yaak in the north—a march
totaling 631 miles.[42] In the general election, Baucus
painted Shoup as an enemy of working Montanans and

pledged to vote for an increase in the minimum wage and Social Security benefits.[43] The conservative Shoup was hurt by his failure to quickly condemn the Nixon administration. (Baucus, 55%; Shoup, 45%)

In the East, Republicans nominated Jack McDonald, a state legislator and cattle rancher from Belt. He changed from the Democrat party to the GOP at a very peculiar time and shocked voters with unscripted, bizarre statements. In one such statement, regarding his opposition to the ERA, McDonald said, "If Christ wanted men and women to be equal, he would have had six women and six men as apostles."[44] His candidacy did nothing to neutralize the Democratic tide and the popular John Melcher. Melcher's slogan was simply, "He is where the action is on vital Montana issues.[45] (Melcher, 63%; McDonald, 37%)

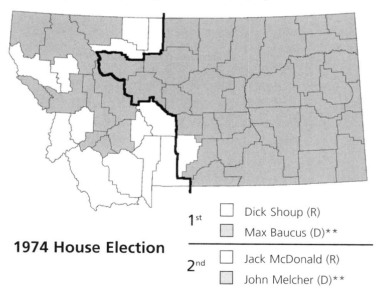

1974 House Election

1st ☐ Dick Shoup (R)
◻ Max Baucus (D)**

2nd ☐ Jack McDonald (R)
◻ John Melcher (D)**

Democrats at the local level also benefited from the nationwide sentiment. They gained three seats in the State Senate and thirteen seats in the State House. (State Senate: 30 Democrats, 20 Republicans; State House: 67 Democrats, 33 Republicans)

The scandals had a big effect on voter interest. The percentage of voters turning out to cast a ballot in Montana dipped below 70% for the first time since 1942. Only 69.7% of registered voters cast ballots in this election.

Hard Times Are Here Again: 1976-1987

The boom of the state's economy took a turn for the worst during this period. High interest rates and inflation slowed growth to a trickle. Later on, agriculture prices fell and demand for coal all but vanished when the foreign oil market stabilized. In 1977, the struggling Anaconda Company was bought out by Atlantic Richfield (ARCO). The new owner quickly closed the smelter in Anaconda and the refinery in Great Falls. Finally, in 1983, ARCO closed the mines in Butte, the heart of the city's economy.

As a result of the bust of the 80's, Montana experienced an exodus of residents moving from rural areas to cities. Many people left the state all together. During this period, 95 out of 137 towns and cities in Montana lost population. The most significant percentages were the decline in rural eastern Montana counties.

A few of Montana's urban areas experienced reasonable growth. Billings, which had already surpassed Great Falls as the largest city in 1970, had more than 14,000 people move into its city limits. In the west, Missoula saw its population grow with an influx of almost 10,000 residents. The further erosion of rural Montana caused candidates to stray less from the urban population centers of the state and focus on different issues.

Ron Marlenee represented Montana's eastern district in the U.S. Congress from 1977-1993.Photo from the Mike Mansfield collection of the K. Ross Toole Archives at the Maureen and Mike Mansfield Library.

This period also marked an era of renewed competition. At the state level, Democrats still held the governor's seat, both Senate seats and the western congressional district, but Republicans regained the eastern congressional seat and often controlled at least one house in the state legislature. Voters also handed Republican presidential candidates large majorities. It seems that political schizophrenia, which is often used to characterize Montana's politics, had returned. In 1984, voters re-elected Democratic governor, Ted Schwinden, with 70% while giving Republican President, Ronald Reagan, the largest majority since FDR.

1976

Watergate was still very much an issue in 1976, but the larger issue was "Who do you trust?" Georgia's Democratic governor, Jimmy Carter, won the party's nomination as a Washington outsider. He ran on a ticket of restoring America's faith in their government. President Ford, on the other hand, still faced questions of the controversial pardoning of the scandal-ridden Nixon. He was behind in most polls as the campaign commenced.

Throughout the campaign, both candidates made numerous gaffs. The most famous were Ford's assertion in a debate that Eastern European countries, like Poland, were free from Soviet domination and Jimmy Carter's interview with Playboy magazine where he admitted to lusting after women other than his wife. Ford closed the gap towards the end, but it wasn't enough. Montana voted like other states in the Rocky

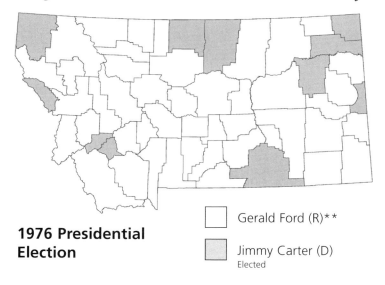

1976 Presidential Election

☐ Gerald Ford (R)**

▨ Jimmy Carter (D)
Elected

Mountain West and gave its four electoral votes to Ford. (Carter, 45%; Ford, 53%)

In 1976, Montana had to decide who would fill the big shoes left by the retiring Mike Mansfield—the longest serving majority leader in history. Stanley Burger, a Republican, faced off with the popular congressman of the East, Democrat John Melcher. Burger, a former executive of the Montana Farm Bureau, was a newcomer to politics. He ran with endorsements from Ford and criticized Melcher for being a big spender. With an endorsement from the outgoing Mansfield, Melcher ran his campaign with the banner, "You know John Melcher stands with Montana." Despite being outspent two to one, Melcher leveled his opponent in the November election.[46] (Melcher, 64%; Burger, 36%)

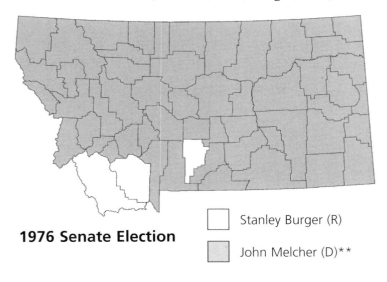

1976 Senate Election

☐ Stanley Burger (R)

▨ John Melcher (D)**

In the seat left by Melcher in the East, Republicans nominated Ron Marlenee, a rancher-businessman from Scobey, to take on Democrat Tom Towe. Marlenee, who had never held public office, voiced a conservative message of lower taxes and less government regulation. His slogan: "One of us for US Congress." Towe was a stark contrast to the Republican. He was a liberal Democrat legislator who practiced law. Towe focused on agricultural issues, but his campaign was not taken seriously by many conservative-minded rural voters. Marlenee recaptured this traditionally Republican district for the GOP. (Marlenee, 55%; Towe, 45%)

Bill Diehl, a Republican, took on one-term congressman, Max Baucus, in Montana's First District. Diehl, a real estate developer from Helena, called Baucus a big spender and an advocate of gun control. At one point during the campaign, the Republican made the fatal mistake of saying Montana was getting too much federal money.[47] Baucus denied the pro-gun control label. After his first year in Congress, he mailed his voting record to every household in the Western District, which brought about a franking abuse charge

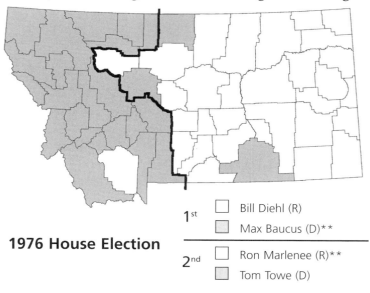

1976 House Election

1st
☐ Bill Diehl (R)
☐ Max Baucus (D)**

2nd
☐ Ron Marlenee (R)**
☐ Tom Towe (D)

from his opponent.[48] Despite these hurdles, Baucus coasted to re-election. (Baucus, 66%; Diehl, 34%)

The race for governor was not unlike the race for president. Candidates charged opponents with scandalous behavior and proclaimed themselves as someone Montanans could trust. The incumbent, Tom Judge, had a stable economy to boast of in his re-election bid.[49] He faced charges of failing to disclose over $94,000 in campaign contributions, however, and his opponent, Attorney General Bob Woodahl, made sure voters knew about it.[50]

But Woodahl, the first Republican Attorney General since the Depression, faced problems of his own. The Supreme Court of Montana found him in contempt of court in a case dealing with worker's compensation. With this dominating any coverage of a campaign message, the Republican had a tough time communicating with voters. Judge won re-election handily. (Judge, 62%; Woodahl, 37%)

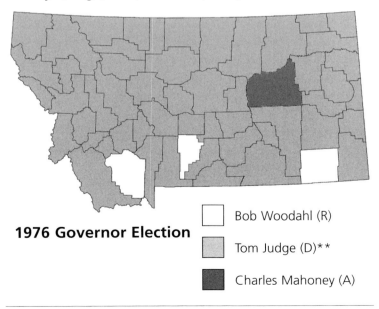

1976 Governor Election

☐ Bob Woodahl (R)

▨ Tom Judge (D)**

■ Charles Mahoney (A)

Republicans cut Democratic majorities in the State Senate by five seats to produce a partisan tie. In the State House, Republicans picked up ten seats. (State Senate: 25 Democrats, 25 Republicans; State House: 57 Democrats, 43 Republicans) 75% of registered voters turned out for the election.

1978

High inflation coupled with skyrocketing interest rates were on all America's mind when voting in 1978. A tax revolt, which started with a citizen movement in California, was seen by many supporters as a way to curb government spending and bringing prosperity back. Candidates voiced their diagnosis and remedies for the economic woes, but it was the electorate who had the final word.

Senator Lee Metcalf died in January of 1978, just one year before his term was up, and Governor Judge appointed Paul Hatfield, the Montana Supreme Court Chief Justice, to fill the vacancy. He wouldn't be there long, however. Western Congressman, Max Baucus, beat Hatfield in the Democratic primary by over 60,000 votes. In the general election, Baucus faced Republican newcomer, Larry Williams.

Williams was a young financial guru who had made his fortune in real estate investments. His campaign called for decreases in foreign aid, term limits for members of Congress and the abolition of Indian reservations.[51] The main focus of the campaign was the growing tax revolt throughout the country. Both candidates tried to prove that they would be they most effective tool in Washington for lowering America's tax burden. Baucus rushed to co-sponsor tax cut legislation for the 1979 Congress, but Williams said it wasn't enough.[52]

The campaign eventually turned ugly. Pictures of a longhaired, love-bead wearing Williams surfaced. The photo contrasted the conservative image the Republican had portrayed throughout his campaign. The Williams camp cried foul. Both candidates accused their opponent of distorting records or statements. After filing complaints, the American Arbitration Association was brought in to settle all disputes. Both were absolved of any wrongdoing, but only Baucus would come out on top on Election Day. (Baucus, 56%; Williams, 44%)

The Western seat left open by Baucus was any-

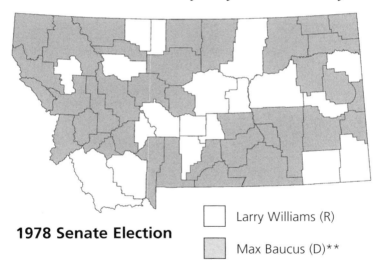

1978 Senate Election

☐ Larry Williams (R)

◼ Max Baucus (D)**

thing but a battleground. Democrat Pat Williams, who ran against Baucus in the 1974 primary, faced off with Republican Jim Waltermire. Williams had strong support from environmental and union groups while Waltermire stuck with the conservative message of fiscal responsibility and tax cuts. In one of the largest door-to-door campaigns in Montana history, the Democrat's campaign visited over 70,000 homes in the western half of the state. Williams won handily on Election Day. (Williams, 57%; Waltermire, 43%)

In the East, incumbent Ron Marlenee was challenged by Democrat Tom Monahan, a former Public Service Commissioner from Billings. Marlenee stuck to his anti-federal message of lower spending and less bureaucracy while Monahan attacked big oil as the cause for rising interest rates and inflation.[53] Marlenee's message resonated well with voters and he was returned to Washington. (Marlenee, 57%; Monahan, 43%)

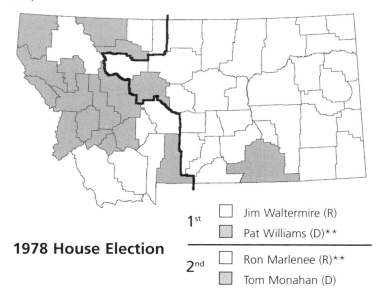

1978 House Election

1st   ☐ Jim Waltermire (R)
    ▨ Pat Williams (D)**

2nd   ☐ Ron Marlenee (R)**
    ▨ Tom Monahan (D)

Few legislative seats shifted in this off-year election, but it was enough to change control of the state Senate. Democrats lost one seat in that body and another three in the State House. (State Senate: 25 Republicans, 24 Democrats; State House: 54 Demo-

*Max Baucus repre-
sented Montana's
western district in the
U.S. Congress from
1975-1979. He was
later elected to the
U.S. Senate in 1979
and has won re-elec-
tion four times. Photo
from the Mike
Mansfield collection
of the K. Ross Toole
Archives at the
Maureen and Mike
Mansfield Library.*

crats, 45 Republicans) 72% of registered voters turned out for the election.

1980

"Are you better off than you were four years ago?" That's the question Republicans were asking voters all over the country in 1980. The resounding answer was usually "no" since inflation and interest rates were still killing the economy. Foreign policy was also on the electorate's mind as a bitter war raged between Iraq and the nation holding American citizens hostage, Iran. The Soviet invasion of Afghanistan added to the image of international insecurity and communist resurgence.

This feeling that America could do better propelled Republican Ronald Reagan, a former actor and two-term governor of California, into the White House. The Republican had made three other attempts at the White House, but this was the first time he had gained the

GOP nomination. Some viewed his old age as a factor, but his warm delivery of a national renewal message attracted many voters. Reagan held on to a sizeable lead after doing well in debates against his opponent, incumbent Democrat Jimmy Carter. In Montana, Reagan won a resounding victory. (Reagan, 57%; Carter, 32%, Anderson 8%)

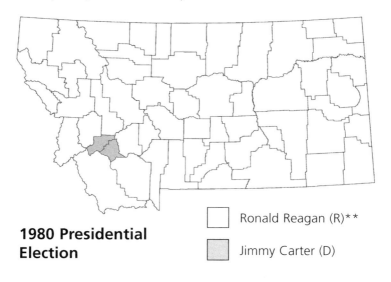

1980 Presidential Election

☐ Ronald Reagan (R)**

▨ Jimmy Carter (D)

The race for Montana governor had an interesting twist. Lieutenant Governor Ted Schwinden ran against his boss, Governor Tom Judge in the Democratic primary. Schwinden launched his campaign and chose a running mate when Judge was out of the country for a month. Schwinden said he made the decision before Judge had decided to run for a third term and only after many Democratic legislators recruited him for the nomination.[54]

The race focused on the candidates' personalities rather than actual issues. Schwinden alluded to mismanagement at the executive level. His campaign efforts were volunteer-heavy at the grassroots level since his war chest was smaller than the incumbent's.[55] Judge, with a late start on re-election, focused his efforts on raising money and buying media time. In the primary election, Schwinden dealt a crushing defeat to Judge who had never lost a race for public office. Schwinden won by 11,105 votes.

But that was only half the battle for Schwinden. Before he could occupy the governor's mansion, he had to beat Republican Jack Ramirez, the House Minority Leader and Billings native. Much of the campaign focused on who could create jobs—a major concern of Montanans who saw one of the largest companies in the state shut down factories and smelters in Great Falls and Anaconda. Ramirez expended much of his media focus on a call for a special session of the legislature to deal with the unemployment problem. His campaign slogan, "More jobs, less taxes," sounded like a generic conservative message, but Ramirez was actu-

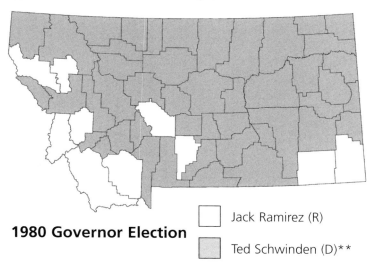

1980 Governor Election

☐ Jack Ramirez (R)

▨ Ted Schwinden (D)**

ally a moderate. He favored passage of the Equal Rights Amendment and opposed right-to-work laws.

The Democrat criticized his opponent's alleged connection to big business. He painted himself as a friend of small business and working class Montanans.[56] The same organization that helped him win the primary helped him mount a strong grassroots campaign in the general election. His personal popularity and organizational superiority helped him keep the governorship in Democratic hands. (Schwinden, 55%; Ramirez, 45%)

Montana's First District stayed solidly in the hands of Democrats as well. One-termer, Pat Williams, soundly defeated a Republican challenge mounted by Jack McDonald. The Republican, who had run in the Eastern Congressional district in 1974, stuck to a conservative pro-life, pro-business and pro-prayer in schools message. Williams coasted to victory in November. (Williams, 61%; McDonald, 39%)

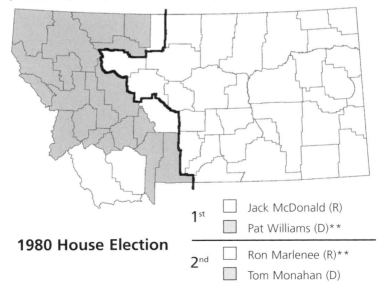

1980 House Election

1st ☐ Jack McDonald (R)
▨ Pat Williams (D)**

2nd ☐ Ron Marlenee (R)**
▨ Tom Monahan (D)

The Eastern District saw a rematch of the previous election. Democrat Tom Monahan echoed his criticisms of the oil industry and other big businesses, but he convinced fewer people this time around.[57] Marlenee was sent back to Washington for a third term. (Marlenee, 59%; Monahan, 41%)

Republicans touting the tax-cutting message won majorities in both houses of the legislature. The GOP picked up twelve seats in the State House and three seats in the State Senate. (State Senate: 28 Republicans, 22 Democrats; State House: 57 Republicans, 43 Democrats) 75% of registered voters turned out for the election.

1982

Interest rates were lowering and inflation was slowing, but in the off-year election of 1982, unemployment was close to ten percent. The President had pushed an economic reform package through Congress, but it was too soon to see any affects of the legislation. Like most off-year elections, however, the White House's party faced history's trend of losing seats in Congress and in state houses.

This meant that Republican Larry Williams faced an up-hill battle in his bid to unseat incumbent John Melcher, who was seen as an endangered Democrat. Williams, who had tried in 1978 to get a Montana Senate seat, focused much of his criticism on Melcher's dependency on out-of-state funds to run his re-election campaign. Despite his pro-choice leanings and calls for dismantling nuclear weapons, Williams had the popular President Reagan stump for him twice—once in Billings and Great Falls.

Many saw his campaign as overly negative, however. In a debate, Williams tried to make issue of a drunk driving arrest Melcher had while serving as a Congressman. This attempt largely backfired on him and the Republican was booed by the crowd.[58] His campaign benefited from large amounts of money from the National Conservative Political Action Committee (NCPAC), an out-of-state organization. These ads, which attacked Melcher, prompted the Democrat to produce ads in response. The Democratic ads, which showed talking cows discussing the money contributions from NCPAC, received national attention and became very popular throughout the state.

Embarrassing photos of a more liberal-looking Williams resurfaced in pamphlets published by the AFL-CIO, but Melcher denied any involvement.[59] The Democrat did, however, raise questions about how Williams aquired his wealth. These problems, coupled with the emergence of the Libertarian Party in Montana, gave Melcher enough votes to win a second

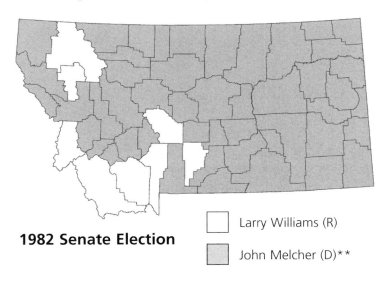

1982 Senate Election

Larry Williams (R)

John Melcher (D)**

term. (Melcher, 55%; Williams, 42%)

Pat Williams was not on any endangered list in his campaign for a third term. He had gained prominence for his fight to protect wilderness areas from oil and gas drilling. His opponent, Bob Davies, was labeled a "John Birch Republican" by many in the liberal First District.[60] Williams won the general election without incident. (Williams, 60%; Davies, 37%)

Eastern Congressman faced a tougher challenge from Democrat Howard Lyman, an agri-businessman with a more conservative-leaning philosophy than other challengers Marlenee had faced in the past. He criticized the Republican's vote to give members of Congress as $19,000 tax exemption and his vote against the 1981 farm bill.[61] Marlenee pointed out Lyman's personal financial difficulties and alluded that he couldn't manage the country's budget if he could handle his own. In November, Marlenee fought off the strong challenge and returned to DC. (Marlenee, 54%;

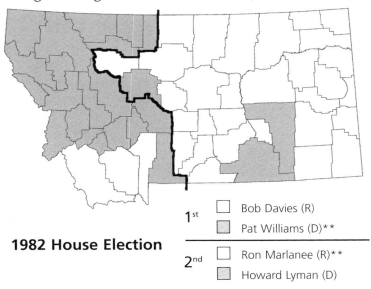

1982 House Election

1st — Bob Davies (R)
— Pat Williams (D)**

2nd — Ron Marlanee (R)**
— Howard Lyman (D)

Lyman, 44%)

In the state legislature, Democrats picked up seats in both chambers including enough seats to take the State House. (State Senate: 26 Republicans, 24 Democrats; State House: 55 Democrats, 45 Republicans) 74% of registered voters turned out for the election.

1984

Four years of cutting taxes and increased spending kept interest rates and inflation under control, but federal deficits had grown immensely. Reagan, who faced a challenge from former Vice-President Walter Mondale, was far ahead in the polls. He claimed that his administration had "given America back her spirit." The Republican neutralized the age issue in a debate and continued his tough on communism rhetoric.

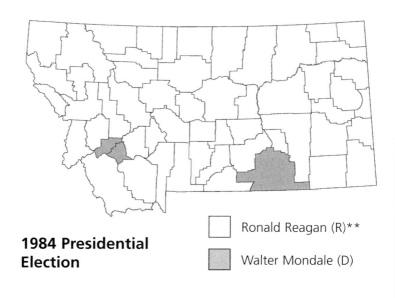

1984 Presidential Election

☐ Ronald Reagan (R)**

▨ Walter Mondale (D)

Mondale took issue with the rising deficits and called for spending cuts to slash them by two-thirds. In his party's convention, the Democrat rather bluntly promised to raise America's taxes. In November, America stuck with Reagan. Montana gave Reagan the largest majority given to a presidential candidate since 1896. (Reagan, 61%; Mondale 38%)

But voters under the Big Sky proved that political party meant little and incumbency meant everything when they supported the status quo of both parties with large pluralities. In the U.S. Senate race, Democrat Max Baucus worked towards a second term as Montana's junior senator. Chuck Cozzens, a Billings businessman and former state legislator, was nominated by the Republicans to oppose Baucus. Cozzens called for fiscal responsibility in spending through a balanced budget amendment to the Constitution. In radio ads, he called Baucus a "wimp"—a label that drew criticism from all corners, including the Reagan camp.[62]

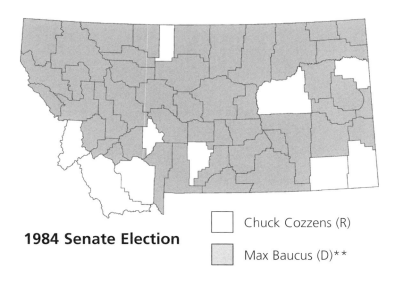

□ Chuck Cozzens (R)

1984 Senate Election

▨ Max Baucus (D)**

Baucus said that a balanced budget amendment was not feasible because it would take seven years to implement.[63] He called for a freeze in federal spending to remedy rising deficits. Voters preferred his option and re-elected him. (Baucus, 57%; Cozzens, 41%)

Republicans denied that their candidate for governor, Pat Goodover, was a sacrificial lamb, but many high ranked GOP officials passed on the opportunity to take on the popular governor, Ted Schwinden.[64] The incumbent had governed conservatively and had even placed his home phone number in the Helena phone directory. Goodover, a Great Falls businessman and state senator, said that Montana's property taxes and severance taxes on key industries where too high. Much of the debate focused on balancing the state's budget, which had become problematic over the past three years. Goodover's campaign did little to convince the electorate and was outspent five to one.[65] (Schwinden, 70%; Goodover, 26%)

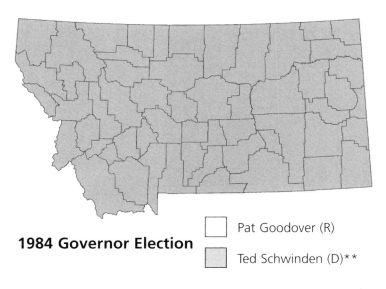

1984 Governor Election

Pat Goodover (R)

Ted Schwinden (D)**

Montana's First Congressional District race was also uneventful. Republican Gary Carlson, the former superintendent of Ravalli County schools, took on Democrat Pat Williams. Carlson focused on his support of President Reagan's policies, but he too was out-spent. Williams campaigned on higher taxes for large corporations and defense spending cuts to shrink the federal deficit. He cruised to victory on this platform. (Williams, 66%; Carlson, 32%)

Republican Ron Marlenee had little opposition in a bid for a fifth term. Democrats chose Chet Blaylock, a veteran state senator and constitutional convention delegate, who favored balancing the budget through tax increases and decreased spending.[66] Marlenee questioned the Democrat's vote in the legislature on a gun control measure and a bill that could lead to the closure of rural schools. Despite a charge of abusing traveling privileges provided by lobbyists, Marlenee was handily re-elected. (Marlenee, 66%; Blaylock, 34%)

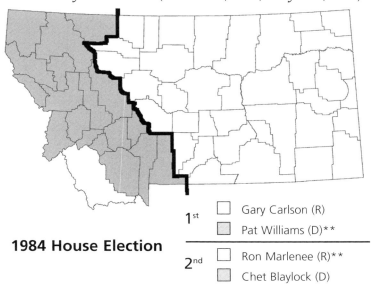

1st ☐ Gary Carlson (R)
   ■ Pat Williams (D)**

1984 House Election

2nd ☐ Ron Marlenee (R)**
   ■ Chet Blaylock (D)

The legislative races were a mixed bag. Democrats took control of the State Senate with a four seat pick-up, but Republicans took four seats from them in the State House. (State Senate: 28 Democrats, 22 Republicans; State House: 51 Democrats, 49 Republicans) 75% of registered voters turned out for the election.

1986

Again satisfied with the status quo, Montana changed little in the off-year election of 1986. Nationally, the focus was still on increased government spending. Americans were also seeing inroads with the Soviets through arms deals and direct talks.

In Eastern Montana, times were tough economically. Many residents of the Second District were either moving to Western Montana or out of the state due to agricultural woes. This gave political newcomer, Richard "Buck" O'Brien much to complain about in his campaign against incumbent Republican Ron Marlenee. O'Brien, a farmer from Conrad and member of the Montana Aeronautics Commission, criticized the administration's farm policies and Marlenee's support of those policies.[67] The Democrat came closer to anyone else, but Marlenee survived the challenge. (Marlenee, 53%; O'Brien, 47%)

Democrat Pat Williams again crushed his Republican opponent. This time Don Allen, a lobbyist for the oil industry, stepped up to the plate for the GOP.[68] Allen moved to Montana in 1975 and ran unsuccessfully for the lieutenant governor position in 1984 with Pat Goodover. He said that Williams had lost touch with the Western District and was sitting comfortably in the pockets of far-left groups.[69] Allen's message failed to touch enough voters. (Williams, 62%; Allen, 38%)

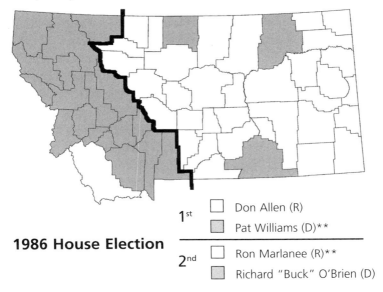

1986 House Election

1st   ☐ Don Allen (R)
      ■ Pat Williams (D)★★

2nd   ☐ Ron Marlanee (R)★★
      ■ Richard "Buck" O'Brien (D)

Some representatives and senators didn't return to Helena, but the number of Republicans and Democrats in each house of the legislature did not change. (State Senate: 28 Democrats, 22 Republicans; State House: 51 Democrats, 49 Republicans) 74% of registered voters turned out for the election.

Conservative Comeback: 1988-2002

Struggling to fit into the new economy, Montana's economic growth continued to be lackluster during this electoral cycle. After over a decade of decline, state industries of agriculture, timber and mining battled drought, fire and low demand. This stagnation proved to be so great that when a census was done in 1990, Montana lost the second congressional seat it had held since 1918. The lone congressional district was and still is the most populous district in all of Congress.

The sales tax resurfaced as an issue and was supported by politicians in both parties. In 1992, both candidates for governor endorsed the idea of a four-percent sales tax. When put to a vote of the people in 1993, the proposal was squashed by a margin of three to one.

Republicans turned the tide in 1988 when they ousted a Democratic incumbent senator and regained the governor's seat for the first time in twenty years. During the 90s, only a handful of Democrats would break the 50% barrier in the major statewide elections. By 1996, Republicans held all major statewide offices but one, and controlled both houses of the state legislature. As of 2002, only Democratic Senator, Max

Conrad Burns (left) was elected to the U.S. Senate from Montana in the election of 1988. He has won re-election twice. Photo courtesy of Senator Burns' Office.

Baucus, had survived political extinction. This new conservative era in statewide politics was the closest thing to political dominance that the Republican Party in Montana had ever seen.

Candidates' campaign expenditures are listed starting with the election of 1992.

1988

America's economic future looked bright after eight years of growth and prosperity. But the federal government was unable to control its appetite for spending, which resulted in record deficits, and a national debt calculated in trillions. Vice-President George Bush stumped for the presidency while Democrats nominated a popular Massachusetts governor, Michael Dukakis.

Surprisingly, as the two battled for the votes of Americans, the Democrat's record as governor became the center of attention. Dukakis' weekend furlough of convicted felons, objections to the death penalty and his advocacy of defense cuts led to a series of damaging commercials produced by the Bush camp. By October, it was clear that he was damaged beyond repair. Montanans threw their support behind Bush, yet the plurality was much smaller than those garnered by Reagan. (Bush, 52%; Dukakis, 46%)

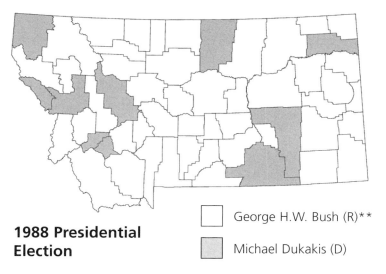

1988 Presidential Election

☐ George H.W. Bush (R)**

▨ Michael Dukakis (D)

The country's economy was healthy, but Montana was looking for political change after a decade of population decline and failing industries. The choice for governor couldn't have been clearer. Democrats nominated former two-term governor, Tom Judge on a platform of new job creation through a government-private sector partnership. He advocated economic development through increased spending on higher education and research. Republicans picked veteran state senator, Stan Stephens, who favored a laissez-faire approach to business and jobs.

The two candidates traded barbs on who could turn the state's economy around. Judge attacked Stephens voting record in the legislature as anti-education and anti-environment. The Republican rebutted by accusing Judge of expanding the bureaucracy and government regulation as governor. In November, Montanans chose to end twenty years of Democratic control in the governor's office by electing Stephens. (Stephens, 52%; Judge, 46%)

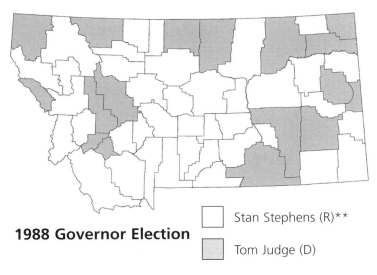

1988 Governor Election

☐ Stan Stephens (R)**

▨ Tom Judge (D)

Republicans created an even bigger upset in the US Senate race. Democrat John Melcher ran a lackluster campaign for re-election against Yellowstone County Commissioner and former Northern Ag

Network broadcaster, Conrad Burns. Melcher was considered a conservative by liberals and a liberal by conservatives. Many saw his voting record as inconsistent; giving Burns plenty of ammunition. The Republican campaigned vigorously on a no new taxes pledge and staunch opposition to the wilderness bill Melcher tried to push through Congress.[70] His personable, folksy style of communication drew many to his candidacy. Burns made history on Election Day by becoming only the second Republican to be popularly elected to the U.S. Senate from Montana. (Burns, 52%; Melcher, 48%)

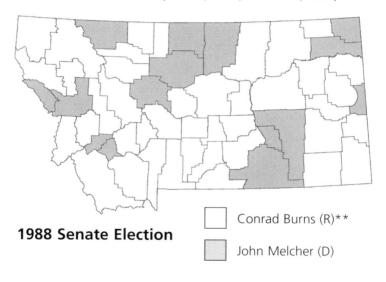

1988 Senate Election

☐ Conrad Burns (R)**

☐ John Melcher (D)

Pat Williams easily won re-election in a race against political novice, Jim Fenlason. The Republican was a twenty-nine year old accountant from Bozeman who ran on an anti-tax platform.[71] He highlighted his campaign with a no new taxes pledge done in front of the Internal Revenue Service building in Missoula. Making little waves, Fenlason's campaign failed to register on the public radar. (Williams, 61%; Fenlason, 39%)

Buck O'Brien tried once again to topple incumbent Ron Marlenee in the Eastern District. The Democrat called Marlenee a "national embarrassment" and "ineffective," but he faired worse in his second bid for the congressional seat.[72] (Marlenee, 56%; O'Brien, 44%)

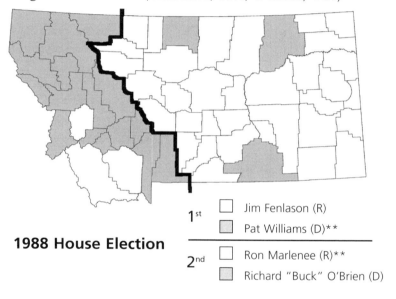

1988 House Election

1st ☐ Jim Fenlason (R)
     ▨ Pat Williams (D)**

2nd ☐ Ron Marlenee (R)**
     ▨ Richard "Buck" O'Brien (D)

The GOP picked up five seats in the state senate to take control. Democrats retained a slim majority in the state House with a gain of one seat. (State Senate: 27 Republicans, 23 Democrats; State House: 52 Democrats, 48 Republicans) 75% of registered voters turned out for the election.

1990

In 1990, Congress worked almost right up until election week on a bill aimed to reduce the deficits largely through tax increases on the wealthy. Every member of the Montana delegation voted against the package. The country was also close to war in the Persian Gulf area after Iraq invaded neighboring Kuwait. President Bush juggled these domestic and foreign affairs as he tried to limit the off-year election losses to GOP incumbents.

Incumbents in Montana's congressional races faced weak challengers with little money and poor name recognition. In the East, Don Burris, a former Social Security administrative judge won the Democratic nomination, but received no support from the DCCC. He rapped Marlenee votes on agricultural and Social Security issues, but he remained relatively unknown to the electorate. Marlenee won handily. (Marlenee, 63%; Burris, 37%)

In the West, Brad Johnson, a businessman from Bozeman, challenged Democrat Pat Williams. Johnson criticized Williams' support of the National Endowment of the Arts funding because of some questionable projects. Conservatives labeled the Democrat "Porno Pat"

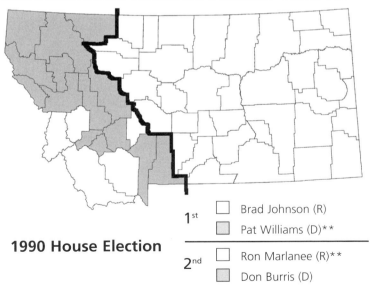

1990 House Election

1st ☐ Brad Johnson (R)
   ▓ Pat Williams (D)**

2nd ☐ Ron Marlanee (R)**
    ▓ Don Burris (D)

in a smear campaign because of the risqué items funded through the NEA.[73] Unmoved by criticism, the Democrat weathered the storm and returned to Washington. (Williams, 61%; Johnson, 39%)

National GOP figures recruited lieutenant governor, Allen Kolstad, to take on incumbent Democrat Max Baucus. Keeping in mind Melcher's overconfidence two years earlier, Baucus raised a sizeable war chest from many PACs. Kolstad tried to replicate Burns' campaign by calling the Democrat a "tax and spend liberal."[74] He also criticized Baucus' votes against cuts in defense spending and his dependence on out of state donors.

Most polls show that Kolstad never came close to Baucus at anytime during the campaign. Baucus accused his opponent of "allowing special interests to roam free in the halls of government" during his time in the state legislature.[75] The Democrat never failed to respond to the attack ads of his opponent. His vote

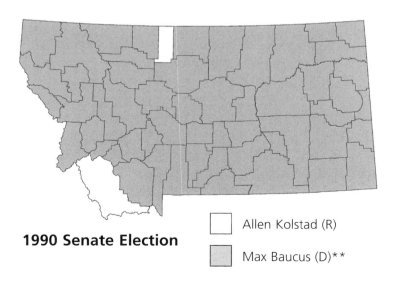

1990 Senate Election

☐ Allen Kolstad (R)

▨ Max Baucus (D)**

Pat Williams represented Montana's western district in the U.S. Congress from 1979-1993. When Montana lost a seat in Congress, Williams was elected to represent the entire state from 1993-1997. Photo from the Mike Mansfield collection of the K. Ross Toole Archives at the Maureen and Mike Mansfield Library.

against the deficit reduction bill, which many considered a heavy burden on Western states, solidified his re-election. (Baucus, 68%; Kolstad, 29%)

Buoyed by a considerable grassroots campaign from the Baucus camp, Democrats made gains in both houses of the legislature. Republicans lost six seats in the state senate and nine seats in the state house. (State Senate: 29 Democrats, 21 Republicans; State House: 61 Democrats, 39 Republicans) 75% of registered voters turned out for the election.

1992

Montana voters were clearly divided in 1992. Candidates running for president, Congress and governor made clear distinctions between their positions and those of their opponents. The race for president was a choice between change, represented by Governor Bill Clinton of Arkansas, and more of the same, advocated by incumbent George Bush. Bush's favorable rating in the polls had dropped considerably from the ninety percent approval he received after the Persian Gulf War. This was due largely to his handling of the nation's economy, which was now bogged down in recession. The country was disinterested in foreign policy victories like the fall of the Berlin Wall and the end of the Soviet Union. Instead voters focused on the candidates' economic positions and plans for the future.

But another factor made the race much like a repeat of the 1912 presidential race. Billionaire Ross Perot threw his hat in the race as an independent with a focus on fiscal discipline. As a political and Washington outsider, Perot captured the support of millions who were looking for a fresh perspective. His candidacy was especially attractive to Montanans who

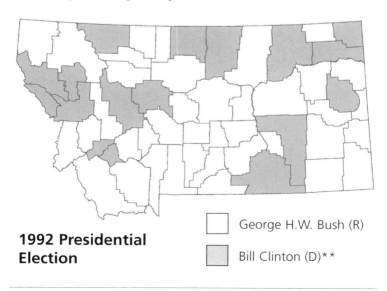

1992 Presidential Election

George H.W. Bush (R)

Bill Clinton (D)**

gave him one of his highest percentages in the country.

Clinton ended up capturing Montana's electoral votes and the presidency on a promise to revive the economy and cut the federal deficit. He was the first Democrat to do so in Montana since 1964. His total, however, was less then impressive in the three-way race. (Clinton, 38%; Bush, 35%; Perot, 26%)

The Congressional race also proved to be an exciting match between two entrenched veterans. In 1990, the census showed that Montana had suffered a large enough population decline to limit the state to one seat in the House of Representatives. This pitted liberal Democrat Pat Williams and conservative Republican Ron Marlenee against each other for the role of Montana's lone voice in Congress. The race was one of the most watched contests in the national press.

Both candidates had a diagnosis for rising deficits—Williams blamed the trickle-down economics of Reagan-Bush while Marlenee said that the tax-and-spend liberals in Congress were to blame. The

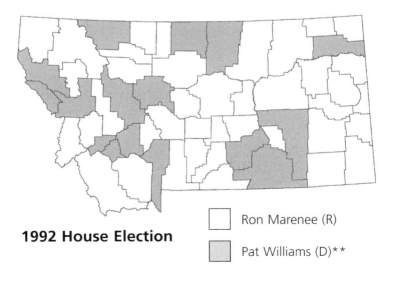

1992 House Election

Ron Marenee (R)

Pat Williams (D)**

Democrat countered by calling the Republican a big spender due to his heavy reliance on the Congressional franking privilege. Marlenee heavily criticized a wilderness bill that Williams had tried to push through.[76]

In this referendum of sorts on Montana's direction, Williams was able to siphon more votes from Marlenee's Eastern District than the Republican could from the West. Williams won every county with large urban populations to give him the edge he needed. (Williams, 51%; Marlenee, 47%) (Williams: $1,534,200; Marlenee: $1,292,583)

The race for governor was also a close contest. One-term governor, Stan Stephens, declined to run again because of health problems. This opened up the race for Republican Attorney General, Marc Racicot, and veteran Democrat legislator, Dorothy Bradley, of Bozeman. Bradley had a slim lead in polls taken at the beginning of the race. This prompted Racicot to go on the attack by labeling Bradley a tax-and-spend liberal for her voting record in the legislature and criticizing

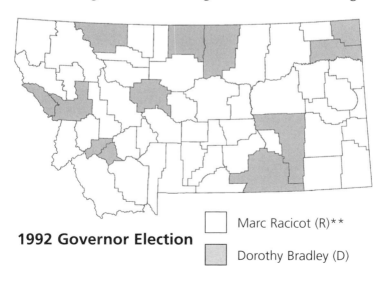

1992 Governor Election

☐ Marc Racicot (R)**

▨ Dorothy Bradley (D)

her for accepting too much out-of-state money.[77]

Most of the campaign focused on the two tax plans presented by the candidates. Surprisingly, both called for a four-percent sales tax. Similarities stopped when the candidates talked about what they would do with the money. Bradley said the state needed the money to balance the budget and give education a shot in the arm. Racicot called for spending cuts and a cut in property and income taxes. The results were close, but Racicot edged Bradley on Election Day. (Racicot, 51%; Bradley, 49%) (Racicot: $1,045,228; Bradley: $998,117)

Republicans lost one seat in the state senate, but they surprised everyone by taking back the state House with a whopping fourteen-seat pick-up. (State Senate: 30 Democrats, 20 Republicans; State House: 53 Republicans, 47 Democrats) 79% of registered voters turned out for the election.

1994

After campaigning as a "New Democrat" in his successful presidential campaign, Bill Clinton took a hard left in his first two years as chief executive. He advocated allowing open homosexuals in the military, proposed new taxes and sent a bill calling for national-ized health care to Congress. Republicans used these unpopular initiatives to their advantage while they campaign in the off-year election of 1994.

378 candidates for Congress around the country signed the GOP's "Contract With America" to show their desire for conservative change. The Contract called for a balanced budget, welfare reform, term lim-its on members of Congress and cuts in government spending. Conservatives and adherents of Ross Perot

stormed the polls to cast their votes for candidates with this message; On Election Day, they gave Republicans control of both houses of Congress for the first time in forty years.

Republican Conrad Burns echoed this conservative message in his quest for a second term. Challenging him was Jack Mudd, a Vietnam veteran and former law school dean from Missoula. Mudd beat two other Democrats in the primary, including former Senator John Melcher, to win the chance to take on Burns.

Mudd attacked Burns' lobbyist-funded trips abroad and his support of items in the Contract With America. Burns criticized Mudd for saying he would have voted for Clinton's tax hikes. He outspent Mudd and overcame a racially insensitive remark at the end of the campaign. Burns was easily re-elected.[78] (Burns, 62%; Mudd, 38%) (Burns: $3,243,392; Mudd: $1,107,591)

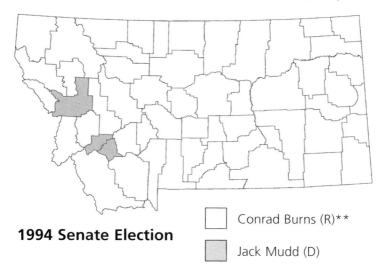

1994 Senate Election

☐ Conrad Burns (R)**

▨ Jack Mudd (D)

Montana's lone congressman, Pat Williams, faced another tough re-election battle. Former U.S. Bureau of Land Management director, Cy Jamison, stepped up to challenge the liberal Democrat.[79] Although Jamison didn't sign the Contract With America, he voiced support for almost every item it contained. He supported term limits and a balanced budget amendment. He criticized Clinton's tax increases and universal health care bill—items that Williams supported in the last session. Williams did, however, go against the president by voting against the Brady gun-control bill.

Independent Steve Kelly, a Bozeman sculptor and environmental activist threw his hat in the ring and focused his attention on wilderness protection. Many Democrats feared that he would be a spoiler in Williams' re-election, but the incumbent managed to win a plurality of votes in November. (Williams, 49%; Jamison, 42%; Kelly, 9%) (Williams: $743,721; Jamison, $436,943; Kelly: $17,382)

The national lean towards the GOP and a favorable redistricting plan helped Republicans in Montana make gains in both houses of the legislature. They picked up fourteen seats in the State House and eleven seats in the State Senate. (State House: 67 Republicans, 33 Democrats; State Senate: 31 Republicans, 19 Democrats) 70% of registered voters turned out for the election.

1996

Many of the items in the Contract With America had passed in one form or another—and that posed a problem for the GOP. Proposals like welfare reform, balancing the budget and spending cuts became reality, which gave Republicans little to campaign for and little to offer.

Bob Dole, the Republican nominee for president and former Senate Majority Leader from Kansas, took shots at dozens of Clinton's positions, but none really seemed to resonate with voters. He finally settled on attacking Clinton's character. But with the economy booming, and no major foreign policy gaffs, Clinton cruised to victory. Although Perot resurfaced under the Reform Party label, he failed to make the same impact as the 1992 election. Montana, like other Rocky Mountain states, voted for Dole. (Dole, 44%; Clinton, 41%; Perot, 14%)

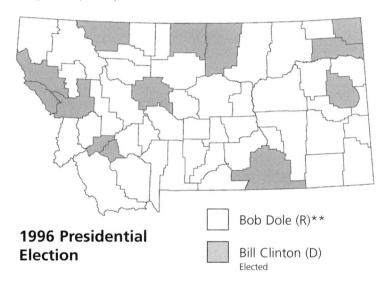

1996 Presidential Election

☐ Bob Dole (R)**

▨ Bill Clinton (D)
Elected

Incumbent Democrat Max Baucus faced a serious challenge from Lieutenant Governor Denny Rehberg. Baucus was seen as the most vulnerable Democratic Senator in national pundits' eyes. This was due largely to his support of gun control measures and Clinton's tax increases. Baucus claimed that he fought off deep cuts in Medicare, Medicaid and education.

But the campaign focused largely on trifle issues, which were communicated through negative attack ads on television and radio. Rehberg claimed that Baucus was out of touch with Montana because he got his haircut at a fancy salon for $100 and voted himself a raise in salary. He also featured an image of Baucus dancing to a tune, "Max Baucus does the wishy-washy"—a charge that the Democrat flip-flopped on issues important to Montana.[80]

The incumbent countered by accusing Rehberg of advocating cuts in programs to the elderly.[81] He also featured an ad quoting Rehberg on cutting AIDS funding.[82] Although Rehberg was outspent, he kept Baucus below 50%. This wasn't enough, however, to take his Senate seat. (Baucus, 49.6%; Rehberg, 45%) (Baucus: $3,748,502; Rehberg: $1,358,165)

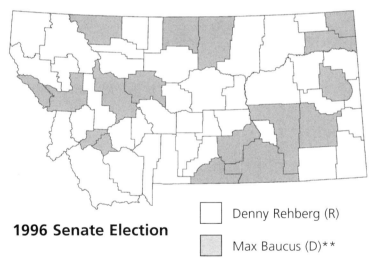

1996 Senate Election

☐ Denny Rehberg (R)

▨ Max Baucus (D)**

After nine-terms in Congress, Pat Williams called it quits in 1996. This opened the gates for many challengers on both sides of the fence. The Republicans nominated Helena businessman and former state party chairman, Rick Hill, while Democrats chose former EPA regional director, Bill Yellowtail.

This race was also highlighted by off-topic jabs.

Revelations surfaced that Yellowtail had burglarized a store in college, slapped his wife, and failed to pay child support. Hill seemingly tried to remain above any personal issues, but his ex-wife revealed that he had indulged in an affair while they were married. When the dust settled, Hill's organization triumphed in the general election. (Hill, 52%; Yellowtail, 43%) (Hill: $943,062; Yellowtail: $641,492)

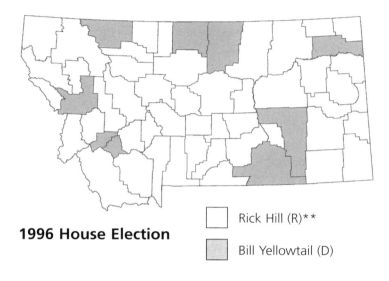

1996 House Election

☐ Rick Hill (R)**

▨ Bill Yellowtail (D)

Incumbent governor Marc Racicot coasted to re-election in a bid for a second term. Chet Blaylock, a twenty-year veteran of the state legislature, ran on the Democratic ticket. A few weeks before the election, Blaylock died of a heart attack on the way to a debate. His running mate, Judy Jacobson, a former legislator from Butte, stepped up to fill Blaylock's spot. Racicot was very popular, however, and the little known Jacobson had no time to mount a campaign of her own. Just before the election, the governor requested the legislature to give tax refunds to Montanans because of a budget surplus. He received one of the largest majorities in Treasure State history. (Racicot, 81%; Jacobson, 19%) (Racicot: $662,278; Jacobson: $72,224)

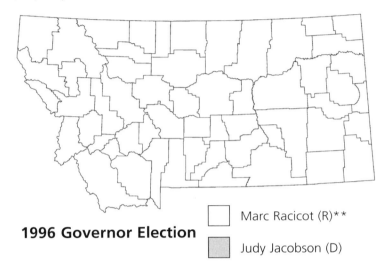

1996 Governor Election

☐ Marc Racicot (R)**

▨ Judy Jacobson (D)

Republicans increased their margin in the State Senate by three seats but lost two in the State House. (State Senate: 34 Republicans, 16 Democrats; State House: 65 Republicans, 35 Democrats) 71% of registered voters turned out for the election.

1998

Many across the county considered the election of 1998 as a national referendum on the impeachment of the president. Clinton was caught in a lie regarding a sexual relationship he had indulged in with White House intern, Monica Lewinsky, and Republicans salivated at the chance to make him only the second chief executive ever to be impeached. Voter disgust was high resulting in record low voter turnouts. Montana was no exception. Voter turnout in Montana reached an all-time low of 53%.

In the only statewide race of the election, Rick Hill faced Democrat Dusty Deschamps, a long-time county attorney from Missoula. The race centered around Social Security.[83] Hill favored a new system allowing younger Americans to have individual accounts. Deschamps criticized this "privatization" idea. The Democrat did better than many thought a newcomer could do against an incumbent, but it wasn't enough. (Hill, 53%; Deschamps, 44%) (Hill: $1,228,097; Deschamps: $705,914)

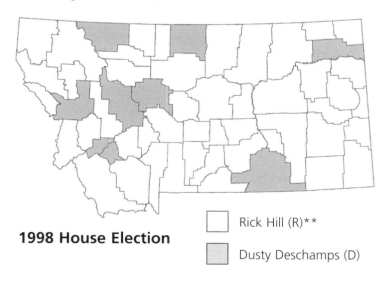

1998 House Election

Rick Hill (R)**

Dusty Deschamps (D)

Democrats cut away at the GOP majorities in the state legislature. Republicans lost six seats in the State House and two seats in the State Senate. (State House: 59 Republicans, 41 Democrats; State Senate: 32 Republicans, 18 Democrats.

2000

It seemed as though Vice President Al Gore had everything going for him in his bid for the presidency in 2000: relative peace in the world, high employment and a growing economy. In the age of television, however, Gore struggled to overcome his wooden image. Republicans nominated the folksy governor of Texas and son of a former chief executive, George W. Bush.

The two battled it out in a close election for the American people's votes, which ended with disputed election results in Florida and a pro-Bush Supreme Court decision. Bush squeaked out a razor-thin Electoral College win, but Al Gore received a majority of the popular vote. Montanans, who were largely angered by the Clinton administration's policies for Western states, supported the Republican. (Bush 58%; Gore 33%; Nader, 6%)

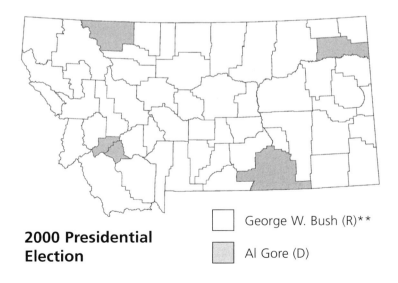

2000 Presidential Election

☐ George W. Bush (R)**

▨ Al Gore (D)

Incumbent Conrad Burns faced a surprisingly strong challenge from Democratic political newcomer, Brian Schweitzer. The Democrat, a mint farmer from Whitefish, went on the attack from the beginning. His populist message centered on a call for the federal government to provide low cost prescription drugs for senior citizens.[84] He also criticized the Freedom to Farm Act and a bill to limit asbestos company's liability.

The Republican had to break a promise to serve only two terms when he sought reelection. Although he had a solid twenty-point lead in most of the early polls, his challenger pulled within the margin of error by late October. His well-funded campaign spent millions on rebuttal ads defending his position and highlighting his seniority in the Senate. Schweitzer came close, but Burns came out on top on Election Day. (Burns, 51%; Schweitzer, 47%) (Burns: $4,337,961; Schweitzer: $2,033,530)

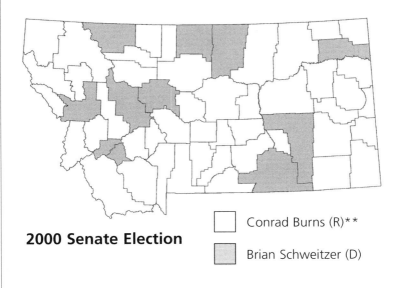

2000 Senate Election

☐ Conrad Burns (R)**

▨ Brian Schweitzer (D)

Rick Hill stepped down from his congressional seat due to health problems, leaving it open for the taking. Two experienced, well-funded candidates were nominated, giving the state a competitive battle for the lone seat. Nancy Keenan, the state superintendent of public instruction, was a liberal Democrat from Anaconda. Denny Rehberg, the former lieutenant governor and legislator, was a conservative Republican from Billings.

Both candidates ran as moderates. Rehberg often pointed out that he was running on the same ticket as George W. Bush and highlighted his experience in agriculture and business. He painted Keenan as a social liberal with values too extreme for someone representing Montana. The Democrat often mentioned her experience in education while attacking Rehberg on Social Security and education issues.[85] Rehberg gained a majority of votes with a slight edge in fundraising and a statewide grassroots campaign. (Rehberg, 51%; Keenan, 46%) (Rehberg: $2,132,364; Keenan: $1,932,099)

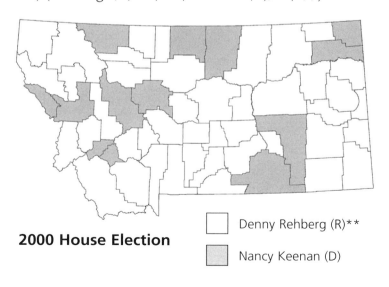

2000 House Election

Denny Rehberg (R)**

Nancy Keenan (D)

In the race for governor, the ever popular Marc Racicot was term limited from running for a third term. His second-in-command, Judy Martz, got the Republican nod. State auditor, Mark O'Keefe, fought off primary challenges from the attorney general and secretary of state in order to gain the Democratic nomination. The general election race centered on the candidates' plans for economic development in the state. Martz favored the conservative approach of cutting taxes and removing regulations impeding business growth. O'Keefe stressed that government had an important role in recruiting businesses and forming a partnership with the private sector.

Although O'Keefe spent millions of his own money on campaign communications, he could not undo the damage done when he made an anti-business statement. In effect, he said that he may be business' biggest nightmare. This statement, along with a strong Republican turnout, made Judy Martz the first female governor elected in Montana. (Martz, 51%; O'Keefe,

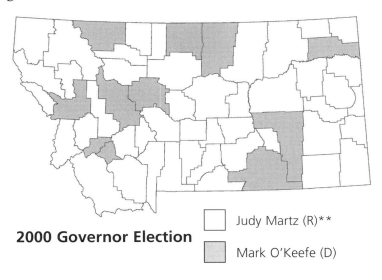

2000 Governor Election

Judy Martz (R)**

Mark O'Keefe (D)

From left to right: Lieutenant Governor Karl Ohs, Congressman Denny Rehberg, Governor Judy Martz, former Governor Marc Racicot, Senator Conrad Burns, Senator Max Baucus and President George W. Bush at a Billings rally in 2001. Photo courtesy of Congressman Rehberg's Office.

47%) (Martz: $989,726; O'Keefe: $3,002,684)

In local legislative races, Democrats again chipped away at Republican majorities, but failed to take over either house. The GOP lost one seat in each house. (State Senate: 31 Republican, 19 Democrats; State House: 58 Republicans, 41 Democrats) 60% of registered voters turned out for the election.

2002

America's outlook had changed profoundly since the last election. On September 11, 2001, terrorists destroyed domestic targets in New York, Washington, DC and Pennsylvania in a day of horror. As a result, the economy was flailing, unemployment was rising and

Americans were increasing concerned with national security. US forces had routed out the terrorist regime in Afghanistan. President Bush now focused on the regime in Iraq as America's next target. Bucking historical trends, Republicans made off-year gains on a ticket of a strong national security.

In Montana, however, the issues were more parochial. Max Baucus, with a record-setting campaign war chest, highlighted his record of job-creation and his chairmanship of the powerful Senate Finance Committee. His challenger was a wealthy legislator from Proctor, Mike Taylor. Taylor painted Baucus as a liberal who changed colors only during election years.

Baucus neutralized a potential damning issue by voting for President Bush's tax relief bill in 2001. He ran commercials showing him at press conferences at the White House next to President Bush and coupled the visual with a recording of words of praise from the popular chief executive. Taylor struggled to find a potent issue and lagged in the polls during the whole

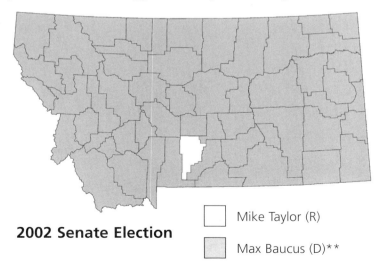

2002 Senate Election

Mike Taylor (R)

Max Baucus (D)**

campaign. The Montana Democratic Party sealed his defeat by running an embarrassing commercial of a younger Mike Taylor, then a hairdresser, wearing disco-like attire while performing a facial massage on another man. Taylor suspended his campaign and more or less conceded victory in October. (Baucus, 63%; Taylor, 32%) (Baucus: $6,189,970; Taylor: $1,839,020)

Denny Rehberg faced a weak challenge from environmental activist Steve Kelly. Democrats failed to find a stronger candidate and largely ignored their own nominee. Kelly had run for Congress earlier as an independent in 1994 against Democrat Pat Williams. He then turned Republican in 1998, and later helped form the Green Party in 2000. Kelly raised little money and little noise. (Rehberg, 65%; Kelly, 33%) (Rehberg: $949,631; Kelly: $18,757)

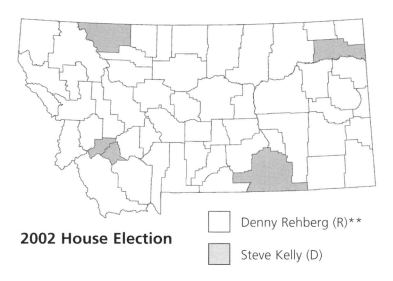

2002 House Election

Denny Rehberg (R)**

Steve Kelly (D)

In the legislative elections Democrats made slight gains, but Republicans maintained their majorities. Democrats added five members to their ranks in the

State House and two in the State Senate. (State House:
53 Republicans, 47 Democrats; State Senate: 29
Republicans, 21 Democrats) 54% of registered voters
turned out for the election.

What the Future Holds: 2004-Future

Montana has proven to be one of the least predictable states in the Rocky Mountain West. It refuses to follow in the steps of neighboring states and often confuses political pundits. There are, however, in the mess of voter turnout results and election statistics, fairly consistent trends that characterize the political landscape of Montana. These same trends will likely continue to shape campaigns and elections to come.

Progressivism still exists in pockets throughout the state. With the university town of Missoula as its Mecca, progressivism is most prevalent in environmental activists, teachers' unions and college students. It continues to be a vocal element hoping to shape state government.

Recent elections have also shown that Montanans still have a strong populist vein. The anti-big mentality of Big Sky voters has remained consistent. Whether it's bashing the big energy and drug companies or trashing a massive federal government, candidates usually can't go wrong if they're taking on the big guys.

For the time being, it is likely that Montanans will stick with Republicans when voting for president. Voters may flirt with a Democratic presidential candidate, but only if the candidate is a moderate from the

South or the West. State politics, however, are very much competitive. Democrats seem to have a better chance at winning statewide elections when the major campaign issues are parochial, such as the environment, education and health care. They run into trouble when the issues are ones where Republicans are considered strong like the Second Amendment, taxes and national security.

Republicans swept the general election in 2000, but the results are somewhat misleading. The margins of victory were relatively small and Democrats can still find hope that electoral majorities are well within reach. Both parties remain competitive and have a chance at shaping the political landscape in the coming years.

It is unclear whether or not Montana will regain a second House seat after the 2010 census. If given another seat, it is unlikely that the western and eastern district elections will be as predictable as they were prior to 1992. Aided by stronger majorities in counties such as Flathead, Gallatin and Ravalli, the GOP is stronger in the western third of the state. On the other hand, the eastern district would also see more competitive races for the U.S. House due to stronger Democratic results in Yellowstone county.

The emptying of rural Montana, especially the east, will likely continue as larger entrepreneurs swallow up smaller farms. Billings, still the largest city, has experienced steady growth and will undoubtedly remain the epicenter of eastern and south-central Montana. Western Montana, aided by the growth of Gallatin, Missoula, Flathead and Ravalli counties, has become a refuge for people seeking outdoor adventure while remaining close to urban areas. These new residents coming to Big Sky Country will likely tilt the political scales giving one of the major parties an electoral edge in elections to come.

Despite its sparse population, Montana has produced a number of legends at the state and national levels. Montanans continue to be active and interested in the political workings of their state and will undoubtedly be important participants in the future of America. No matter who controls the electoral reigns of the state, it is clear that democracy will remain alive and well in Big Sky Country.

Appendix

County Profiles

Montana Counties

Beaverhead

Founded: *1865*
County Seat: *Dillon*
Registered Voters in 2002: *5,855*
Voter Turnout in 2002: *56%*
Voter Turnout in 2000: *66%*
Current Political Preference: *Solid Republican*
Interesting Political Facts: *Beaverhead county is Montana's largest county in area.*

Big Horn

Founded: *1913*
County Seat: *Hardin*
Registered Voters in 2002: *7,323*
Voter Turnout in 2002: *56%*
Voter Turnout in 2000: *58%*
Historical Political Preference: *Solid Republican*
Current Political Preference: *Solid Democrat*

Blaine

Founded: *1912*
County Seat: *Chinook*
Registered Voters in 2002: *4,167*
Voter Turnout in 2002: *60%*
Voter Turnout in 2000: *61%*
Historical Political Preference: *Swing*
Current Political Preference: *Leans Democrat*
Interesting Political Facts: *Blaine county is one of the most accurate counties in presidential elections. It was named after James G. Blaine, former U.S. Secretary of State.*

Broadwater

Founded: *1897*
County Seat: *Townsend*
Registered Voters in 2002: *3,192*
Voter Turnout in 2002: *60%*
Voter Turnout in 2000: *60%*
Current Political Preference: *Solid Republican*

Carbon

Founded: *1895*
County Seat: *Red Lodge*
Registered Voters in 2002: *7,229*
Voter Turnout in 2002: *61%*
Voter Turnout in 2000: *63%*
Current Political Preference: *Leans Republican*

Carter

Founded: *1917*
County Seat: *Ekalaka*
Registered Voters in 2002: *907*
Voter Turnout in 2002: *73%*
Voter Turnout in 2000: *64%*
Current Political Preference: *Solid Republican*
Interesting Political Facts: *Carter county was named after Thomas H. Carter, Montana's first congressman.*

Cascade

Founded: *1887*
County Seat: *Great Falls*
Registered Voters in 2002: *48,894*
Voter Turnout in 2002: *54%*
Voter Turnout in 2000: *59%*
Historical Political Preference: *Solid Democrat*
Current Political Preference: *Leans Democrat*
Interesting Political Facts: *Cascade County is Montana's third most populated county.*

Chouteau

Founded: *1865*
County Seat: *Fort Benton*
Registered Voters in 2002: *3,938*
Voter Turnout in 2002: *68%*
Voter Turnout in 2000: *77%*
Historical Political Preference: *Leaned Democrat*
Current Political Preference: *Solid Republican*
Interesting Facts: *Fort Benton was named after U.S. Senator Thomas H. Benton of Missouri.*

Custer

Founded: *1877*
County Seat: *Miles City*
Registered Voters in 2002: *7,021*
Voter Turnout in 2002: *59%*
Voter Turnout in 2000: *56%*
Current Political Preference: *Leans Republican*

Daniels

Founded: *1920*
County Seat: *Scobey*
Registered Voters in 2002: *1,552*
Voter Turnout in 2002: *70%*
Voter Turnout in 2000: *70%*
Historical Political Preference: *Swing*
Current Political Preference: *Solid Republican*
Interesting Political Facts: *Daniel's county was home of Congressman Ron Marlenee.*

Dawson

Founded: *1869*
County Seat: *Glendive*
Registered Voters in 2002: *6,595*
Voter Turnout in 2002: *56%*
Voter Turnout in 2000: *65%*
Current Political Preference: *Leans Republican*

Deer Lodge

Founded: *1865*
County Seat: *Anaconda*
Registered Voters in 2002: *6,481*
Voter Turnout in 2002: *60%*
Voter Turnout in 2000: *62%*
Current Political Preference: *Solid Democrat*
Interesting Political Facts: *Anaconda is the former capitol of Montana. Since World War II, Deer Lodge County has been the most consistently Democratic county in the state. It is the least accurate county in presidential and governor elections. It is the second smallest county in area.*

Fallon

Founded: *1913*
County Seat: *Baker*
Registered Voters in 2002: *1,811*
Voter Turnout in 2002: *74%*
Voter Turnout in 2000: *66%*
Current Political Preference: *Solid Republican*

Fergus

Founded: *1885*
County Seat: *Lewistown*
Registered Voters in 2002: *8,385*
Voter Turnout in 2002: *63%*
Voter Turnout in 2000: *67%*
Historical Political Preference: *Leaned Republican*
Current Political Preference: *Solid Republican*
Interesting Political Facts: *Fergus County is named after James Fergus, a pioneer, miner, cattleman and territorial legislator.*

Flathead

Founded: *1893*
County Seat: *Kalispell*
Registered Voters in 2002: *53,175*
Voter Turnout in 2002: *51%*
Voter Turnout in 2000: *58%*
Historical Political Preference: *Leaned Democrat*
Current Political Preference: *Solid Republican*
Interesting Facts: *Flathead county is Montana's fourth most populated county.*

Gallatin

Founded: *1865*
County Seat: *Bozeman*
Voter Turnout in 2002: *49%*
Voter Turnout in 2000: *58%*
Current Political Preference: *Solid Republican*
Interesting Political Facts: *Gallatin county was named after the Gallatin river which got its name from former U.S. Secretary of the Treasury, Albert Gallatin. It was the home of Senator Zales Ecton. It is Montana's fifth most populated county.*

Garfield

Founded: *1919*
County Seat: *Jordan*
Registered Voters in 2002: *914*
Voter Turnout in 2002: *67%*
Voter Turnout in 2000: *69%*
Current Political Preference: *Solid Republican*
Interesting Political Facts: *Garfield county was named after former U.S. President, James A. Garfield. It is the only county that gave a majority of votes to a third-party candidate in the post-war era (1976 governor's race).*

Glacier

Founded: *1919*
County Seat: *Cut Bank*
Registered Voters in 2002: *7,821*
Voter Turnout in 2002: *45%*
Voter Turnout in 2000: *50%*
Historical Political Preference: *Leaned Democrat*
Current Political Preference: *Solid Democrat*
Interesting Political Facts: *Glacier county was home of Governor Hugo Aronson, the "Galloping Swede."*

Golden Valley

Founded: *1920*
County Seat: *Ryegate*
Registered Voters in 2002: *641*
Voter Turnout in 2002: *71%*
Voter Turnout in 2000: *81%*
Current Political Preference: *Solid Republican*
Interesting Political Facts: *The first female sheriff in Montana had her office in Ryegate.*

Granite

Founded: *1893*
County Seat: *Philipsburg*
Registered Voters in 2002: *2,207*
Voter Turnout in 2002: *62%*
Voter Turnout in 2000: *68%*
Current Political Preference: *Solid Republican*

Hill

Founded: *1912*
County Seat: *Havre*
Registered Voters in 2002: *9,922*
Voter Turnout in 2002: *55%*
Voter Turnout in 2000: *57%*
Current Political Preference: *Leans Democrat*
Interesting Political Facts: *Hill County is one of the most accurate counties in presidential elections. It was home of Governor Stan Stephens.*

Jefferson

Founded: *1865*
County Seat: *Boulder*
Registered Voters in 2002: *7,499*
Voter Turnout in 2002: *60%*
Voter Turnout in 2000: *65%*
Historical Political Preference: *Swing*
Current Political Preference: *Solid Republican*
Interesting Political Facts: *Jefferson county was named after the Jefferson River, which got its name from President Thomas Jefferson.*

Judith Basin

Founded: *1920*
County Seat: *Stanford*
Registered Voters in 2002: *1,676*
Voter Turnout in 2002: *71%*
Voter Turnout in 2000: *79%*
Historical Political Preference: *Leaned Democrat*
Current Political Preference: *Solid Republican*

Lake

Founded: *1923*
County Seat: *Polson*
Registered Voters in 2002: *17,472*
Voter Turnout in 2002: *55%*
Voter Turnout in 2000: *61%*
Current Political Preference: *Solid Republican*

Lewis & Clark

Founded: *1865*
County Seat: *Helena*
Registered Voters in 2002: *35,600*
Voter Turnout in 2002: *66%*
Voter Turnout in 2000: *63%*
Historical Political Preference: *Leaned Republican*
Current Political Preference: *Leans Democrat*
Interesting Political Facts: *Lewis & Clark county was originally named Edgerton county, which was named after Montana's first territorial governor. It was home of Governor Forrest Anderson, Senator Max Baucus and Congressman Rick Hill.*

Liberty

Founded: *1920*
County Seat: *Chester*
Registered Voters in 2002: *1,335*
Voter Turnout in 2002: *80%*
Voter Turnout in 2000: *75%*
Current Political Preference: *Solid Republican*

Lincoln

Founded: *1909*
County Seat: *Libby*
Registered Voters in 2002: *12,286*
Voter Turnout in 2002: *57%*
Voter Turnout in 2000: *58%*
Historical Political Preference: *Solid Democrat*
Current Political Preference: *Leans Republican*
Interesting Political Facts: *Lincoln county was named after U.S. President, Abraham Lincoln. It was home of Governor Marc Racicot.*

Madison

Founded: *1865*
County Seat: *Virginia City*
Registered Voters in 2002: *5,347*
Voter Turnout in 2002: *60%*
Voter Turnout in 2000: *61%*
Current Political Preference: *Solid Republican*
Interesting Political Facts: *Madison county was named after the Madison river, which got its name from former U.S. Secretary of State and future U.S. President, James Madison.*

McCone

Founded: *1919*
County Seat: *Circle*
Registered Voters in 2002: *1,477*
Voter Turnout in 2002: *75%*
Voter Turnout in 2000: *73%*
Historical Political Preference: *Leaned Democrat*
Current Political Preference: *Solid Republican*
Interesting Political Facts: *McCone county was named after State Senator George McCone.*

Meagher

Founded: *1866*
County Seat: *White Sulphur Springs*
Registered Voters in 2002: *1,277*
Voter Turnout in 2002: *62%*
Voter Turnout in 2000: *69%*
Current Political Preference: *Solid Republican*
Interesting Political Facts: *Meagher county was named after acting Montana territorial governor, Thomas Francis Meagher.*

Mineral

Founded: *1914*
County Seat: *Superior*
Registered Voters in 2002: *2,688*
Voter Turnout in 2002: *53%*
Voter Turnout in 2000: *57%*
Historical Political Preference: *Solid Democrat*
Current Political Preference: *Swing*
Interesting Political Facts: *Mineral County is one of the most accurate counties in senate elections.*

Missoula

Founded: *1865*
County Seat: *Missoula*
Registered Voters in 2002: *76,671*
Voter Turnout in 2002: *45%*
Voter Turnout in 2000: *54%*
Historical Political Preference: *Swing*
Current Political Preference: *Solid Democrat*
Interesting Political Facts: *Missoula county is Montana's second most populated county. It was home of Congressman Dick Shoup.*

Musselshell

Founded: *1911*
County Seat: *Roundup*
Registered Voters in 2002: *3,107*
Voter Turnout in 2002: *62%*
Voter Turnout in 2000: *66%*
Historical Political Preference: *Leaned Democrat*
Current Political Preference: *Solid Republican*

Park

Founded: *1887*
County Seat: *Livingston*
Registered Voters in 2002: *11,224*
Voter Turnout in 2002: *56%*
Voter Turnout in 2000: *59%*
Current Political Preference: *Solid Republican*
Interesting Political Facts: *Park County was home of Congressman Wesley D'Ewart.*

Petroleum

Founded: *1925*
County Seat: *Winnett*
Registered Voters in 2002: *397*
Voter Turnout in 2002: *66%*
Voter Turnout in 2000: *70%*
Current Political Preference: *Solid Republican*
Interesting Political Facts: *Petroleum has the smallest population of any Montana county.*

Phillips

Founded: *1915*
County Seat: *Malta*
Registered Voters in 2002: *2,997*
Voter Turnout in 2002: *62%*
Voter Turnout in 2000: *66%*
Historical Political Preference: *Swing*
Current Political Preference: *Solid Republican*
Interesting Political Facts: *Phillips county was named after State Senator, Ben D. Phillips.*

Pondera

Founded: *1919*
County Seat: *Conrad*
Registered Voters in 2002: *4,155*
Voter Turnout in 2002: *64%*
Voter Turnout in 2000: *69%*
Historical Political Preference: *Leaned Democrat*
Current Political Preference: *Solid Republican*
Interesting Political Facts: *Pondera county is one of the most accurate counties overall. Conrad was named after W.G. Conrad, a local politician.*

Powder River

Founded: *1919*
County Seat: *Broadus*
Registered Voters in 2002: *1,349*
Voter Turnout in 2002: *73%*
Voter Turnout in 2000: *76%*
Current Political Preference: *Solid Republican*

Powell

Founded: *1901*
County Seat: *Deer Lodge*
Registered Voters in 2002: *3,783*
Voter Turnout in 2002: *65%*
Voter Turnout in 2000: *67%*
Historical Political Preference: *Swing*
Current Political Preference: *Solid Republican*
Interesting Political Facts: *Powell county is one of the most accurate for senate elections and is also one of the most accurate counties overall.*

Prairie

Founded: *1915*
County Seat: *Terry*
Registered Voters in 2002: *965*
Voter Turnout in 2002: *73%*
Voter Turnout in 2000: *78%*
Current Political Preference: *Solid Republican*

Ravalli

Founded: *1893*
County Seat: *Hamilton*
Registered Voters in 2002: *26,802*
Voter Turnout in 2002: *53%*
Voter Turnout in 2000: *60%*
Historical Political Preference: *Swing*
Current Political Preference: *Solid Republican*
Interesting Political Facts: *Ravalli was home of Senator Lee Metcalf.*

Richland

Founded: *1914*
County Seat: *Sidney*
Registered Voters in 2002: *6,899*
Voter Turnout in 2002: *53%*
Voter Turnout in 2000: *52%*
Current Political Preference: *Solid Republican*
Interesting Political Facts: *Richland county was home of Governor Donald Nutter.*

Roosevelt

Founded: *1919*
County Seat: *Wolf Point*
Registered Voters in 2002: *6,584*
Voter Turnout in 2002: *48%*
Voter Turnout in 2000: *54%*
Historical Political Preference: *Leaned Democrat*
Current Political Preference: *Solid Democrat*
Interesting Political Facts: *Roosevelt county was named after U.S. President, Theodore Roosevelt. It was home of Governor Ted Schwinden.*

Rosebud

Founded: *1901*
County Seat: *Forsyth*
Registered Voters in 2002: *5,917*
Voter Turnout in 2002: *52%*
Voter Turnout in 2000: *50%*
Historical Political Preference: *Solid Republican*
Current Political Preference: *Leans Democrat*
Interesting Political Facts: *Rosebud county was home of Senator John Melcher.*

Sanders

Founded: *1905*
County Seat: *Thompson Falls*
Registered Voters in 2002: *7,294*
Voter Turnout in 2002: *57%*
Voter Turnout in 2000: *58%*
Historical Political Preference: *Solid Democrat*
Current Political Preference: *Leans Republican*
Interesting Political Facts: *Sanders county was named after Wilbur F. Sanders, U.S. Senator from Montana. It is one of the most accurate counties overall.*

Sheridan

Founded: *1913*
County Seat: *Plentywood*
Registered Voters in 2002: *2,997*
Voter Turnout in 2002: *58%*
Voter Turnout in 2000: *59%*
Current Political Preference: *Swing*

Silver Bow

Founded: *1881*
County Seat: *Butte*
Registered Voters in 2002: *23,874*
Voter Turnout in 2002: *53%*
Voter Turnout in 2000: *63%*
Current Political Preference: *Solid Democrat*
Interesting Political Facts: *Silver Bow county is Montana's smallest county in area. It was home to numerous Montana politicians: Senator Burton K. Wheeler, Senator James Murray, Senator Mike Mansfield, Governor John Bonner, Congressman Arnold Olsen, Congressman Pat Williams and Governor Judy Martz.*

Stillwater

Founded: *1913*
County Seat: *Columbus*
Registered Voters in 2002: *5,637*
Voter Turnout in 2002: *60%*
Voter Turnout in 2000: *64%*
Current Political Preference: *Solid Republican*

Sweet Grass

Founded: *1865*
County Seat: *Big Timber*
Registered Voters in 2002: *2,854*
Voter Turnout in 2002: *54%*
Voter Turnout in 2000: *68%*
Current Political Preference: *Solid Republican*
Interesting Political Facts: *Sweet Grass is Montana's most Republican county. It is the least accurate county in senate elections. It was home of Congressman Orvin Fjare.*

Teton

Founded: *1893*
County Seat: *Choteau*
Registered Voters in 2002: *4,236*
Voter Turnout in 2002: *69%*
Voter Turnout in 2000: *70%*
Historical Political Preference: *Leaned Democrat*
Current Political Preference: *Solid Republican*

Toole

Founded: *1914*
County Seat: *Shelby*
Registered Voters in 2002: *3,346*
Voter Turnout in 2002: *61%*
Voter Turnout in 2000: *67%*
Historical Political Preference: *Leaned Democrat*
Current Political Preference: Solid Republican
Interesting Political Facts: Toole county was named after the first governor of the state, Joseph K. Toole.

Treasure

Founded: *1919*
County Seat: *Hysham*
Registered Voters in 2002: *630*
Voter Turnout in 2002: *68%*
Voter Turnout in 2000: *74%*
Current Political Preference: *Solid Republican*
Interesting Political Facts: *Treasure county is Montana's second least populated county.*

Valley

Founded: *1893*
County Seat: *Glasgow*
Registered Voters in 2002: *6,005*
Voter Turnout in 2002: *60%*
Voter Turnout in 2000: *69%*
Historical Political Preference: *Leaned Democrat*
Current Political Preference: *Leans Republican*

Wheatland

Founded: *1917*
County Seat: *Harlowton*
Registered Voters in 2002: *1,525*
Voter Turnout in 2002: *56%*
Voter Turnout in 2000: *66%*
Current Political Preference: *Solid Republican*
Interesting Political Facts: *Wheatland county is the most accurate county in governor elections.*

Wibaux

Founded: *1914*
County Seat: *Wibaux*
Registered Voters in 2002: *835*
Voter Turnout in 2002: *69%*
Voter Turnout in 2000: *57%*
Historical Political Preference: *Swing*
Current Political Preference: *Solid Republican*

Yellowstone

Founded: *1883*
County Seat: *Billings*
Registered Voters in 2002: *88,334*
Voter Turnout in 2002: *54%*
Voter Turnout in 2000: *61%*
Historical Political Preference: *Solid Republican*
Current Political Preference: *Leans Republican*
Interesting Political Facts: *Yellowstone has the largest
population of any county in the state. It was home to
numerous politicians: Governor Tim Babcock,
Congressman "Big Jim" Battin, Senator Conrad Burns and
Congressman Denny Rehberg.*

Election Statistics

1946 U.S. Senate Election

COUNTIES	Leif Erickson (D)		Zales Ecton (R)		Other
Beaverhead	979	35.8%	1732	63.4%	23
Big Horn	824	33.9%	1589	65.3%	19
Blaine	1152	51.8%	1061	47.7%	13
Broadwater	368	29.9%	855	69.4%	9
Carbon	1614	42.4%	2141	56.3%	48
Carter	444	44.0%	549	54.4%	17
Cascade	9039	55.2%	7120	43.5%	206
Chouteau	1524	52.1%	1381	47.2%	19
Custer	1447	39.6%	2164	59.3%	39
Daniels	582	40.6%	831	58.0%	19
Dawson	877	35.2%	1573	63.2%	39
Deer Lodge	3527	62.2%	2062	36.4%	78
Fallon	420	34.4%	781	64.0%	19
Fergus	2367	45.5%	2799	53.8%	38
Flathead	3116	43.9%	3875	54.5%	113
Gallatin	1830	29.1%	4416	70.3%	35
Garfield	397	42.0%	545	57.7%	3
Glacier	1516	53.1%	1323	46.4%	14
Golden Valley	147	26.1%	415	73.6%	2
Granite	379	32.3%	782	66.7%	11
Hill	2043	50.5%	1959	48.4%	42
Jefferson	668	45.3%	795	53.9%	13
Judith Basin	897	50.5%	868	48.9%	10
Lake	1594	39.0%	2463	60.2%	35
Lewis & Clark	3750	43.9%	4713	55.2%	77
Liberty	397	47.2%	436	51.8%	8
Lincoln	1375	53.2%	1158	44.8%	51
Madison	630	31.9%	1325	67.2%	18
McCone	663	51.1%	609	47.0%	25
Meagher	337	33.7%	650	65.1%	12
Mineral	339	47.5%	357	50.1%	17
Missoula	4350	42.2%	5793	56.2%	160
Musselshell	1154	49.6%	1126	48.4%	45
Park	1583	37.0%	2613	61.0%	86
Petroleum	182	46.5%	205	52.4%	4
Phillips	1027	44.4%	1254	54.2%	34
Pondera	1174	57.2%	857	41.8%	21
Powder River	352	33.4%	697	66.2%	4
Powell	1006	40.7%	1433	58.0%	33
Prairie	344	33.3%	678	65.6%	12
Ravalli	1559	40.0%	2316	59.4%	26
Richland	1264	45.1%	1523	54.3%	18
Roosevelt	1504	47.0%	1667	52.1%	29
Rosebud	624	31.6%	1317	66.8%	31
Sanders	1005	43.2%	1257	54.0%	66
Sheridan	1330	55.5%	1040	43.4%	28
Silver Bow	11442	59.7%	7442	38.8%	289
Stillwater	641	33.6%	1256	65.9%	10
Sweet Grass	334	26.0%	941	73.3%	9
Teton	1172	50.3%	1143	49.1%	13
Toole	1416	51.3%	1325	48.0%	19
Treasure	217	35.9%	383	63.3%	5
Valley	1664	46.8%	1859	52.3%	31
Wheatland	422	36.3%	732	63.0%	7
Wibaux	313	39.5%	471	59.4%	9
Yellowstone	5155	35.5%	9246	63.6%	127
TOTALS	**86476**	**45.4%**	**101901**	**53.5%**	**2189**

1946 U.S. House Election, 1st District

COUNTIES	Mike Mansfied (D)		Walter Rankin (R)		Other
Beaverhead	1265	46.3%	1470	53.7%	
Big Horn					
Blaine					
Broadwater	530	42.8%	707	57.2%	
Carbon					
Carter					
Cascade					
Chouteau					
Custer					
Daniels					
Dawson					
Deer Lodge	4081	71.3%	1642	28.7%	
Fallon					
Fergus					
Flathead	4034	55.9%	3178	44.1%	
Gallatin	2639	41.8%	3667	58.2%	
Garfield					
Glacier					
Golden Valley					
Granite	553	51.6%	518	48.4%	
Hill					
Jefferson	806	53.8%	692	46.2%	
Judith Basin					
Lake	1976	48.1%	2128	51.9%	
Lewis & Clark	4524	52.7%	4053	47.3%	
Liberty					
Lincoln	1546	59.6%	1048	40.4%	
Madison	793	40.9%	1147	59.1%	
McCone					
Meagher					
Mineral	414	57.8%	302	42.2%	
Missoula	6489	61.9%	3993	38.1%	
Musselshell					
Park					
Petroleum					
Phillips					
Pondera					
Powder River					
Powell	1475	59.1%	1022	40.9%	
Prairie					
Ravalli	1789	45.6%	2134	54.4%	
Richland					
Roosevelt					
Rosebud					
Sanders	1280	54.8%	1055	45.2%	
Sheridan					
Silver Bow	13224	68.4%	6102	31.6%	
Stillwater					
Sweet Grass					
Teton					
Toole					
Treasure					
Valley					
Wheatland					
Wibaux					
Yellowstone					
TOTALS	**47418**	**57.6%**	**34958**	**42.4%**	

1946 U.S. House Election, 2nd District

COUNTIES	John Holmes (D)		Wesley D'Ewart		Other
Beaverhead					
Big Horn	773	32.0%	1605	66.5%	34
Blaine	1169	53.1%	1020	46.4%	11
Broadwater					
Carbon	1573	41.8%	2145	57.0%	45
Carter	393	41.2%	556	58.3%	5
Cascade	8914	54.4%	7305	44.6%	165
Chouteau	1550	53.7%	1329	46.0%	10
Custer	1495	41.4%	2093	57.9%	27
Daniels	629	45.3%	749	53.9%	12
Dawson	1006	40.7%	1454	58.8%	12
Deer Lodge					
Fallon	466	38.6%	730	60.5%	10
Fergus	2462	47.7%	2656	51.5%	40
Flathead					
Gallatin					
Garfield	359	38.9%	561	60.8%	3
Glacier	1379	49.7%	1385	50.0%	8
Golden Valley	172	30.3%	392	69.1%	3
Granite					
Hill	2058	50.8%	1967	48.5%	30
Jefferson					
Judith Basin	953	53.9%	804	45.5%	10
Lake					
Lewis & Clark					
Liberty	403	49.7%	405	49.9%	3
Lincoln					
Madison					
McCone	679	53.5%	568	44.8%	21
Meagher	300	30.5%	676	68.7%	8
Mineral					
Missoula					
Musselshell	1213	52.9%	1046	45.6%	34
Park	1309	30.4%	2945	68.4%	54
Petroleum	166	43.7%	211	55.5%	3
Phillips	1068	47.3%	1171	51.9%	19
Pondera	1210	59.8%	802	39.7%	10
Powder River	309	29.8%	724	69.7%	5
Powell					
Prairie	341	33.5%	665	65.4%	11
Ravalli					
Richland	1211	44.6%	1484	54.6%	21
Roosevelt	1542	49.2%	1575	50.2%	19
Rosebud	606	31.0%	1330	68.1%	17
Sanders					
Sheridan	1366	58.7%	929	39.9%	31
Silver Bow					
Stillwater	657	34.6%	1238	65.2%	5
Sweet Grass	298	23.5%	967	76.1%	5
Teton	1214	52.8%	1078	46.9%	7
Toole	1358	50.6%	1315	49.0%	10
Treasure	209	34.9%	385	64.4%	4
Valley	1806	51.2%	1692	47.9%	31
Wheatland	422	36.5%	730	63.1%	4
Wibaux	336	44.3%	421	55.5%	2
Yellowstone	5190	35.8%	9199	63.5%	92
TOTALS	**48564**	**45.1%**	**58307**	**54.1%**	**841**

1948 Presidential Election

COUNTIES	Harry Truman (D)		Thomas Dewey (R)		Other
Beaverhead	1356	45.1%	1583	52.7%	66
Big Horn	1328	49.1%	1334	49.4%	40
Blaine	1669	60.7%	997	36.3%	82
Broadwater	539	42.5%	704	55.5%	26
Carbon	1997	47.9%	1901	45.6%	271
Carter	568	52.4%	501	46.2%	15
Cascade	12082	61.0%	6830	34.5%	905
Chouteau	1832	58.4%	1181	37.6%	125
Custer	2359	55.3%	1845	43.3%	59
Daniels	829	54.3%	624	40.9%	73
Dawson	1397	46.3%	1555	51.5%	65
Deer Lodge	3862	62.2%	2036	32.8%	314
Fallon	623	46.9%	678	51.0%	28
Fergus	3059	54.1%	2411	42.7%	182
Flathead	4546	49.5%	4240	46.1%	407
Gallatin	3548	44.6%	4220	53.1%	182
Garfield	451	46.4%	501	51.5%	21
Glacier	2238	63.8%	1238	35.3%	32
Golden Valley	295	44.5%	352	53.1%	16
Granite	567	44.7%	659	52.0%	42
Hill	3321	64.1%	1645	31.8%	215
Jefferson	836	50.9%	750	45.6%	58
Judith Basin	934	56.2%	609	36.6%	119
Lake	2177	46.8%	2295	49.4%	178
Lewis & Clark	4745	46.6%	5174	50.8%	257
Liberty	542	58.5%	354	38.2%	30
Lincoln	1689	58.4%	1079	37.3%	125
Madison	1006	42.7%	1300	55.2%	51
McCone	702	51.2%	518	37.8%	151
Meagher	497	48.0%	518	50.0%	20
Mineral	475	55.2%	338	39.3%	47
Missoula	7005	50.5%	6426	46.3%	442
Musselshell	1188	47.6%	1010	40.5%	298
Park	2222	45.9%	2461	50.8%	162
Petroleum	235	51.0%	214	46.4%	12
Phillips	1506	58.6%	964	37.5%	99
Pondera	1555	61.0%	902	35.4%	93
Powder River	480	36.8%	784	60.2%	39
Powell	1427	53.4%	1163	43.5%	84
Prairie	527	50.6%	499	47.9%	16
Ravalli	2159	45.7%	2354	49.8%	210
Richland	1673	54.1%	1332	43.1%	85
Roosevelt	1820	58.2%	1142	36.5%	166
Rosebud	1031	47.3%	1106	50.7%	44
Sanders	1425	51.5%	1191	43.0%	151
Sheridan	1515	61.8%	699	28.5%	239
Silver Bow	12715	59.6%	7305	34.2%	1315
Stillwater	890	42.6%	1137	54.5%	60
Sweet Grass	499	36.5%	843	61.7%	24
Teton	1632	60.0%	1005	36.9%	83
Toole	1756	60.8%	1092	37.8%	40
Treasure	291	52.0%	253	45.2%	16
Valley	2535	61.7%	1375	33.5%	200
Wheatland	733	47.8%	780	50.9%	20
Wibaux	471	52.0%	421	46.5%	13
Yellowstone	9718	47.7%	10342	50.7%	324
TOTALS	**119071**	**53.1%**	**96770**	**43.1%**	**8437**

1948 Gubernatorial Election

COUNTIES	John Bonner (D)		Sam Ford (R)		Other
Beaverhead	1690	57.0%	1271	42.9%	4
Big Horn	1172	43.8%	1486	55.6%	16
Blaine	1585	58.1%	1134	41.6%	9
Broadwater	682	54.1%	578	45.8%	1
Carbon	2388	57.3%	1763	42.3%	14
Carter	464	43.8%	593	56.0%	2
Cascade	12146	61.3%	7601	38.3%	80
Chouteau	1705	55.3%	1367	44.4%	10
Custer	2004	47.4%	2208	52.3%	13
Daniels	660	43.2%	865	56.6%	4
Dawson	1346	44.8%	1651	54.9%	10
Deer Lodge	4526	73.5%	1611	26.1%	24
Fallon	513	38.7%	809	61.0%	4
Fergus	2931	52.1%	2678	47.6%	17
Flathead	5185	56.9%	3902	42.8%	33
Gallatin	3520	44.6%	4350	55.1%	23
Garfield	483	49.3%	495	50.6%	1
Glacier	2132	61.3%	1329	38.2%	15
Golden Valley	313	47.7%	342	52.1%	1
Granite	681	53.5%	592	46.5%	1
Hill	2865	55.1%	2315	44.6%	15
Jefferson	911	55.5%	727	44.3%	4
Judith Basin	991	59.1%	679	40.5%	6
Lake	2350	50.8%	2265	48.9%	13
Lewis & Clark	4975	48.9%	5150	50.7%	41
Liberty	497	54.0%	422	45.8%	2
Lincoln	1834	64.8%	983	34.7%	15
Madison	1166	49.0%	1202	50.5%	11
McCone	768	56.2%	591	43.2%	8
Meagher	527	49.9%	530	50.1%	0
Mineral	523	60.5%	338	39.1%	3
Missoula	7650	55.4%	6094	44.1%	72
Musselshell	1456	58.2%	1005	40.2%	39
Park	2307	48.0%	2467	51.4%	29
Petroleum	243	52.9%	216	47.1%	0
Phillips	1505	59.0%	1034	40.5%	11
Pondera	1625	64.4%	886	35.1%	11
Powder River	478	43.8%	608	55.7%	5
Powell	1555	58.0%	1116	41.7%	8
Prairie	431	41.2%	616	58.8%	0
Ravalli	2417	51.6%	2246	47.9%	22
Richland	1498	49.3%	1529	50.3%	10
Roosevelt	1543	50.3%	1513	49.3%	11
Rosebud	1017	46.4%	1170	53.4%	6
Sanders	1775	64.5%	949	34.5%	27
Sheridan	1306	53.7%	1115	45.9%	9
Silver Bow	15099	71.1%	6005	28.3%	125
Stillwater	955	45.4%	1141	54.2%	9
Sweet Grass	602	44.5%	744	55.0%	7
Teton	1491	55.2%	1194	44.2%	15
Toole	1738	60.3%	1129	39.1%	17
Treasure	255	46.8%	288	52.8%	2
Valley	2274	55.9%	1778	43.7%	16
Wheatland	852	55.3%	686	44.5%	2
Wibaux	413	49.2%	425	50.7%	1
Yellowstone	10249	50.5%	10011	49.3%	51
TOTALS	**124267**	**55.7%**	**97792**	**43.9%**	**905**

1948 U.S. Senate Election

COUNTIES	James Murray (D)		Tom Davis (R)		Other
Beaverhead	1360	46.2%	1575	53.5%	11
Big Horn	1273	47.4%	1396	52.0%	18
Blaine	1706	63.2%	980	36.3%	13
Broadwater	545	43.2%	711	56.3%	7
Carbon	2287	55.3%	1820	44.0%	27
Carter	548	53.2%	477	46.3%	6
Cascade	12881	65.4%	6579	33.4%	222
Chouteau	1904	61.9%	1147	37.3%	26
Custer	2248	53.7%	1915	45.8%	20
Daniels	840	55.6%	662	43.8%	8
Dawson	1582	51.7%	1462	47.8%	14
Deer Lodge	4283	69.4%	1860	30.1%	32
Fallon	619	48.1%	662	51.4%	7
Fergus	3125	56.1%	2413	43.3%	31
Flathead	5065	55.7%	3993	43.9%	33
Gallatin	3559	45.6%	4200	53.8%	51
Garfield	478	50.5%	466	49.2%	3
Glacier	2149	62.4%	1289	37.4%	7
Golden Valley	322	50.0%	318	49.4%	4
Granite	627	49.4%	636	50.1%	7
Hill	3302	63.7%	1838	35.4%	45
Jefferson	882	53.9%	744	45.5%	10
Judith Basin	1029	62.1%	617	37.3%	10
Lake	2310	50.6%	2237	49.0%	21
Lewis & Clark	4904	49.3%	4994	50.2%	47
Liberty	560	62.4%	331	36.9%	7
Lincoln	1822	64.9%	971	34.6%	13
Madison	1036	43.9%	1311	55.6%	11
McCone	852	63.7%	475	35.5%	11
Meagher	481	46.7%	541	52.6%	7
Mineral	549	64.5%	300	35.3%	2
Missoula	7412	54.0%	6263	45.6%	56
Musselshell	1513	61.1%	951	38.4%	11
Park	2348	49.0%	2421	50.5%	24
Petroleum	272	59.4%	186	40.6%	0
Phillips	1552	61.8%	947	37.7%	12
Pondera	1641	64.9%	873	34.5%	16
Powder River	498	46.3%	563	52.3%	15
Powell	1529	57.6%	1116	42.1%	8
Prairie	551	53.9%	470	45.9%	2
Ravalli	2378	51.0%	2231	47.9%	50
Richland	1728	57.8%	1194	39.9%	67
Roosevelt	1869	61.9%	1118	37.0%	32
Rosebud	1088	50.3%	1062	49.1%	11
Sanders	1598	58.9%	1103	40.7%	10
Sheridan	1611	68.4%	730	31.0%	14
Silver Bow	13783	65.4%	7182	34.1%	94
Stillwater	967	46.6%	1100	53.0%	10
Sweet Grass	496	36.7%	847	62.7%	8
Teton	1678	62.1%	1007	37.3%	16
Toole	1765	61.3%	1090	37.9%	22
Treasure	272	50.7%	261	48.6%	4
Valley	2669	65.9%	1349	33.3%	34
Wheatland	761	50.2%	748	49.4%	6
Wibaux	427	52.8%	370	45.8%	11
Yellowstone	9659	48.0%	10356	51.5%	88
TOTALS	**125193**	**56.6%**	**94458**	**42.7%**	**1352**

1948 U.S. House Election, 1st District

COUNTIES	Mike Mansfield (D)		Al Angstman (R)		Other
Beaverhead	1679	58.4%	1185	41.2%	13
Big Horn					
Blaine					
Broadwater	685	55.7%	543	44.1%	2
Carbon					
Carter					
Cascade					
Chouteau					
Custer					
Daniels					
Dawson					
Deer Lodge	4820	78.7%	1261	20.6%	44
Fallon					
Fergus					
Flathead	6155	67.6%	2897	31.8%	53
Gallatin	4750	61.3%	2971	38.4%	26
Garfield					
Glacier					
Golden Valley					
Granite	766	61.9%	465	37.6%	7
Hill					
Jefferson	1041	64.1%	578	35.6%	4
Judith Basin					
Lake	2848	62.9%	1658	36.6%	21
Lewis & Clark	5963	59.8%	3973	39.9%	30
Liberty					
Lincoln	2113	75.8%	654	23.5%	19
Madison	1289	56.2%	985	43.0%	19
McCone					
Meagher					
Mineral	607	74.2%	205	25.1%	6
Missoula	9580	69.8%	4089	29.8%	59
Musselshell					
Park					
Petroleum					
Phillips					
Pondera					
Powder River					
Powell	1807	68.7%	812	30.9%	10
Prairie					
Ravalli	2807	61.0%	1771	38.5%	20
Richland					
Roosevelt					
Rosebud					
Sanders	1870	70.7%	753	28.5%	21
Sheridan					
Silver Bow	15496	74.6%	5137	24.7%	147
Stillwater					
Sweet Grass					
Teton					
Toole					
Treasure					
Valley					
Wheatland					
Wibaux					
Yellowstone					
TOTALS	**64276**	**68.2%**	**29937**	**31.8%**	

1948 U.S. House Election, 2nd District

COUNTIES	Willard Fraser (D)		Wesley D'Ewart (R)	
Beaverhead				
Big Horn	989	39.0%	1547	61.0%
Blaine	1334	52.5%	1209	47.5%
Broadwater				
Carbon	1879	47.7%	2060	52.3%
Carter	400	41.8%	558	58.2%
Cascade	11249	59.3%	7735	40.7%
Chouteau	1514	51.7%	1416	48.3%
Custer	1856	46.6%	2124	53.4%
Daniels	624	44.7%	771	55.3%
Dawson	1139	40.2%	1695	59.8%
Deer Lodge				
Fallon	471	38.8%	744	61.2%
Fergus	2636	49.2%	2719	50.8%
Flathead				
Gallatin				
Garfield	339	37.6%	563	62.4%
Glacier	1732	53.3%	1518	46.7%
Golden Valley	225	36.2%	397	63.8%
Granite				
Hill	2773	55.5%	2223	44.5%
Jefferson				
Judith Basin	823	51.7%	768	48.3%
Lake				
Lewis & Clark				
Liberty	400	48.3%	428	51.7%
Lincoln				
Madison				
McCone	624	49.7%	631	50.3%
Meagher	341	34.8%	639	65.2%
Mineral				
Missoula				
Musselshell	1332	56.8%	1015	43.2%
Park	1912	40.6%	2792	59.4%
Petroleum	214	49.0%	223	51.0%
Phillips	1157	48.9%	1207	51.1%
Pondera	1360	56.9%	1031	43.1%
Powder River	338	33.7%	665	66.3%
Powell				
Prairie	384	39.7%	583	60.3%
Ravalli				
Richland	1308	46.4%	1510	53.6%
Roosevelt	1322	47.3%	1473	52.7%
Rosebud	793	39.2%	1232	60.8%
Sanders				
Sheridan	1274	57.7%	934	42.3%
Silver Bow				
Stillwater	762	37.6%	1266	62.4%
Sweet Grass	336	26.1%	949	73.9%
Teton	1353	52.7%	1216	47.3%
Toole	1427	52.8%	1275	47.2%
Treasure	210	41.7%	293	58.3%
Valley	2187	57.1%	1642	42.9%
Wheatland	622	43.1%	820	56.9%
Wibaux	342	45.0%	418	55.0%
Yellowstone	8730	44.6%	10835	55.4%
TOTALS	**58711**	**49.0%**	**61124**	**51.0%**

1950 U.S. House Election, 1st District

COUNTIES	Mike Mansfield (D)		Ralph McGinnis (R)		
Beaverhead	1628	59.4%	1111	40.6%	
Big Horn					
Blaine					
Broadwater	714	51.1%	683	48.9%	
Carbon					
Carter					
Cascade					
Chouteau					
Custer					
Daniels					
Dawson					
Deer Lodge	4262	74.7%	1446	25.3%	
Fallon					
Fergus					
Flathead	5353	59.6%	3623	40.4%	
Gallatin	3537	48.9%	3694	51.1%	
Garfield					
Glacier					
Golden Valley					
Granite	598	49.0%	622	51.0%	
Hill					
Jefferson	926	60.8%	596	39.2%	
Judith Basin					
Lake	2159	47.7%	2370	52.3%	
Lewis & Clark	5053	54.2%	4263	45.8%	
Liberty					
Lincoln	1762	66.4%	890	33.6%	
Madison	1170	52.3%	1067	47.7%	
McCone					
Meagher					
Mineral	648	67.9%	307	32.1%	
Missoula	7535	60.9%	4847	39.1%	
Musselshell					
Park					
Petroleum					
Phillips					
Pondera					
Powder River					
Powell	1636	65.4%	867	34.6%	
Prairie					
Ravalli	2160	51.3%	2048	48.7%	
Richland					
Roosevelt					
Rosebud					
Sanders	1671	63.6%	958	36.4%	
Sheridan					
Silver Bow	13582	71.0%	5553	29.0%	
Stillwater					
Sweet Grass					
Teton					
Toole					
Treasure					
Valley					
Wheatland					
Wibaux					
Yellowstone					
TOTALS	**54394**	**60.9%**	**34945**	**39.1%**	

1950 U.S. House Election, 2nd District

COUNTIES	John Holmes (D)		Wesley D'Ewart (R)		
Beaverhead					
Big Horn	888	34.9%	1658	65.1%	
Blaine	1338	50.1%	1335	49.9%	
Broadwater					
Carbon	1561	41.2%	2224	58.8%	
Carter	410	39.9%	618	60.1%	
Cascade	9462	55.7%	7513	44.3%	
Chouteau	1496	49.8%	1511	50.2%	
Custer	1756	42.8%	2350	57.2%	
Daniels	715	46.3%	828	53.7%	
Dawson	1166	41.0%	1677	59.0%	
Deer Lodge					
Fallon	535	39.2%	830	60.8%	
Fergus	2458	46.2%	2860	53.8%	
Flathead					
Gallatin					
Garfield	343	35.8%	615	64.2%	
Glacier	1340	45.7%	1591	54.3%	
Golden Valley	174	31.4%	380	68.6%	
Granite					
Hill	2429	50.8%	2351	49.2%	
Jefferson					
Judith Basin	796	51.8%	740	48.2%	
Lake					
Lewis & Clark					
Liberty	461	52.3%	421	47.7%	
Lincoln					
Madison					
McCone	669	49.9%	671	50.1%	
Meagher	291	31.1%	645	68.9%	
Mineral					
Missoula					
Musselshell	1217	53.4%	1061	46.6%	
Park	1775	35.5%	3225	64.5%	
Petroleum	166	40.0%	249	60.0%	
Phillips	1213	47.0%	1369	53.0%	
Pondera	1357	57.3%	1010	42.7%	
Powder River	299	33.1%	603	66.9%	
Powell					
Prairie	322	34.7%	606	65.3%	
Ravalli					
Richland	1391	46.3%	1616	53.7%	
Roosevelt	1408	51.0%	1352	49.0%	
Rosebud	796	34.9%	1484	65.1%	
Sanders					
Sheridan	1370	60.1%	908	39.9%	
Silver Bow					
Stillwater	760	35.2%	1400	64.8%	
Sweet Grass	283	22.6%	967	77.4%	
Teton	1361	49.7%	1375	50.3%	
Toole	1305	48.2%	1400	51.8%	
Treasure	211	38.6%	335	61.4%	
Valley	1870	48.1%	2020	51.9%	
Wheatland	498	39.2%	771	60.8%	
Wibaux	389	47.1%	437	52.9%	
Yellowstone	7575	38.7%	11997	61.3%	
TOTALS	**53854**	**45.3%**	**65003**	**54.7%**	

1952 Presidential Election

COUNTIES	Adlai Stevenson (D)		Dwight Eisenhower (R)		Other
Beaverhead	920	29.4%	2196	70.2%	12
Big Horn	1114	33.9%	2165	65.9%	6
Blaine	1207	38.9%	1890	60.8%	9
Broadwater	435	31.1%	962	68.9%	0
Carbon	1713	38.3%	2734	61.2%	23
Carter	351	27.5%	921	72.1%	5
Cascade	11051	47.3%	12176	52.1%	146
Chouteau	1423	40.3%	2098	59.3%	14
Custer	2050	37.0%	3461	62.5%	24
Daniels	649	37.1%	1092	62.5%	7
Dawson	1247	34.1%	2396	65.5%	15
Deer Lodge	4162	57.7%	3001	41.6%	54
Fallon	440	29.5%	1046	70.0%	8
Fergus	2271	33.9%	4402	65.8%	18
Flathead	4994	40.0%	7372	59.1%	110
Gallatin	2697	27.7%	6998	71.9%	34
Garfield	269	27.1%	723	72.7%	2
Glacier	1698	45.1%	2061	54.7%	10
Golden Valley	198	29.6%	471	70.4%	0
Granite	473	33.8%	923	65.9%	5
Hill	2748	43.9%	3474	55.4%	44
Jefferson	687	38.5%	1084	60.8%	13
Judith Basin	746	40.3%	1074	58.0%	33
Lake	1893	33.7%	3651	65.1%	65
Lewis & Clark	4563	37.3%	7663	62.6%	20
Liberty	411	37.8%	671	61.7%	6
Lincoln	1907	49.9%	1881	49.2%	33
Madison	751	27.3%	1993	72.4%	8
McCone	674	42.2%	900	56.3%	24
Meagher	326	29.1%	792	70.7%	2
Mineral	491	46.6%	553	52.5%	10
Missoula	6901	40.5%	10053	59.0%	87
Musselshell	1240	49.6%	1253	50.1%	9
Park	1969	32.0%	4152	67.5%	29
Petroleum	155	32.7%	319	67.3%	0
Phillips	1224	40.6%	1771	58.7%	22
Pondera	1246	41.6%	1719	57.5%	27
Powder River	327	26.8%	888	72.7%	7
Powell	1281	41.6%	1783	57.9%	18
Prairie	338	30.3%	771	69.2%	5
Ravalli	1750	32.8%	3537	66.4%	42
Richland	1196	32.1%	2506	67.3%	23
Roosevelt	1466	42.1%	1998	57.4%	19
Rosebud	805	31.5%	1734	67.9%	14
Sanders	1311	42.6%	1724	56.0%	43
Sheridan	1347	49.7%	1339	49.4%	25
Silver Bow	13114	55.9%	10196	43.5%	148
Stillwater	816	32.4%	1689	67.0%	15
Sweet Grass	372	21.8%	1315	77.2%	17
Teton	1389	41.1%	1978	58.6%	11
Toole	1426	43.3%	1853	56.3%	15
Treasure	205	34.3%	392	65.7%	0
Valley	2130	46.1%	2462	53.3%	29
Wheatland	572	35.6%	1026	63.8%	9
Wibaux	324	36.6%	556	62.8%	5
Yellowstone	8750	33.2%	17556	66.6%	51
TOTALS	**106213**	**40.1%**	**157394**	**59.4%**	**1430**

1952 Gubernatorial Election

COUNTIES	John Bonner (D)		Hugo Aronson (R)		Other
Beaverhead	1430	46.5%	1633	53.1%	13
Big Horn	1429	43.3%	1872	56.7%	
Blaine	1424	46.1%	1668	53.9%	
Broadwater	653	45.9%	765	53.7%	6
Carbon	2096	47.0%	2368	53.0%	
Carter	466	37.3%	783	62.7%	
Cascade	12848	55.5%	10296	44.5%	
Chouteau	1762	49.5%	1797	50.5%	
Custer	2256	41.7%	3149	58.3%	
Daniels	726	41.7%	1014	58.3%	
Dawson	1922	52.9%	1709	47.1%	
Deer Lodge	4811	66.7%	2360	32.7%	40
Fallon	641	42.8%	856	57.2%	
Fergus	2994	44.6%	3715	55.4%	
Flathead	6357	50.8%	6076	48.5%	89
Gallatin	3002	31.0%	6659	68.7%	28
Garfield	400	40.9%	577	59.1%	
Glacier	2124	55.9%	1679	44.1%	
Golden Valley	271	40.4%	399	59.6%	
Granite	579	40.4%	844	58.9%	9
Hill	3343	53.3%	2930	46.7%	
Jefferson	831	45.8%	972	53.6%	11
Judith Basin	942	51.2%	897	48.8%	
Lake	2478	44.4%	3073	55.1%	31
Lewis & Clark	6084	49.6%	6119	49.9%	70
Liberty	530	48.7%	559	51.3%	
Lincoln	2402	62.9%	1395	36.5%	23
Madison	1149	41.3%	1611	57.9%	20
McCone	942	58.9%	656	41.1%	
Meagher	391	34.9%	728	65.1%	
Mineral	547	50.6%	526	48.6%	9
Missoula	8045	47.0%	8887	51.9%	200
Musselshell	1349	54.1%	1144	45.9%	
Park	2293	37.4%	3831	62.6%	
Petroleum	230	48.6%	243	51.4%	
Phillips	1541	51.3%	1463	48.7%	
Pondera	1657	55.5%	1328	44.5%	
Powder River	472	38.9%	742	61.1%	
Powell	1398	45.3%	1666	53.9%	25
Prairie	417	37.2%	705	62.8%	
Ravalli	2262	42.5%	3040	57.1%	26
Richland	1995	54.0%	1699	46.0%	
Roosevelt	1784	51.3%	1693	48.7%	
Rosebud	1083	42.2%	1483	57.8%	
Sanders	1575	50.5%	1492	47.8%	54
Sheridan	1619	60.2%	1070	39.8%	
Silver Bow	14282	60.7%	9002	38.3%	234
Stillwater	973	38.4%	1562	61.6%	
Sweet Grass	433	25.5%	1263	74.5%	
Teton	1678	49.9%	1685	50.1%	
Toole	1912	58.1%	1380	41.9%	
Treasure	288	48.1%	311	51.9%	
Valley	2569	55.9%	2027	44.1%	
Wheatland	734	45.7%	871	54.3%	
Wibaux	506	56.8%	385	43.2%	
Yellowstone	10444	39.8%	15766	60.2%	
TOTALS	**129369**	**48.9%**	**134423**	**50.8%**	**888**

1952 U.S. Senate Election

COUNTIES	Mike Mansfield (D)		Zales Ecton (R)		Other
Beaverhead	1318	43.3%	1709	56.1%	19
Big Horn	1252	38.0%	2019	61.3%	24
Blaine	1471	47.8%	1593	51.7%	16
Broadwater	554	40.1%	816	59.0%	13
Carbon	2008	45.5%	2368	53.7%	33
Carter	426	34.9%	786	64.4%	9
Cascade	13312	57.3%	9692	41.7%	217
Chouteau	1818	51.0%	1727	48.5%	18
Custer	2503	46.6%	2830	52.7%	37
Daniels	736	42.7%	974	56.5%	13
Dawson	1632	45.4%	1946	54.1%	17
Deer Lodge	5278	73.6%	1834	25.6%	62
Fallon	526	35.6%	937	63.5%	13
Fergus	2980	44.9%	3632	54.7%	28
Flathead	7266	58.3%	5119	41.1%	79
Gallatin	3324	34.4%	6290	65.0%	58
Garfield	378	38.8%	594	61.0%	1
Glacier	2020	54.1%	1701	45.5%	15
Golden Valley	257	38.6%	407	61.1%	2
Granite	652	46.8%	730	52.4%	10
Hill	3380	54.3%	2798	44.9%	50
Jefferson	923	51.4%	861	48.0%	10
Judith Basin	920	50.5%	871	47.9%	29
Lake	2471	44.8%	3003	54.5%	39
Lewis & Clark	6045	49.8%	6012	49.6%	71
Liberty	568	52.6%	508	47.0%	4
Lincoln	2468	65.2%	1302	34.4%	18
Madison	1113	41.1%	1583	58.5%	10
McCone	807	51.2%	753	47.8%	16
Meagher	417	37.8%	677	61.4%	8
Mineral	639	60.1%	414	38.9%	11
Missoula	9411	55.5%	7486	44.1%	67
Musselshell	1386	55.9%	1083	43.7%	11
Park	2515	41.1%	3548	58.0%	50
Petroleum	210	44.1%	266	55.9%	0
Phillips	1497	50.7%	1432	48.5%	22
Pondera	1666	56.1%	1278	43.1%	24
Powder River	361	32.5%	740	66.5%	11
Powell	1711	55.6%	1351	43.9%	14
Prairie	405	36.1%	710	63.3%	6
Ravalli	2394	45.5%	2835	53.9%	34
Richland	1490	40.9%	2122	58.2%	33
Roosevelt	1675	48.2%	1766	50.8%	35
Rosebud	931	36.9%	1574	62.4%	19
Sanders	1645	53.9%	1371	44.9%	36
Sheridan	1478	55.6%	1152	43.4%	27
Silver Bow	15776	68.2%	7123	30.8%	243
Stillwater	940	37.4%	1562	62.1%	13
Sweet Grass	492	29.1%	1183	70.0%	14
Teton	1688	50.6%	1619	48.6%	26
Toole	1815	55.9%	1422	43.8%	9
Treasure	248	42.7%	331	57.0%	2
Valley	2460	54.0%	2068	45.4%	26
Wheatland	710	44.3%	887	55.4%	5
Wibaux	381	44.1%	477	55.3%	5
Yellowstone	10362	39.9%	15488	59.6%	146
TOTALS	**133109**	**50.7%**	**127360**	**48.6%**	**1828**

1952 U.S. House Election, 1st District

COUNTIES	Wellington Rankin (R)		Lee Metcalf (D)		Other
Beaverhead	1214	40.8%	1752	58.8%	13
Big Horn					
Blaine					
Broadwater	495	36.1%	871	63.5%	6
Carbon					
Carter					
Cascade					
Chouteau					
Custer					
Daniels					
Dawson					
Deer Lodge	4511	64.7%	2417	34.7%	40
Fallon					
Fergus					
Flathead	6032	49.6%	6043	49.7%	89
Gallatin	3638	38.5%	5791	61.2%	28
Garfield					
Glacier					
Golden Valley					
Granite	552	41.0%	785	58.3%	9
Hill					
Jefferson	816	46.5%	928	52.9%	11
Judith Basin					
Lake	2172	40.8%	3123	58.6%	31
Lewis & Clark	5743	48.4%	6043	51.0%	70
Liberty					
Lincoln	2169	59.0%	1483	40.4%	23
Madison	1049	39.7%	1576	59.6%	20
McCone					
Meagher					
Mineral	582	57.5%	422	41.7%	9
Missoula	8164	49.4%	8169	49.4%	200
Musselshell					
Park					
Petroleum					
Phillips					
Pondera					
Powder River					
Powell	1466	49.5%	1470	49.6%	25
Prairie					
Ravalli	2331	44.7%	2857	54.8%	26
Richland					
Roosevelt					
Rosebud					
Sanders	1528	51.6%	1377	46.5%	54
Sheridan					
Silver Bow	13217	58.9%	8979	40.0%	234
Stillwater					
Sweet Grass					
Teton					
Toole					
Treasure					
Valley					
Wheatland					
Wibaux					
Yellowstone					
TOTALS	**55679**	**50.3%**	**54086**	**48.9%**	**888**

1952 U.S. House Election, 2nd District

COUNTIES	Willard Fraser (D)		Wesley D'Ewart (R)		Other
Beaverhead					
Big Horn	975	30.4%	2232	69.6%	
Blaine	1158	38.7%	1834	61.3%	
Broadwater					
Carbon	1585	36.9%	2705	63.1%	
Carter	326	27.4%	864	72.6%	
Cascade	10750	47.3%	11955	52.7%	
Chouteau	1417	40.5%	2078	59.5%	
Custer	1932	36.7%	3339	63.3%	
Daniels	668	39.8%	1010	60.2%	
Dawson	1208	34.7%	2277	65.3%	
Deer Lodge					
Fallon	440	30.4%	1009	69.6%	
Fergus	2252	34.6%	4257	65.4%	
Flathead					
Gallatin					
Garfield	260	27.5%	686	72.5%	
Glacier	1490	41.5%	2103	58.5%	
Golden Valley	185	28.5%	463	71.5%	
Granite					
Hill	2665	43.6%	3454	56.4%	
Jefferson					
Judith Basin	748	42.0%	1032	58.0%	
Lake					
Lewis & Clark					
Liberty	431	41.4%	611	58.6%	
Lincoln					
Madison					
McCone	671	44.6%	833	55.4%	
Meagher	276	25.9%	791	74.1%	
Mineral					
Missoula					
Musselshell	1196	49.7%	1211	50.3%	
Park	1908	31.3%	4181	68.7%	
Petroleum	153	32.6%	316	67.4%	
Phillips	1141	39.7%	1730	60.3%	
Pondera	1246	43.2%	1636	56.8%	
Powder River	314	26.7%	860	73.3%	
Powell					
Prairie	299	27.5%	790	72.5%	
Ravalli					
Richland	1213	34.7%	2287	65.3%	
Roosevelt	1339	40.1%	2000	59.9%	
Rosebud	729	29.6%	1731	70.4%	
Sanders					
Sheridan	1265	49.1%	1311	50.9%	
Silver Bow					
Stillwater	743	30.3%	1708	69.7%	
Sweet Grass	329	19.9%	1324	80.1%	
Teton	1293	39.7%	1962	60.3%	
Toole	1323	42.2%	1814	57.8%	
Treasure	184	34.3%	353	65.7%	
Valley	1924	43.4%	2514	56.6%	
Wheatland	572	36.7%	987	63.3%	
Wibaux	316	38.3%	510	61.7%	
Yellowstone	8279	32.2%	17452	67.8%	
TOTALS	**55203**	**38.0%**	**90210**	**62.0%**	

1954 U.S. Senate Election

COUNTIES	James Murray (D)		WesleyD'Ewart (R)		Other
Beaverhead	1161	42.1%	1597	57.9%	
Big Horn	1133	42.9%	1509	57.1%	
Blaine	1438	53.4%	1254	46.6%	
Broadwater	580	44.8%	714	55.2%	
Carbon	1832	47.3%	2043	52.7%	
Carter	454	41.6%	638	58.4%	
Cascade	10955	57.5%	8105	42.5%	
Chouteau	1748	53.5%	1519	46.5%	
Custer	2227	46.9%	2518	53.1%	
Daniels	858	50.8%	830	49.2%	
Dawson	1671	49.7%	1690	50.3%	
Deer Lodge	4552	68.7%	2072	31.3%	
Fallon	667	47.4%	741	52.6%	
Fergus	2702	48.1%	2912	51.9%	
Flathead	4663	46.0%	5481	54.0%	
Gallatin	2892	36.2%	5090	63.8%	
Garfield	446	46.6%	511	53.4%	
Glacier	1837	54.4%	1541	45.6%	
Golden Valley	284	44.8%	350	55.2%	
Granite	578	45.2%	701	54.8%	
Hill	2770	52.9%	2462	47.1%	
Jefferson	730	47.3%	813	52.7%	
Judith Basin	945	55.8%	749	44.2%	
Lake	1919	41.4%	2721	58.6%	
Lewis & Clark	4752	46.1%	5559	53.9%	
Liberty	518	51.2%	493	48.8%	
Lincoln	1904	60.3%	1254	39.7%	
Madison	974	41.4%	1380	58.6%	
McCone	857	54.7%	711	45.3%	
Meagher	437	41.6%	614	58.4%	
Mineral	602	59.3%	413	40.7%	
Missoula	6407	48.2%	6890	51.8%	
Musselshell	1244	56.4%	960	43.6%	
Park	2401	46.0%	2820	54.0%	
Petroleum	207	48.5%	220	51.5%	
Phillips	1638	55.8%	1295	44.2%	
Pondera	1449	56.6%	1109	43.4%	
Powder River	405	40.1%	604	59.9%	
Powell	1540	55.5%	1234	44.5%	
Prairie	391	39.9%	590	60.1%	
Ravalli	1997	45.0%	2444	55.0%	
Richland	1608	47.3%	1789	52.7%	
Roosevelt	1938	57.1%	1454	42.9%	
Rosebud	986	41.3%	1400	58.7%	
Sanders	1310	52.7%	1177	47.3%	
Sheridan	1575	62.6%	942	37.4%	
Silver Bow	12634	65.0%	6803	35.0%	
Stillwater	1075	43.4%	1403	56.6%	
Sweet Grass	431	28.3%	1094	71.7%	
Teton	1560	52.6%	1408	47.4%	
Toole	1535	51.9%	1424	48.1%	
Treasure	270	47.1%	303	52.9%	
Valley	2530	58.2%	1820	41.8%	
Wheatland	672	46.3%	780	53.7%	
Wibaux	365	48.9%	382	51.1%	
Yellowstone	9337	40.8%	13533	59.2%	
TOTALS	**114591**	**50.4%**	**112863**	**49.6%**	

1954 U.S. House Election, 1st District

COUNTIES	Lee Metcalf (D)		Winfield Page (R)		Other
Beaverhead	1294	47.4%	1434	52.6%	
Big Horn					
Blaine					
Broadwater	645	50.4%	636	49.6%	
Carbon					
Carter					
Cascade					
Chouteau					
Custer					
Daniels					
Dawson					
Deer Lodge	4711	71.9%	1841	28.1%	
Fallon					
Fergus					
Flathead	5395	53.1%	4768	46.9%	
Gallatin	3537	44.6%	4390	55.4%	
Garfield					
Glacier					
Golden Valley					
Granite	602	47.9%	655	52.1%	
Hill					
Jefferson	840	55.3%	679	44.7%	
Judith Basin					
Lake	2110	45.9%	2486	54.1%	
Lewis & Clark	5482	53.2%	4822	46.8%	
Liberty					
Lincoln	2082	66.3%	1057	33.7%	
Madison	1069	45.8%	1263	54.2%	
McCone					
Meagher					
Mineral	658	64.9%	356	35.1%	
Missoula	6623	49.9%	6639	50.1%	
Musselshell					
Park					
Petroleum					
Phillips					
Pondera					
Powder River					
Powell	1653	60.0%	1100	40.0%	
Prairie					
Ravalli	2252	50.9%	2176	49.1%	
Richland					
Roosevelt					
Rosebud					
Sanders	1403	57.3%	1047	42.7%	
Sheridan					
Silver Bow	12258	67.0%	6026	33.0%	
Stillwater					
Sweet Grass					
Teton					
Toole					
Treasure					
Valley					
Wheatland					
Wibaux					
Yellowstone					
TOTALS	**52614**	**56.0%**	**41375**	**44.0%**	

1954 U.S. House Election, 2nd District

COUNTIES	LeRoy Anderson (D)		Orvin Fjare (R)		Other
Beaverhead					
Big Horn	1125	42.9%	1498	57.1%	
Blaine	1549	58.5%	1099	41.5%	
Broadwater					
Carbon	1795	46.6%	2054	53.4%	
Carter	482	46.1%	563	53.9%	
Cascade	10059	53.9%	8612	46.1%	
Chouteau	1721	52.8%	1539	47.2%	
Custer	2378	50.7%	2316	49.3%	
Daniels	867	52.4%	788	47.6%	
Dawson	1653	50.4%	1630	49.6%	
Deer Lodge					
Fallon	638	46.1%	746	53.9%	
Fergus	2720	49.0%	2831	51.0%	
Flathead					
Gallatin					
Garfield	455	49.2%	470	50.8%	
Glacier	1802	54.5%	1507	45.5%	
Golden Valley	260	41.1%	372	58.9%	
Granite					
Hill	2839	54.9%	2335	45.1%	
Jefferson					
Judith Basin	907	53.7%	781	46.3%	
Lake					
Lewis & Clark					
Liberty	532	52.6%	480	47.4%	
Lincoln					
Madison					
McCone	903	58.3%	645	41.7%	
Meagher	401	38.8%	632	61.2%	
Mineral					
Missoula					
Musselshell	1172	54.2%	989	45.8%	
Park	2263	43.4%	2956	56.6%	
Petroleum	201	47.1%	226	52.9%	
Phillips	1671	57.8%	1218	42.2%	
Pondera	1549	60.2%	1024	39.8%	
Powder River	421	42.2%	577	57.8%	
Powell					
Prairie	424	43.8%	545	56.2%	
Ravalli					
Richland	1670	50.0%	1670	50.0%	
Roosevelt	1894	56.8%	1440	43.2%	
Rosebud	951	41.3%	1350	58.7%	
Sanders					
Sheridan	1605	64.9%	867	35.1%	
Silver Bow					
Stillwater	1011	41.0%	1455	59.0%	
Sweet Grass	406	26.4%	1133	73.6%	
Teton	1522	51.3%	1443	48.7%	
Toole	1471	50.2%	1462	49.8%	
Treasure	274	48.8%	288	51.2%	
Valley	2533	59.5%	1726	40.5%	
Wheatland	582	39.8%	882	60.2%	
Wibaux	364	51.0%	350	49.0%	
Yellowstone	9425	40.9%	13604	59.1%	
TOTALS	**64495**	**49.4%**	**66103**	**50.6%**	

1956 Presidential Election

COUNTIES	Adlai Stevenson (D)		Dwight Eisenhower (R)		Other
Beaverhead	1029	34.5%	1955	65.5%	
Big Horn	1342	43.6%	1739	56.4%	
Blaine	1438	49.6%	1460	50.4%	
Broadwater	449	34.1%	869	65.9%	
Carbon	1820	43.7%	2345	56.3%	
Carter	435	38.4%	698	61.6%	
Cascade	11098	47.1%	12455	52.9%	
Chouteau	1794	51.0%	1721	49.0%	
Custer	2317	41.7%	3240	58.3%	
Daniels	946	49.1%	982	50.9%	
Dawson	1929	43.9%	2463	56.1%	
Deer Lodge	3792	51.6%	3551	48.4%	
Fallon	612	38.8%	967	61.2%	
Fergus	2757	42.2%	3771	57.8%	
Flathead	6003	42.6%	8088	57.4%	
Gallatin	3260	32.8%	6680	67.2%	
Garfield	424	43.2%	558	56.8%	
Glacier	1822	47.0%	2054	53.0%	
Golden Valley	256	40.1%	383	59.9%	
Granite	533	37.3%	896	62.7%	
Hill	2999	46.8%	3415	53.2%	
Jefferson	660	38.6%	1049	61.4%	
Judith Basin	848	51.8%	789	48.2%	
Lake	2253	40.1%	3363	59.9%	
Lewis & Clark	4397	35.6%	7959	64.4%	
Liberty	488	44.8%	601	55.2%	
Lincoln	2286	49.6%	2321	50.4%	
Madison	925	35.8%	1662	64.2%	
McCone	889	54.2%	752	45.8%	
Meagher	355	33.3%	712	66.7%	
Mineral	552	47.7%	606	52.3%	
Missoula	6760	38.9%	10627	61.1%	
Musselshell	1115	48.9%	1165	51.1%	
Park	2151	36.6%	3733	63.4%	
Petroleum	205	44.3%	258	55.7%	
Phillips	1427	47.1%	1605	52.9%	
Pondera	1438	46.6%	1651	53.4%	
Powder River	456	39.4%	700	60.6%	
Powell	1214	41.9%	1683	58.1%	
Prairie	403	38.8%	637	61.3%	
Ravalli	2161	38.6%	3437	61.4%	
Richland	1884	44.3%	2366	55.7%	
Roosevelt	2205	52.6%	1985	47.4%	
Rosebud	890	37.0%	1516	63.0%	
Sanders	1519	47.9%	1649	52.1%	
Sheridan	1857	61.7%	1153	38.3%	
Silver Bow	11475	49.7%	11619	50.3%	
Stillwater	1013	39.7%	1540	60.3%	
Sweet Grass	455	28.7%	1129	71.3%	
Teton	1622	48.4%	1728	51.6%	
Toole	1460	43.1%	1927	56.9%	
Treasure	252	42.8%	337	57.2%	
Valley	2511	51.6%	2357	48.4%	
Wheatland	578	38.3%	932	61.7%	
Wibaux	390	47.5%	431	52.5%	
Yellowstone	10088	35.1%	18664	64.9%	
TOTALS	**116238**	**42.9%**	**154933**	**57.1%**	

1956 Gubernatorial Election

COUNTIES	Arnold Olsen (D)		Hugo Aronson (R)		Other
Beaverhead	1139	38.3%	1835	61.7%	
Big Horn	1396	45.7%	1656	54.3%	
Blaine	1568	53.8%	1349	46.2%	
Broadwater	508	38.6%	808	61.4%	
Carbon	2047	49.3%	2106	50.7%	
Carter	410	36.3%	718	63.7%	
Cascade	11685	51.2%	11155	48.8%	
Chouteau	1770	50.6%	1725	49.4%	
Custer	2554	45.6%	3052	54.4%	
Daniels	947	48.8%	994	51.2%	
Dawson	2005	45.7%	2381	54.3%	
Deer Lodge	5184	70.8%	2143	29.2%	
Fallon	701	44.4%	879	55.6%	
Fergus	2579	39.5%	3955	60.5%	
Flathead	6389	45.5%	7638	54.5%	
Gallatin	4016	40.4%	5926	59.6%	
Garfield	424	43.4%	552	56.6%	
Glacier	1633	41.9%	2261	58.1%	
Golden Valley	268	42.1%	369	57.9%	
Granite	696	49.2%	719	50.8%	
Hill	3256	50.7%	3169	49.3%	
Jefferson	877	51.3%	832	48.7%	
Judith Basin	847	50.7%	822	49.3%	
Lake	2612	46.7%	2984	53.3%	
Lewis & Clark	5323	43.0%	7068	57.0%	
Liberty	480	44.1%	608	55.9%	
Lincoln	2878	62.7%	1711	37.3%	
Madison	1123	43.6%	1454	56.4%	
McCone	951	57.9%	692	42.1%	
Meagher	411	38.5%	656	61.5%	
Mineral	617	53.3%	541	46.7%	
Missoula	7825	45.2%	9503	54.8%	
Musselshell	1187	52.1%	1092	47.9%	
Park	2638	45.0%	3229	55.0%	
Petroleum	206	44.6%	256	55.4%	
Phillips	1503	48.2%	1616	51.8%	
Pondera	1532	50.1%	1528	49.9%	
Powder River	454	39.3%	702	60.7%	
Powell	1719	59.2%	1185	40.8%	
Prairie	434	41.4%	615	58.6%	
Ravalli	2467	44.5%	3081	55.5%	
Richland	1833	43.5%	2376	56.5%	
Roosevelt	2035	49.1%	2111	50.9%	
Rosebud	946	39.2%	1466	60.8%	
Sanders	1748	55.1%	1426	44.9%	
Sheridan	1849	61.5%	1156	38.5%	
Silver Bow	16259	70.1%	6951	29.9%	
Stillwater	1127	44.1%	1428	55.9%	
Sweet Grass	588	36.7%	1014	63.3%	
Teton	1743	51.9%	1613	48.1%	
Toole	1281	38.1%	2082	61.9%	
Treasure	233	39.6%	355	60.4%	
Valley	2523	52.2%	2311	47.8%	
Wheatland	623	41.3%	885	58.7%	
Wibaux	386	48.6%	409	51.4%	
Yellowstone	11055	38.4%	17730	61.6%	
TOTALS	**131488**	**48.6%**	**138878**	**51.4%**	

1956 U.S. House Election, 1st District

COUNTIES	Lee Metcalf (D)		W.D. McDonald (R)		Other
Beaverhead	1499	51.9%	1390	48.1%	
Big Horn					
Blaine					
Broadwater	654	50.8%	634	49.2%	
Carbon					
Carter					
Cascade					
Chouteau					
Custer					
Daniels					
Dawson					
Deer Lodge	5418	75.9%	1721	24.1%	
Fallon					
Fergus					
Flathead	8312	60.1%	5507	39.9%	
Gallatin	5175	52.8%	4633	47.2%	
Garfield					
Glacier					
Golden Valley					
Granite	763	55.9%	603	44.1%	
Hill					
Jefferson	996	60.3%	657	39.7%	
Judith Basin					
Lake	3058	55.8%	2422	44.2%	
Lewis & Clark	7222	58.9%	5049	41.1%	
Liberty					
Lincoln	3172	70.5%	1327	29.5%	
Madison	1318	53.2%	1160	46.8%	
McCone					
Meagher					
Mineral	780	69.5%	342	30.5%	
Missoula	9988	58.5%	7094	41.5%	
Musselshell					
Park					
Petroleum					
Phillips					
Pondera					
Powder River					
Powell	1879	66.3%	957	33.7%	
Prairie					
Ravalli	3233	59.5%	2203	40.5%	
Richland					
Roosevelt					
Rosebud					
Sanders	2011	65.1%	1077	34.9%	
Sheridan					
Silver Bow	14166	70.9%	5815	29.1%	
Stillwater					
Sweet Grass					
Teton					
Toole					
Treasure					
Valley					
Wheatland					
Wibaux					
Yellowstone					
TOTALS	**69644**	**62.1%**	**42591**	**37.9%**	

1956 U.S. House Election, 2nd District

COUNTIES	LeRoy Anderson (D)		Orvin Fjare (R)		Other
Beaverhead					
Big Horn	1693	55.8%	1341	44.2%	
Blaine	1613	55.6%	1287	44.4%	
Broadwater					
Carbon	2195	53.3%	1921	46.7%	
Carter	468	43.6%	605	56.4%	
Cascade	12109	54.5%	10095	45.5%	
Chouteau	1981	56.2%	1547	43.8%	
Custer	2609	48.5%	2766	51.5%	
Daniels	1002	52.9%	892	47.1%	
Dawson	2230	51.4%	2112	48.6%	
Deer Lodge					
Fallon	704	45.8%	833	54.2%	
Fergus	3233	49.8%	3263	50.2%	
Flathead					
Gallatin					
Garfield	445	46.9%	503	53.1%	
Glacier	2075	53.8%	1783	46.2%	
Golden Valley	265	41.7%	371	58.3%	
Granite					
Hill	3452	54.1%	2926	45.9%	
Jefferson					
Judith Basin	920	55.2%	747	44.8%	
Lake					
Lewis & Clark					
Liberty	545	50.4%	537	49.6%	
Lincoln					
Madison					
McCone	918	56.4%	709	43.6%	
Meagher	406	38.7%	644	61.3%	
Mineral					
Missoula					
Musselshell	1259	55.4%	1013	44.6%	
Park	2632	45.1%	3206	54.9%	
Petroleum	251	55.2%	204	44.8%	
Phillips	1693	55.3%	1367	44.7%	
Pondera	1860	60.5%	1215	39.5%	
Powder River	458	41.0%	660	59.0%	
Powell					
Prairie	449	43.8%	577	56.2%	
Ravalli					
Richland	2028	48.8%	2131	51.2%	
Roosevelt	2212	54.2%	1871	45.8%	
Rosebud	1041	43.2%	1369	56.8%	
Sanders					
Sheridan	1938	65.7%	1010	34.3%	
Silver Bow					
Stillwater	1143	45.2%	1385	54.8%	
Sweet Grass	465	28.7%	1154	71.3%	
Teton	1712	51.1%	1639	48.9%	
Toole	1793	53.4%	1562	46.6%	
Treasure	285	49.3%	293	50.7%	
Valley	2688	56.6%	2062	43.4%	
Wheatland	626	41.8%	871	58.2%	
Wibaux	375	48.1%	404	51.9%	
Yellowstone	13034	46.0%	15289	54.0%	
TOTALS	**76805**	**50.9%**	**74164**	**49.1%**	

1958 U.S. Senate Election

COUNTIES	Mike Mansfield (D)		Lou Welch (R)		Other
Beaverhead	2086	76.4%	646	23.6%	
Big Horn	1672	65.8%	868	34.2%	
Blaine	1962	77.4%	574	22.6%	
Broadwater	897	72.5%	341	27.5%	
Carbon	2503	69.7%	1087	30.3%	
Carter	631	68.9%	285	31.1%	
Cascade	16132	81.0%	3776	19.0%	
Chouteau	2505	79.6%	642	20.4%	
Custer	3410	75.0%	1137	25.0%	
Daniels	1302	74.9%	436	25.1%	
Dawson	2759	73.3%	1007	26.7%	
Deer Lodge	6125	87.1%	910	12.9%	
Fallon	1038	69.2%	463	30.8%	
Fergus	4439	76.9%	1333	23.1%	
Flathead	9191	77.9%	2612	22.1%	
Gallatin	5560	67.8%	2643	32.2%	
Garfield	580	75.4%	189	24.6%	
Glacier	2381	75.6%	768	24.4%	
Golden Valley	378	65.5%	199	34.5%	
Granite	979	73.6%	351	26.4%	
Hill	4283	80.2%	1055	19.8%	
Jefferson	1185	79.5%	305	20.5%	
Judith Basin	1137	77.5%	330	22.5%	
Lake	3244	68.8%	1471	31.2%	
Lewis & Clark	8047	75.2%	2653	24.8%	
Liberty	740	77.2%	218	22.8%	
Lincoln	3031	83.0%	620	17.0%	
Madison	1739	73.1%	639	26.9%	
McCone	1087	77.4%	318	22.6%	
Meagher	553	62.5%	332	37.5%	
Mineral	869	82.8%	180	17.2%	
Missoula	11727	79.2%	3072	20.8%	
Musselshell	1548	77.1%	461	22.9%	
Park	3458	71.9%	1350	28.1%	
Petroleum	315	75.0%	105	25.0%	
Phillips	2186	76.4%	677	23.6%	
Pondera	2150	80.4%	523	19.6%	
Powder River	652	64.6%	357	35.4%	
Powell	2365	82.5%	502	17.5%	
Prairie	576	65.2%	307	34.8%	
Ravalli	3423	74.1%	1199	25.9%	
Richland	2812	75.4%	919	24.6%	
Roosevelt	2905	78.1%	813	21.9%	
Rosebud	1523	69.2%	678	30.8%	
Sanders	2245	79.8%	569	20.2%	
Sheridan	2236	84.6%	408	15.4%	
Silver Bow	15805	84.7%	2852	15.3%	
Stillwater	1554	65.3%	825	34.7%	
Sweet Grass	800	58.1%	577	41.9%	
Teton	2107	72.4%	802	27.6%	
Toole	2133	76.6%	651	23.4%	
Treasure	411	72.7%	154	27.3%	
Valley	3249	81.8%	725	18.2%	
Wheatland	906	68.0%	427	32.0%	
Wibaux	516	70.4%	217	29.6%	
Yellowstone	14863	67.9%	7015	32.1%	
TOTALS	**174910**	**76.2%**	**54573**	**23.8%**	

1958 U.S. House Election, 1st District

COUNTIES	Lee Metcalf (D)		Jean Walterskirchen (R)		Other
Beaverhead	1733	64.0%	975	36.0%	
Big Horn					
Blaine					
Broadwater	800	64.9%	432	35.1%	
Carbon					
Carter					
Cascade					
Chouteau					
Custer					
Daniels					
Dawson					
Deer Lodge	5560	80.0%	1387	20.0%	
Fallon					
Fergus					
Flathead	7885	67.0%	3878	33.0%	
Gallatin	5134	63.5%	2953	36.5%	
Garfield					
Glacier					
Golden Valley					
Granite	868	66.1%	446	33.9%	
Hill					
Jefferson	1043	70.6%	435	29.4%	
Judith Basin					
Lake	2970	63.2%	1730	36.8%	
Lewis & Clark	7277	68.6%	3329	31.4%	
Liberty					
Lincoln	2771	76.8%	838	23.2%	
Madison	1505	63.6%	863	36.4%	
McCone					
Meagher					
Mineral	805	77.6%	233	22.4%	
Missoula	9699	65.9%	5013	34.1%	
Musselshell					
Park					
Petroleum					
Phillips					
Pondera					
Powder River					
Powell	2073	73.1%	764	26.9%	
Prairie					
Ravalli	3155	68.8%	1432	31.2%	
Richland					
Roosevelt					
Rosebud					
Sanders	2067	74.2%	718	25.8%	
Sheridan					
Silver Bow	13241	73.9%	4685	26.1%	
Stillwater					
Sweet Grass					
Teton					
Toole					
Treasure					
Valley					
Wheatland					
Wibaux					
Yellowstone					
TOTALS	**68586**	**69.5%**	**30111**	**30.5%**	

1958 U.S. House Election, 2nd District

COUNTIES	LeRoy Anderson (D)		Ashton Jones (R)		Other
Beaverhead					
Big Horn	1507	58.7%	1062	41.3%	
Blaine	1681	66.5%	846	33.5%	
Broadwater					
Carbon	2096	58.4%	1490	41.6%	
Carter	377	40.7%	550	59.3%	
Cascade	13089	66.0%	6741	34.0%	
Chouteau	2065	65.6%	1085	34.4%	
Custer	2616	57.5%	1933	42.5%	
Daniels	1119	64.7%	611	35.3%	
Dawson	2384	62.9%	1407	37.1%	
Deer Lodge					
Fallon	843	55.5%	677	44.5%	
Fergus	3616	62.7%	2152	37.3%	
Flathead					
Gallatin					
Garfield	450	58.5%	319	41.5%	
Glacier	1955	62.4%	1176	37.6%	
Golden Valley	326	55.8%	258	44.2%	
Granite					
Hill	3649	69.0%	1640	31.0%	
Jefferson					
Judith Basin	920	63.2%	536	36.8%	
Lake					
Lewis & Clark					
Liberty	603	62.8%	357	37.2%	
Lincoln					
Madison					
McCone	931	66.1%	478	33.9%	
Meagher	430	48.6%	455	51.4%	
Mineral					
Missoula					
Musselshell	1305	64.7%	712	35.3%	
Park	2717	56.2%	2118	43.8%	
Petroleum	248	58.9%	173	41.1%	
Phillips	1822	63.9%	1028	36.1%	
Pondera	1935	71.8%	760	28.2%	
Powder River	397	37.7%	657	62.3%	
Powell					
Prairie	454	51.3%	431	48.7%	
Ravalli					
Richland	2317	62.2%	1407	37.8%	
Roosevelt	2440	66.2%	1247	33.8%	
Rosebud	1167	52.3%	1066	47.7%	
Sanders					
Sheridan	1980	74.8%	668	25.2%	
Silver Bow					
Stillwater	1279	53.0%	1133	47.0%	
Sweet Grass	582	41.0%	836	59.0%	
Teton	1774	60.2%	1175	39.8%	
Toole	1805	64.9%	978	35.1%	
Treasure	355	61.2%	225	38.8%	
Valley	2818	71.3%	1133	28.7%	
Wheatland	727	53.3%	636	46.7%	
Wibaux	451	61.6%	281	38.4%	
Yellowstone	11910	53.9%	10196	46.1%	
TOTALS	**79140**	**61.0%**	**50633**	**39.0%**	

1960 Presidential Election

COUNTIES	John Kennedy (D)		Richard Nixon (R)		Other
Beaverhead	1307	43.0%	1731	56.9%	5
Big Horn	1497	46.4%	1724	53.5%	3
Blaine	1569	54.6%	1290	44.9%	17
Broadwater	631	48.1%	680	51.9%	0
Carbon	1903	48.0%	2050	51.8%	8
Carter	383	35.6%	688	64.0%	4
Cascade	14117	54.1%	11928	45.7%	45
Chouteau	1708	50.4%	1672	49.3%	9
Custer	2393	44.7%	2943	55.0%	15
Daniels	960	55.7%	763	44.3%	1
Dawson	2108	46.0%	2460	53.7%	14
Deer Lodge	5149	70.1%	2188	29.8%	7
Fallon	597	39.4%	918	60.6%	1
Fergus	2999	47.6%	3294	52.2%	13
Flathead	6689	46.9%	7554	52.9%	24
Gallatin	3761	35.3%	6870	64.5%	21
Garfield	363	41.3%	515	58.5%	2
Glacier	2260	56.0%	1775	43.9%	4
Golden Valley	277	43.3%	362	56.7%	0
Granite	592	44.7%	722	54.6%	9
Hill	3741	54.1%	3163	45.7%	12
Jefferson	769	48.4%	817	51.4%	4
Judith Basin	842	53.8%	721	46.1%	1
Lake	2462	43.1%	3240	56.8%	7
Lewis & Clark	6008	45.2%	7260	54.6%	17
Liberty	501	45.5%	597	54.3%	2
Lincoln	2623	57.7%	1902	41.8%	21
Madison	1010	40.9%	1456	59.0%	3
McCone	764	50.4%	743	49.0%	8
Meagher	431	41.1%	613	58.5%	4
Mineral	686	55.3%	549	44.3%	5
Missoula	8876	45.9%	10396	53.8%	65
Musselshell	1100	49.8%	1107	50.1%	3
Park	2249	40.2%	3329	59.4%	23
Petroleum	221	46.4%	255	53.6%	0
Phillips	1455	49.7%	1457	49.8%	13
Pondera	1653	53.2%	1452	46.8%	0
Powder River	438	39.6%	665	60.2%	2
Powell	1522	50.3%	1497	49.5%	6
Prairie	338	34.2%	649	65.8%	0
Ravalli	2381	43.1%	3121	56.5%	26
Richland	1863	43.6%	2395	56.1%	11
Roosevelt	2227	53.9%	1876	45.4%	29
Rosebud	1002	41.8%	1386	57.8%	11
Sanders	1469	49.2%	1497	50.2%	18
Sheridan	1549	56.2%	1196	43.4%	9
Silver Bow	13754	64.9%	7290	34.4%	146
Stillwater	1036	41.6%	1455	58.4%	0
Sweet Grass	521	32.2%	1096	67.8%	0
Teton	1648	50.3%	1623	49.5%	5
Toole	1767	52.8%	1577	47.1%	4
Treasure	270	47.4%	300	52.6%	0
Valley	2953	55.2%	2387	44.7%	6
Wheatland	724	47.7%	793	52.2%	1
Wibaux	419	52.0%	387	48.0%	0
Yellowstone	12356	38.6%	19467	60.8%	183
TOTALS	**134891**	**48.6%**	**141841**	**51.1%**	**847**

1960 Gubernatorial Election

COUNTIES	Paul Cannon (D)		Donald Nutter (R)		Other
Beaverhead	1145	36.9%	1962	63.1%	
Big Horn	1427	43.7%	1842	56.3%	
Blaine	1431	49.7%	1447	50.3%	
Broadwater	505	38.1%	821	61.9%	
Carbon	1976	48.0%	2143	52.0%	
Carter	308	28.4%	777	71.6%	
Cascade	11377	45.6%	13576	54.4%	
Chouteau	1710	48.9%	1788	51.1%	
Custer	2396	43.0%	3173	57.0%	
Daniels	938	53.1%	830	46.9%	
Dawson	1979	41.5%	2785	58.5%	
Deer Lodge	5096	67.3%	2479	32.7%	
Fallon	617	37.5%	1027	62.5%	
Fergus	2730	42.2%	3739	57.8%	
Flathead	6652	46.0%	7802	54.0%	
Gallatin	3426	31.7%	7378	68.3%	
Garfield	383	42.6%	517	57.4%	
Glacier	2234	53.0%	1984	47.0%	
Golden Valley	276	43.2%	363	56.8%	
Granite	583	41.9%	808	58.1%	
Hill	3432	49.4%	3509	50.6%	
Jefferson	767	46.3%	889	53.7%	
Judith Basin	787	49.2%	811	50.8%	
Lake	2550	43.5%	3308	56.5%	
Lewis & Clark	4968	37.4%	8326	62.6%	
Liberty	434	39.1%	676	60.9%	
Lincoln	2896	61.4%	1821	38.6%	
Madison	902	36.2%	1593	63.8%	
McCone	824	52.7%	741	47.3%	
Meagher	379	35.2%	698	64.8%	
Mineral	722	55.7%	574	44.3%	
Missoula	7853	40.4%	11577	59.6%	
Musselshell	1175	51.2%	1122	48.8%	
Park	2412	42.0%	3327	58.0%	
Petroleum	201	41.7%	281	58.3%	
Phillips	1526	50.5%	1496	49.5%	
Pondera	1478	46.5%	1698	53.5%	
Powder River	391	35.1%	722	64.9%	
Powell	1559	50.8%	1512	49.2%	
Prairie	347	35.3%	636	64.7%	
Ravalli	2298	40.2%	3415	59.8%	
Richland	1829	41.0%	2634	59.0%	
Roosevelt	2182	51.5%	2052	48.5%	
Rosebud	978	39.5%	1499	60.5%	
Sanders	1440	46.8%	1640	53.2%	
Sheridan	1543	55.1%	1259	44.9%	
Silver Bow	12542	60.1%	8320	39.9%	
Stillwater	1032	39.9%	1554	60.1%	
Sweet Grass	509	31.9%	1089	68.1%	
Teton	1487	44.8%	1835	55.2%	
Toole	1434	41.1%	2055	58.9%	
Treasure	260	44.3%	327	55.7%	
Valley	2779	53.2%	2441	46.8%	
Wheatland	693	45.9%	818	54.1%	
Wibaux	337	42.8%	450	57.2%	
Yellowstone	11516	36.2%	20284	63.8%	
TOTALS	**125651**	**44.9%**	**154230**	**55.1%**	

1960 U.S. Senate Election

COUNTIES	Lee Metcalf (D)		Orvin Fjare (R)		Other
Beaverhead	1477	47.4%	1640	52.6%	
Big Horn	1666	50.2%	1652	49.8%	
Blaine	1603	55.0%	1311	45.0%	
Broadwater	630	46.9%	712	53.1%	
Carbon	2056	51.0%	1978	49.0%	
Carter	423	41.7%	591	58.3%	
Cascade	12525	51.9%	11585	48.1%	
Chouteau	1754	50.8%	1700	49.2%	
Custer	2737	50.0%	2739	50.0%	
Daniels	1022	58.0%	741	42.0%	
Dawson	2279	47.8%	2488	52.2%	
Deer Lodge	5188	68.2%	2415	31.8%	
Fallon	754	46.8%	857	53.2%	
Fergus	3249	50.0%	3250	50.0%	
Flathead	7388	50.5%	7236	49.5%	
Gallatin	4441	42.0%	6141	58.0%	
Garfield	444	49.8%	448	50.2%	
Glacier	2319	56.8%	1765	43.2%	
Golden Valley	272	42.3%	371	57.7%	
Granite	666	48.3%	712	51.7%	
Hill	3671	54.3%	3090	45.7%	
Jefferson	819	49.9%	821	50.1%	
Judith Basin	875	54.3%	735	45.7%	
Lake	2715	46.2%	3163	53.8%	
Lewis & Clark	6341	48.1%	6844	51.9%	
Liberty	497	44.3%	624	55.7%	
Lincoln	3163	67.2%	1543	32.8%	
Madison	1145	45.3%	1380	54.7%	
McCone	856	54.7%	709	45.3%	
Meagher	407	37.7%	674	62.3%	
Mineral	849	65.1%	456	34.9%	
Missoula	10002	51.4%	9450	48.6%	
Musselshell	1215	52.9%	1082	47.1%	
Park	2581	44.8%	3179	55.2%	
Petroleum	230	47.5%	254	52.5%	
Phillips	1620	56.5%	1247	43.5%	
Pondera	1695	53.3%	1487	46.7%	
Powder River	447	39.7%	678	60.3%	
Powell	1747	56.8%	1329	43.2%	
Prairie	409	41.2%	584	58.8%	
Ravalli	2842	49.5%	2897	50.5%	
Richland	2149	48.6%	2269	51.4%	
Roosevelt	2433	57.4%	1805	42.6%	
Rosebud	1049	43.4%	1370	56.6%	
Sanders	1686	56.7%	1287	43.3%	
Sheridan	1786	64.1%	999	35.9%	
Silver Bow	11572	58.4%	8247	41.6%	
Stillwater	1085	41.7%	1518	58.3%	
Sweet Grass	469	28.9%	1152	71.1%	
Teton	1649	49.2%	1700	50.8%	
Toole	1839	52.9%	1637	47.1%	
Treasure	294	49.2%	304	50.8%	
Valley	3138	60.0%	2093	40.0%	
Wheatland	687	44.8%	847	55.2%	
Wibaux	416	52.3%	379	47.7%	
Yellowstone	13062	41.9%	18116	58.1%	
TOTALS	**140331**	**50.7%**	**136281**	**49.3%**	

1960 U.S. House Election, 1st District

COUNTIES	Arnold Olsen (D)		George Sarsfield (R)		Other
Beaverhead	1283	41.4%	1813	58.6%	
Big Horn					
Blaine					
Broadwater	640	48.2%	687	51.8%	
Carbon					
Carter					
Cascade					
Chouteau					
Custer					
Daniels					
Dawson					
Deer Lodge	5261	69.5%	2308	30.5%	
Fallon					
Fergus					
Flathead	7359	51.1%	7056	48.9%	
Gallatin	4334	41.3%	6160	58.7%	
Garfield					
Glacier					
Golden Valley					
Granite	660	48.3%	706	51.7%	
Hill					
Jefferson	886	54.2%	748	45.8%	
Judith Basin					
Lake	2708	47.0%	3058	53.0%	
Lewis & Clark	6748	51.5%	6361	48.5%	
Liberty					
Lincoln	3048	66.4%	1544	33.6%	
Madison	1075	43.4%	1402	56.6%	
McCone					
Meagher			.		
Mineral	837	65.1%	449	34.9%	
Missoula	9287	48.3%	9960	51.7%	
Musselshell					
Park					
Petroleum					
Phillips					
Pondera					
Powder River					
Powell	1741	57.1%	1310	42.9%	
Prairie					
Ravalli	2571	45.9%	3027	54.1%	
Richland					
Roosevelt					
Rosebud					
Sanders	1657	56.7%	1263	43.3%	
Sheridan					
Silver Bow	12986	63.4%	7495	36.6%	
Stillwater					
Sweet Grass					
Teton					
Toole					
Treasure					
Valley					
Wheatland					
Wibaux					
Yellowstone					
TOTALS	**63081**	**53.3%**	**55347**	**46.7%**	

189

1960 U.S. House Election, 2nd District

COUNTIES	Leo Graybill (D)		James "Big Jim" Battin (R)	
Beaverhead				
Big Horn	1538	48.5%	1636	51.5%
Blaine	1607	56.0%	1264	44.0%
Broadwater				
Carbon	2061	51.9%	1909	48.1%
Carter	407	40.1%	608	59.9%
Cascade	10325	45.1%	12555	54.9%
Chouteau	1787	51.9%	1655	48.1%
Custer	2672	49.6%	2720	50.4%
Daniels	1011	58.5%	718	41.5%
Dawson	2114	45.8%	2500	54.2%
Deer Lodge				
Fallon	747	47.3%	833	52.7%
Fergus	3306	51.5%	3115	48.5%
Flathead				
Gallatin				
Garfield	410	47.1%	460	52.9%
Glacier	2438	60.6%	1585	39.4%
Golden Valley	291	46.9%	330	53.1%
Granite				
Hill	3789	56.7%	2888	43.3%
Jefferson				
Judith Basin	863	54.2%	728	45.8%
Lake				
Lewis & Clark				
Liberty	530	47.7%	581	52.3%
Lincoln				
Madison				
McCone	868	56.9%	657	43.1%
Meagher	411	38.9%	645	61.1%
Mineral				
Missoula				
Musselshell	1221	54.1%	1034	45.9%
Park	2721	48.0%	2951	52.0%
Petroleum	235	49.5%	240	50.5%
Phillips	1597	56.5%	1230	43.5%
Pondera	1775	56.2%	1384	43.8%
Powder River	443	40.9%	641	59.1%
Powell				
Prairie	366	38.2%	591	61.8%
Ravalli				
Richland	2138	49.4%	2189	50.6%
Roosevelt	2446	59.1%	1693	40.9%
Rosebud	1082	45.5%	1298	54.5%
Sanders				
Sheridan	1806	66.3%	917	33.7%
Silver Bow				
Stillwater	1191	46.3%	1382	53.7%
Sweet Grass	575	36.3%	1008	63.7%
Teton	1677	50.9%	1616	49.1%
Toole	1804	52.7%	1620	47.3%
Treasure	293	51.0%	282	49.0%
Valley	3181	61.5%	1988	38.5%
Wheatland	744	49.1%	770	50.9%
Wibaux	398	52.9%	354	47.1%
Yellowstone	12594	41.6%	17702	58.4%
TOTALS	**75507**	**49.1%**	**78277**	**50.9%**

1962 U.S. House Election, 1st District

COUNTIES	Arnold Olsen (D)		Wayne Montgomery (R)		Other
Beaverhead	1027	36.0%	1829	64.0%	
Big Horn					
Blaine					
Broadwater	514	42.9%	683	57.1%	
Carbon					
Carter					
Cascade					
Chouteau					
Custer					
Daniels					
Dawson					
Deer Lodge	4423	69.6%	1934	30.4%	
Fallon					
Fergus					
Flathead	6222	48.9%	6503	51.1%	
Gallatin	3776	41.1%	5411	58.9%	
Garfield					
Glacier					
Golden Valley					
Granite	584	47.8%	637	52.2%	
Hill					
Jefferson	785	50.7%	764	49.3%	
Judith Basin					
Lake	2082	40.0%	3129	60.0%	
Lewis & Clark	5988	51.1%	5734	48.9%	
Liberty					
Lincoln	2562	60.0%	1710	40.0%	
Madison	988	41.3%	1404	58.7%	
McCone					
Meagher					
Mineral	702	64.2%	392	35.8%	
Missoula	7905	47.7%	8663	52.3%	
Musselshell					
Park					
Petroleum					
Phillips					
Pondera					
Powder River					
Powell	1495	53.3%	1308	46.7%	
Prairie					
Ravalli	2381	48.0%	2576	52.0%	
Richland					
Roosevelt					
Rosebud					
Sanders	1515	54.4%	1269	45.6%	
Sheridan					
Silver Bow	12662	68.5%	5814	31.5%	
Stillwater					
Sweet Grass					
Teton					
Toole					
Treasure					
Valley					
Wheatland					
Wibaux					
Yellowstone					
TOTALS	**55611**	**52.8%**	**49760**	**47.2%**	

1962 U.S. House Election, 2nd District

COUNTIES	Leo Graybill (D)		James "Big Jim" Battin (R)		Other
Beaverhead					
Big Horn	1358	43.9%	1738	56.1%	
Blaine	1447	52.9%	1286	47.1%	
Broadwater					
Carbon	1790	48.8%	1875	51.2%	
Carter	294	29.6%	698	70.4%	
Cascade	10324	44.9%	12652	55.1%	
Chouteau	1341	42.3%	1826	57.7%	
Custer	2226	44.4%	2782	55.6%	
Daniels	864	50.0%	863	50.0%	
Dawson	1889	43.2%	2482	56.8%	
Deer Lodge					
Fallon	672	42.1%	925	57.9%	
Fergus	2505	41.8%	3484	58.2%	
Flathead					
Gallatin					
Garfield	309	35.6%	560	64.4%	
Glacier	1674	47.6%	1843	52.4%	
Golden Valley	242	42.5%	328	57.5%	
Granite					
Hill	3194	52.7%	2871	47.3%	
Jefferson					
Judith Basin	680	46.2%	792	53.8%	
Lake					
Lewis & Clark					
Liberty	459	40.9%	663	59.1%	
Lincoln					
Madison					
McCone	740	51.9%	687	48.1%	
Meagher	291	32.3%	611	67.7%	
Mineral					
Missoula					
Musselshell	1004	48.6%	1062	51.4%	
Park	2092	44.5%	2609	55.5%	
Petroleum	187	44.4%	234	55.6%	
Phillips	1228	45.1%	1494	54.9%	
Pondera	1320	48.0%	1430	52.0%	
Powder River	367	32.6%	759	67.4%	
Powell					
Prairie	346	34.0%	671	66.0%	
Ravalli					
Richland	1946	46.2%	2266	53.8%	
Roosevelt	1949	49.1%	2024	50.9%	
Rosebud	947	41.6%	1332	58.4%	
Sanders					
Sheridan	1522	58.5%	1078	41.5%	
Silver Bow					
Stillwater	856	39.7%	1299	60.3%	
Sweet Grass	466	33.2%	936	66.8%	
Teton	1350	43.4%	1761	56.6%	
Toole	1305	44.0%	1658	56.0%	
Treasure	219	41.2%	312	58.8%	
Valley	2469	52.0%	2278	48.0%	
Wheatland	693	48.8%	726	51.2%	
Wibaux	378	47.9%	411	52.1%	
Yellowstone	10812	40.3%	16008	59.7%	
TOTALS	**63755**	**44.6%**	**79315**	**55.4%**	

1964 Presidential Election

COUNTIES	Lyndon Johnson (D)		Barry Goldwater (R)		Other
Beaverhead	1469	45.5%	1754	54.3%	8
Big Horn	2509	62.8%	1481	37.1%	3
Blaine	1742	64.4%	961	35.6%	0
Broadwater	595	49.4%	609	50.6%	0
Carbon	2098	57.7%	1535	42.3%	0
Carter	453	44.0%	576	56.0%	0
Cascade	17609	65.9%	8986	33.6%	119
Chouteau	1827	55.8%	1444	44.1%	5
Custer	2790	54.7%	2302	45.1%	9
Daniels	987	57.1%	742	42.9%	1
Dawson	2691	58.0%	1938	41.8%	8
Deer Lodge	4835	77.2%	1415	22.6%	9
Fallon	765	48.0%	827	51.8%	3
Fergus	3300	52.4%	2980	47.4%	13
Flathead	8015	55.8%	6325	44.0%	30
Gallatin	5600	49.8%	5621	50.0%	27
Garfield	384	42.9%	509	56.8%	3
Glacier	2218	60.0%	1458	39.4%	21
Golden Valley	352	58.3%	252	41.7%	0
Granite	658	55.4%	527	44.4%	2
Hill	4491	68.0%	2101	31.8%	12
Jefferson	967	59.3%	662	40.6%	2
Judith Basin	822	54.7%	678	45.1%	2
Lake	3148	52.6%	2828	47.2%	10
Lewis & Clark	7506	54.8%	6155	45.0%	26
Liberty	619	53.6%	533	46.1%	3
Lincoln	3140	66.7%	1554	33.0%	15
Madison	1125	46.8%	1276	53.1%	2
McCone	891	59.1%	615	40.8%	1
Meagher	405	44.4%	506	55.4%	2
Mineral	901	70.7%	368	28.9%	5
Missoula	12900	61.4%	8065	38.4%	39
Musselshell	1189	59.1%	823	40.9%	0
Park	2824	51.8%	2619	48.0%	10
Petroleum	210	52.4%	190	47.4%	1
Phillips	1612	56.4%	1242	43.5%	3
Pondera	1759	61.1%	1110	38.6%	8
Powder River	449	40.9%	649	59.1%	1
Powell	1896	62.4%	1140	37.5%	4
Prairie	488	46.6%	555	53.0%	5
Ravalli	3300	58.3%	2350	41.5%	12
Richland	2320	56.2%	1784	43.2%	27
Roosevelt	2463	60.4%	1612	39.5%	3
Rosebud	1212	52.2%	1105	47.6%	4
Sanders	1836	60.9%	1163	38.6%	14
Sheridan	1905	69.2%	837	30.4%	12
Silver Bow	15751	74.2%	4873	22.9%	615
Stillwater	1130	49.8%	1140	50.2%	1
Sweet Grass	653	43.1%	856	56.5%	5
Teton	1808	56.5%	1388	43.4%	3
Toole	1649	57.4%	1223	42.6%	2
Treasure	285	53.2%	251	46.8%	0
Valley	3032	59.2%	2077	40.5%	16
Wheatland	790	57.5%	583	42.5%	0
Wibaux	427	57.9%	308	41.8%	2
Yellowstone	17446	52.5%	15571	46.8%	222
TOTALS	**164246**	**58.9%**	**113032**	**40.6%**	**1350**

1964 Gubernatorial Election

COUNTIES	Roland Renne (D)		Tim Babcock (R)		Other
Beaverhead	1190	36.2%	2093	63.8%	
Big Horn	1956	48.1%	2110	51.9%	
Blaine	1291	46.8%	1469	53.2%	
Broadwater	441	35.4%	804	64.6%	
Carbon	1792	46.9%	2029	53.1%	
Carter	371	34.9%	693	65.1%	
Cascade	15038	56.7%	11506	43.3%	
Chouteau	1406	42.0%	1943	58.0%	
Custer	2155	40.3%	3189	59.7%	
Daniels	786	44.6%	976	55.4%	
Dawson	1913	40.1%	2852	59.9%	
Deer Lodge	4442	70.5%	1858	29.5%	
Fallon	696	41.4%	984	58.6%	
Fergus	2969	46.1%	3465	53.9%	
Flathead	7527	51.9%	6988	48.1%	
Gallatin	4828	42.9%	6419	57.1%	
Garfield	247	26.8%	675	73.2%	
Glacier	1898	49.8%	1912	50.2%	
Golden Valley	281	45.1%	342	54.9%	
Granite	511	42.5%	690	57.5%	
Hill	3489	53.2%	3064	46.8%	
Jefferson	804	49.5%	819	50.5%	
Judith Basin	728	46.5%	836	53.5%	
Lake	2637	43.3%	3449	56.7%	
Lewis & Clark	6206	45.1%	7545	54.9%	
Liberty	469	39.6%	715	60.4%	
Lincoln	3091	63.4%	1785	36.6%	
Madison	764	31.6%	1656	68.4%	
McCone	766	49.5%	782	50.5%	
Meagher	284	30.4%	651	69.6%	
Mineral	784	62.4%	472	37.6%	
Missoula	10569	50.3%	10424	49.7%	
Musselshell	951	45.9%	1122	54.1%	
Park	2205	40.2%	3281	59.8%	
Petroleum	162	40.1%	242	59.9%	
Phillips	1266	43.8%	1622	56.2%	
Pondera	1296	44.6%	1608	55.4%	
Powder River	356	32.0%	755	68.0%	
Powell	1469	48.8%	1540	51.2%	
Prairie	347	33.1%	702	66.9%	
Ravalli	2649	45.9%	3122	54.1%	
Richland	2070	48.0%	2241	52.0%	
Roosevelt	2178	51.4%	2059	48.6%	
Rosebud	875	36.7%	1512	63.3%	
Sanders	1471	49.2%	1520	50.8%	
Sheridan	1657	60.0%	1105	40.0%	
Silver Bow	14131	67.7%	6730	32.3%	
Stillwater	821	35.4%	1498	64.6%	
Sweet Grass	432	28.1%	1108	71.9%	
Teton	1505	47.0%	1695	53.0%	
Toole	1285	43.7%	1657	56.3%	
Treasure	203	37.7%	336	62.3%	
Valley	2591	50.2%	2572	49.8%	
Wheatland	620	43.7%	798	56.3%	
Wibaux	358	46.5%	412	53.5%	
Yellowstone	13635	40.9%	19681	59.1%	
TOTALS	**136862**	**48.7%**	**144113**	**51.3%**	

1964 U.S. Senate Election

COUNTIES	Mike Mansfield (D)		Alex Blewett (R)		Other
Beaverhead	1666	50.8%	1616	49.2%	
Big Horn	2777	68.2%	1292	31.8%	
Blaine	1928	69.7%	837	30.3%	
Broadwater	655	52.7%	589	47.3%	
Carbon	2424	63.2%	1412	36.8%	
Carter	522	52.3%	476	47.7%	
Cascade	18693	70.7%	7749	29.3%	
Chouteau	1976	58.7%	1392	41.3%	
Custer	3181	62.1%	1942	37.9%	
Daniels	1065	61.0%	680	39.0%	
Dawson	3245	67.8%	1544	32.2%	
Deer Lodge	4606	72.4%	1755	27.6%	
Fallon	905	58.5%	642	41.5%	
Fergus	3860	59.7%	2604	40.3%	
Flathead	9405	64.1%	5258	35.9%	
Gallatin	6273	56.2%	4884	43.8%	
Garfield	423	46.2%	493	53.8%	
Glacier	2513	65.8%	1309	34.2%	
Golden Valley	352	57.1%	264	42.9%	
Granite	666	54.8%	549	45.2%	
Hill	4719	72.0%	1831	28.0%	
Jefferson	1005	60.7%	652	39.3%	
Judith Basin	956	61.6%	596	38.4%	
Lake	3419	55.7%	2717	44.3%	
Lewis & Clark	8566	62.8%	5080	37.2%	
Liberty	651	54.6%	541	45.4%	
Lincoln	3655	75.0%	1219	25.0%	
Madison	1187	48.7%	1252	51.3%	
McCone	1002	64.5%	551	35.5%	
Meagher	442	47.2%	495	52.8%	
Mineral	998	78.0%	282	22.0%	
Missoula	14834	69.4%	6531	30.6%	
Musselshell	1305	62.8%	772	37.2%	
Park	3241	57.9%	2356	42.1%	
Petroleum	242	59.6%	164	40.4%	
Phillips	1721	59.8%	1156	40.2%	
Pondera	1841	63.2%	1072	36.8%	
Powder River	518	46.9%	587	53.1%	
Powell	1989	64.9%	1078	35.1%	
Prairie	557	53.4%	487	46.6%	
Ravalli	3494	62.6%	2089	37.4%	
Richland	2796	65.2%	1493	34.8%	
Roosevelt	2969	70.1%	1265	29.9%	
Rosebud	1358	57.0%	1024	43.0%	
Sanders	2078	69.3%	919	30.7%	
Sheridan	2109	75.9%	671	24.1%	
Silver Bow	15064	73.4%	5454	26.6%	
Stillwater	1268	54.5%	1059	45.5%	
Sweet Grass	708	46.0%	831	54.0%	
Teton	1922	60.0%	1282	40.0%	
Toole	1837	63.2%	1071	36.8%	
Treasure	325	60.3%	214	39.7%	
Valley	3520	69.6%	1537	30.4%	
Wheatland	866	61.1%	552	38.9%	
Wibaux	512	66.8%	255	33.2%	
Yellowstone	19834	60.5%	12945	39.5%	
TOTALS	**180643**	**64.5%**	**99367**	**35.5%**	

1964 U.S. House Election, 1st District

COUNTIES	Arnold Olsen (D)		Wayne Montgomery (R)		Other
Beaverhead	1088	33.1%	2181	66.4%	17
Big Horn					
Blaine					
Broadwater	563	49.0%	583	50.7%	3
Carbon					
Carter					
Cascade					
Chouteau					
Custer					
Daniels					
Dawson					
Deer Lodge	3881	61.3%	2415	38.2%	31
Fallon					
Fergus					
Flathead	7413	50.8%	7090	48.6%	79
Gallatin	4933	44.7%	6077	55.0%	30
Garfield					
Glacier					
Golden Valley					
Granite	566	47.0%	636	52.9%	1
Hill					
Jefferson	855	51.4%	795	47.8%	12
Judith Basin					
Lake	2689	44.2%	3370	55.4%	22
Lewis & Clark	7207	53.6%	6176	45.9%	62
Liberty					
Lincoln	3044	63.2%	1755	36.5%	14
Madison	985	40.8%	1422	58.8%	10
McCone					
Meagher					
Mineral	833	66.1%	421	33.4%	7
Missoula	11052	52.1%	10062	47.4%	92
Musselshell					
Park					
Petroleum					
Phillips					
Pondera					
Powder River					
Powell	1626	52.9%	1440	46.9%	6
Prairie					
Ravalli	2640	47.4%	2910	52.2%	23
Richland					
Roosevelt					
Rosebud					
Sanders	1631	54.8%	1326	44.6%	19
Sheridan					
Silver Bow	13841	66.8%	6658	32.1%	216
Stillwater					
Sweet Grass					
Teton					
Toole					
Treasure					
Valley					
Wheatland					
Wibaux					
Yellowstone					
TOTALS	**64847**	**53.6%**	**55417**	**45.8%**	**644**

1964 U.S. House Election, 2nd District

COUNTIES	Jack Toole (D)		James "Big Jim"Battin (R)		Othe
Beaverhead					
Big Horn	1818	45.1%	2216	54.9%	
Blaine	1379	50.3%	1360	49.7%	
Broadwater					
Carbon	1803	47.7%	1978	52.3%	
Carter	381	36.2%	671	63.8%	
Cascade	13563	53.9%	11619	46.1%	
Chouteau	1563	46.6%	1789	53.4%	
Custer	1992	39.0%	3112	61.0%	
Daniels	841	48.6%	888	51.4%	
Dawson	1931	40.8%	2802	59.2%	
Deer Lodge					
Fallon	706	42.6%	952	57.4%	
Fergus	2862	44.6%	3550	55.4%	
Flathead					
Gallatin					
Garfield	303	33.3%	607	66.7%	
Glacier	1839	48.7%	1935	51.3%	
Golden Valley	290	46.3%	337	53.7%	
Granite					
Hill	3567	54.9%	2927	45.1%	
Jefferson					
Judith Basin	716	46.3%	829	53.7%	
Lake					
Lewis & Clark					
Liberty	455	38.9%	714	61.1%	
Lincoln					
Madison					
McCone	804	52.6%	724	47.4%	
Meagher	320	34.7%	601	65.3%	
Mineral					
Missoula					
Musselshell	970	47.1%	1090	52.9%	
Park	2397	43.2%	3158	56.8%	
Petroleum	169	42.1%	232	57.9%	
Phillips	1293	45.2%	1570	54.8%	
Pondera	1353	46.6%	1549	53.4%	
Powder River	356	32.4%	742	67.6%	
Powell					
Prairie	344	32.8%	704	67.2%	
Ravalli					
Richland	2017	47.5%	2230	52.5%	
Roosevelt	2271	53.8%	1954	46.2%	
Rosebud	968	41.1%	1390	58.9%	
Sanders					
Sheridan	1579	58.1%	1140	41.9%	
Silver Bow					
Stillwater	863	37.6%	1431	62.4%	
Sweet Grass	458	29.9%	1076	70.1%	
Teton	1510	47.4%	1675	52.6%	
Toole	1217	42.1%	1671	57.9%	
Treasure	219	40.9%	316	59.1%	
Valley	2603	53.0%	2308	47.0%	
Wheatland	641	45.9%	755	54.1%	
Wibaux	387	51.0%	372	49.0%	
Yellowstone	12713	39.8%	19267	60.2%	
TOTALS	**71461**	**46.5%**	**82241**	**53.5%**	

1966 U.S. Senate Election

COUNTIES	Lee Metcalf (D)		Tim Babcock (R)		Other
Beaverhead	1126	39.9%	1699	60.1%	
Big Horn	1826	52.0%	1685	48.0%	
Blaine	1629	60.3%	1074	39.7%	
Broadwater	488	41.9%	676	58.1%	
Carbon	1894	52.1%	1739	47.9%	
Carter	436	47.6%	480	52.4%	
Cascade	15013	60.8%	9667	39.2%	
Chouteau	1533	49.7%	1551	50.3%	
Custer	2372	50.1%	2358	49.9%	
Daniels	827	51.1%	791	48.9%	
Dawson	2272	51.3%	2159	48.7%	
Deer Lodge	4286	72.0%	1665	28.0%	
Fallon	699	45.7%	830	54.3%	
Fergus	2647	46.7%	3025	53.3%	
Flathead	7346	53.0%	6508	47.0%	
Gallatin	4765	45.0%	5824	55.0%	
Garfield	300	36.8%	515	63.2%	
Glacier	1930	56.5%	1488	43.5%	
Golden Valley	264	46.2%	307	53.8%	
Granite	565	48.1%	610	51.9%	
Hill	4018	61.8%	2480	38.2%	
Jefferson	840	53.2%	738	46.8%	
Judith Basin	752	50.5%	738	49.5%	
Lake	2528	44.8%	3116	55.2%	
Lewis & Clark	6409	48.7%	6750	51.3%	
Liberty	545	51.3%	518	48.7%	
Lincoln	2894	63.0%	1700	37.0%	
Madison	891	39.4%	1369	60.6%	
McCone	784	55.1%	639	44.9%	
Meagher	302	35.8%	542	64.2%	
Mineral	734	64.5%	404	35.5%	
Missoula	10623	54.8%	8762	45.2%	
Musselshell	978	52.5%	885	47.5%	
Park	2302	47.2%	2570	52.8%	
Petroleum	197	50.8%	191	49.2%	
Phillips	1410	50.8%	1368	49.2%	
Pondera	1626	54.4%	1363	45.6%	
Powder River	376	36.9%	644	63.1%	
Powell	1641	58.9%	1145	41.1%	
Prairie	434	43.1%	574	56.9%	
Ravalli	2607	48.2%	2799	51.8%	
Richland	2106	52.9%	1874	47.1%	
Roosevelt	2197	56.2%	1715	43.8%	
Rosebud	1022	47.3%	1138	52.7%	
Sanders	1511	54.8%	1246	45.2%	
Sheridan	1609	63.0%	944	37.0%	
Silver Bow	12607	66.6%	6309	33.4%	
Stillwater	957	44.4%	1200	55.6%	
Sweet Grass	497	34.9%	926	65.1%	
Teton	1546	51.0%	1484	49.0%	
Toole	1397	52.9%	1244	47.1%	
Treasure	264	48.9%	276	51.1%	
Valley	2629	55.6%	2097	44.4%	
Wheatland	639	49.6%	650	50.4%	
Wibaux	375	54.3%	316	45.7%	
Yellowstone	13701	45.6%	16332	54.4%	
TOTALS	**138166**	**53.2%**	**121697**	**46.8%**	

1966 U.S. House Election, 1st District

COUNTIES	Arnold Olsen (D)		Dick Smiley (R)		Other
Beaverhead	998	35.0%	1851	65.0%	
Big Horn					
Blaine					
Broadwater	463	39.5%	709	60.5%	
Carbon					
Carter					
Cascade					
Chouteau					
Custer					
Daniels					
Dawson					
Deer Lodge	4060	68.2%	1889	31.8%	
Fallon					
Fergus					
Flathead	6586	47.4%	7297	52.6%	
Gallatin	4470	43.0%	5923	57.0%	
Garfield					
Glacier	1743	51.5%	1641	48.5%	
Golden Valley					
Granite	519	43.7%	669	56.3%	
Hill					
Jefferson	832	52.0%	768	48.0%	
Judith Basin					
Lake	2255	39.7%	3426	60.3%	
Lewis & Clark	6218	47.6%	6846	52.4%	
Liberty	509	47.7%	559	52.3%	
Lincoln	2723	59.4%	1864	40.6%	
Madison	881	38.6%	1402	61.4%	
McCone					
Meagher	280	32.9%	570	67.1%	
Mineral	703	61.8%	434	38.2%	
Missoula	9984	51.1%	9541	48.9%	
Musselshell					
Park	2102	43.2%	2769	56.8%	
Petroleum					
Phillips					
Pondera	1544	51.8%	1439	48.2%	
Powder River					
Powell	1407	49.9%	1412	50.1%	
Prairie					
Ravalli	2225	41.0%	3207	59.0%	
Richland					
Roosevelt					
Rosebud					
Sanders	1481	53.2%	1302	46.8%	
Sheridan					
Silver Bow	12299	65.3%	6526	34.7%	
Stillwater					
Sweet Grass					
Teton	1504	49.6%	1527	50.4%	
Toole	1337	49.7%	1354	50.3%	
Treasure					
Valley					
Wheatland					
Wibaux					
Yellowstone					
TOTALS	**67123**	**50.8%**	**64925**	**49.2%**	

1968 U.S. House Election, 2nd District

COUNTIES	John Melcher (D)		James "Big Jim" Battin (R)		Other
Beaverhead					
Big Horn	1234	35.6%	2229	64.4%	
Blaine	1270	47.2%	1422	52.8%	
Broadwater					
Carbon	1450	40.0%	2173	60.0%	
Carter	300	33.0%	608	67.0%	
Cascade	11309	47.6%	12428	52.4%	
Chouteau	1224	39.4%	1886	60.6%	
Custer	1587	33.6%	3139	66.4%	
Daniels	711	44.4%	889	55.6%	
Dawson	1448	32.8%	2968	67.2%	
Deer Lodge					
Fallon	544	35.8%	975	64.2%	
Fergus	2057	36.3%	3604	63.7%	
Flathead					
Gallatin					
Garfield	214	26.3%	600	73.7%	
Glacier					
Golden Valley	213	37.0%	362	63.0%	
Granite					
Hill	3052	46.8%	3472	53.2%	
Jefferson					
Judith Basin	617	41.2%	879	58.8%	
Lake					
Lewis & Clark					
Liberty					
Lincoln					
Madison					
McCone	625	44.4%	783	55.6%	
Meagher					
Mineral					
Missoula					
Musselshell	817	43.9%	1045	56.1%	
Park					
Petroleum	141	36.0%	251	64.0%	
Phillips	1147	41.1%	1643	58.9%	
Pondera					
Powder River	311	30.8%	700	69.2%	
Powell					
Prairie	289	28.9%	711	71.1%	
Ravalli					
Richland	1473	36.5%	2564	63.5%	
Roosevelt	1759	45.0%	2151	55.0%	
Rosebud	1101	50.9%	1063	49.1%	
Sanders					
Sheridan	1221	48.1%	1318	51.9%	
Silver Bow					
Stillwater	672	30.9%	1504	69.1%	
Sweet Grass	387	27.3%	1033	72.7%	
Teton					
Toole					
Treasure	274	50.0%	274	50.0%	
Valley	1954	42.9%	2598	57.1%	
Wheatland	512	39.7%	777	60.3%	
Wibaux	303	44.0%	386	56.0%	
Yellowstone	10092	34.0%	19580	66.0%	
TOTALS	**50308**	**39.8%**	**76015**	**60.2%**	

1968 Presidential Election

COUNTIES	Hubert Humphrey (D)		Richard Nixon (R)		Other
Beaverhead	853	27.5%	1896	61.0%	357
Big Horn	1319	39.7%	1789	53.9%	213
Blaine	1198	45.1%	1291	48.6%	166
Broadwater	439	35.5%	671	54.3%	126
Carbon	1353	37.7%	1972	55.0%	262
Carter	269	26.8%	624	62.2%	110
Cascade	13507	50.4%	11588	43.2%	1708
Chouteau	1216	38.5%	1695	53.7%	248
Custer	1760	36.1%	2831	58.1%	285
Daniels	688	43.4%	826	52.1%	70
Dawson	1695	37.1%	2650	58.0%	223
Deer Lodge	4208	69.3%	1554	25.6%	312
Fallon	477	30.5%	990	63.3%	98
Fergus	2070	34.2%	3367	55.6%	620
Flathead	5253	37.5%	7215	51.5%	1532
Gallatin	3818	31.9%	7433	62.1%	727
Garfield	190	22.5%	542	64.2%	112
Glacier	1732	47.1%	1643	44.6%	305
Golden Valley	194	35.1%	332	60.0%	27
Granite	502	39.7%	626	49.6%	135
Hill	3386	50.8%	2970	44.5%	313
Jefferson	820	46.3%	798	45.1%	153
Judith Basin	606	40.0%	804	53.0%	106
Lake	1956	32.6%	3358	56.0%	685
Lewis & Clark	5379	38.1%	7979	56.5%	757
Liberty	390	34.1%	670	58.6%	84
Lincoln	2677	46.1%	2355	40.6%	775
Madison	734	32.1%	1289	56.4%	263
McCone	589	41.9%	733	52.2%	83
Meagher	218	25.3%	543	62.9%	102
Mineral	576	49.3%	483	41.3%	110
Missoula	8398	41.4%	9745	48.0%	2149
Musselshell	795	42.7%	953	51.2%	115
Park	1815	34.0%	3063	57.4%	462
Petroleum	98	29.3%	211	63.0%	26
Phillips	1100	41.8%	1353	51.4%	179
Pondera	1149	39.8%	1530	53.0%	209
Powder River	258	24.0%	699	65.0%	119
Powell	1206	44.0%	1301	47.5%	232
Prairie	270	28.8%	635	67.8%	32
Ravalli	2080	34.8%	3183	53.3%	714
Richland	1399	34.8%	2381	59.3%	236
Roosevelt	1771	45.6%	1947	50.1%	167
Rosebud	711	33.7%	1190	56.4%	208
Sanders	1242	41.5%	1459	48.7%	295
Sheridan	1275	49.5%	1180	45.8%	121
Silver Bow	12626	64.4%	5488	28.0%	1503
Stillwater	676	30.7%	1347	61.2%	178
Sweet Grass	336	22.6%	1043	70.0%	111
Teton	1228	39.5%	1697	54.6%	184
Toole	1048	38.7%	1407	52.0%	253
Treasure	188	35.7%	298	56.5%	41
Valley	1926	41.6%	2290	49.4%	416
Wheatland	525	40.4%	673	51.8%	102
Wibaux	252	38.5%	347	53.0%	56
Yellowstone	11682	34.5%	19898	58.8%	2277
TOTALS	**114117**	**41.6%**	**138835**	**50.6%**	**21452**

1968 Gubernatorial Election

COUNTIES	Forrest Anderson (D)		Tim Babcock(R)		Other
Beaverhead	1373	43.9%	1580	50.5%	175
Big Horn	1779	51.5%	1548	44.8%	129
Blaine	1622	60.4%	978	36.4%	84
Broadwater	611	48.5%	604	47.9%	46
Carbon	2010	54.9%	1556	42.5%	94
Carter	487	50.1%	451	46.4%	35
Cascade	15447	57.8%	10397	38.9%	904
Chouteau	1755	54.8%	1303	40.7%	147
Custer	2515	49.8%	2403	47.6%	128
Daniels	875	55.1%	673	42.4%	41
Dawson	2541	54.3%	2013	43.0%	129
Deer Lodge	4583	74.6%	1246	20.3%	316
Fallon	902	56.9%	650	41.0%	32
Fergus	3158	51.2%	2790	45.2%	220
Flathead	8259	54.9%	5983	39.8%	798
Gallatin	5139	42.9%	6369	53.2%	472
Garfield	408	48.3%	411	48.7%	25
Glacier	2300	61.3%	1333	35.5%	117
Golden Valley	287	51.1%	265	47.2%	10
Granite	679	52.9%	536	41.8%	68
Hill	4165	61.6%	2410	35.6%	188
Jefferson	1034	57.3%	690	38.2%	81
Judith Basin	821	54.4%	624	41.4%	64
Lake	2962	48.7%	2749	45.2%	373
Lewis & Clark	6368	44.3%	7491	52.1%	530
Liberty	610	54.0%	463	41.0%	56
Lincoln	3920	66.7%	1613	27.4%	347
Madison	1164	50.4%	1065	46.1%	81
McCone	873	61.7%	512	36.2%	29
Meagher	382	43.8%	449	51.4%	42
Mineral	760	64.5%	342	29.0%	77
Missoula	10276	48.2%	9150	42.9%	1895
Musselshell	1076	57.4%	767	40.9%	32
Park	2730	50.5%	2494	46.1%	181
Petroleum	173	50.7%	157	46.0%	11
Phillips	1545	57.8%	1052	39.4%	75
Pondera	1692	57.6%	1092	37.2%	152
Powder River	459	43.7%	569	54.2%	22
Powell	1578	57.8%	988	36.2%	163
Prairie	459	47.9%	485	50.6%	15
Ravalli	3034	51.2%	2583	43.6%	306
Richland	2335	57.2%	1676	41.1%	69
Roosevelt	2375	60.4%	1486	37.8%	69
Rosebud	1121	51.5%	975	44.8%	80
Sanders	1688	55.2%	1213	39.7%	157
Sheridan	1753	68.0%	775	30.1%	51
Silver Bow	13545	70.0%	4978	25.7%	840
Stillwater	1083	48.7%	1064	47.8%	79
Sweet Grass	625	41.4%	832	55.2%	51
Teton	1669	53.4%	1325	42.4%	134
Toole	1609	58.9%	980	35.9%	143
Treasure	287	53.1%	237	43.9%	16
Valley	2673	58.1%	1823	39.6%	107
Wheatland	735	55.9%	540	41.0%	41
Wibaux	427	64.2%	231	34.7%	7
Yellowstone	15745	46.5%	17463	51.6%	665
TOTALS	**150481**	**54.1%**	**116432**	**41.9%**	**11199**

1968 U.S. House Election, 1st District

COUNTIES	Arnold Olsen (D)		Dick Smiley (R)		Other
Beaverhead	1120	36.4%	1959	63.6%	
Big Horn					
Blaine					
Broadwater	606	48.0%	656	52.0%	
Carbon					
Carter					
Cascade					
Chouteau					
Custer					
Daniels					
Dawson					
Deer Lodge	4496	73.9%	1585	26.1%	
Fallon					
Fergus					
Flathead	7673	52.0%	7074	48.0%	
Gallatin	5149	43.9%	6591	56.1%	
Garfield					
Glacier	1964	55.0%	1605	45.0%	
Golden Valley					
Granite	626	48.7%	660	51.3%	
Hill					
Jefferson	996	56.4%	769	43.6%	
Judith Basin					
Lake	2668	44.2%	3366	55.8%	
Lewis & Clark	6853	50.2%	6802	49.8%	
Liberty	500	45.0%	610	55.0%	
Lincoln	3710	64.3%	2056	35.7%	
Madison	985	42.7%	1320	57.3%	
McCone					
Meagher	294	33.8%	577	66.2%	
Mineral	725	61.8%	449	38.2%	
Missoula	11407	53.8%	9790	46.2%	
Musselshell					
Park	2574	48.1%	2773	51.9%	
Petroleum					
Phillips					
Pondera	1469	50.3%	1451	49.7%	
Powder River					
Powell	1497	55.6%	1197	44.4%	
Prairie					
Ravalli	2646	44.4%	3308	55.6%	
Richland					
Roosevelt					
Rosebud					
Sanders	1643	54.7%	1362	45.3%	
Sheridan					
Silver Bow	12655	68.4%	5856	31.6%	
Stillwater					
Sweet Grass					
Teton	1487	48.3%	1591	51.7%	
Toole	1231	45.8%	1455	54.2%	
Treasure					
Valley					
Wheatland					
Wibaux					
Yellowstone					
TOTALS	**74974**	**53.6%**	**64862**	**46.4%**	

1968 U.S. House Election, 2nd District

COUNTIES	Robert Kelleher (D)		James "Big Jim" Battin (R)		Other
Beaverhead					
Big Horn	1050	31.3%	2305	68.7%	
Blaine	888	34.0%	1723	66.0%	
Broadwater					
Carbon	1237	34.5%	2352	65.5%	
Carter	215	22.5%	740	77.5%	
Cascade	8111	36.8%	13922	63.2%	
Chouteau	1003	31.8%	2154	68.2%	
Custer	1276	29.1%	3102	70.9%	
Daniels	555	35.9%	992	64.1%	
Dawson	1308	28.5%	3288	71.5%	
Deer Lodge					
Fallon	443	29.4%	1062	70.6%	
Fergus	1718	28.5%	4309	71.5%	
Flathead					
Gallatin					
Garfield	164	19.9%	661	80.1%	
Glacier					
Golden Valley	161	29.0%	394	71.0%	
Granite					
Hill	2460	38.1%	4005	61.9%	
Jefferson					
Judith Basin	471	32.2%	990	67.8%	
Lake					
Lewis & Clark					
Liberty					
Lincoln					
Madison					
McCone	503	36.4%	877	63.6%	
Meagher					
Mineral					
Missoula					
Musselshell	715	39.0%	1116	61.0%	
Park					
Petroleum	84	25.1%	250	74.9%	
Phillips	839	32.9%	1714	67.1%	
Pondera					
Powder River	228	22.2%	797	77.8%	
Powell					
Prairie	224	24.1%	704	75.9%	
Ravalli					
Richland	1131	28.8%	2802	71.2%	
Roosevelt	1363	35.8%	2440	64.2%	
Rosebud	625	29.4%	1503	70.6%	
Sanders					
Sheridan	962	38.8%	1519	61.2%	
Silver Bow					
Stillwater	597	27.3%	1592	72.7%	
Sweet Grass	308	20.8%	1174	79.2%	
Teton					
Toole					
Treasure	139	26.4%	388	73.6%	
Valley	1400	34.8%	2620	65.2%	
Wheatland	447	34.7%	841	65.3%	
Wibaux	229	35.9%	409	64.1%	
Yellowstone	8898	29.6%	21143	70.4%	
TOTALS	**39752**	**32.2%**	**83888**	**67.8%**	

1970 U.S. Senate Election

COUNTIES	Mike Mansfield (D)		Harold Wallace (R)		Other
Beaverhead	1414	51.9%	1311	48.1%	
Big Horn	1780	57.7%	1306	42.3%	
Blaine	1623	65.3%	862	34.7%	
Broadwater	595	52.2%	544	47.8%	
Carbon	2082	59.3%	1430	40.7%	
Carter	486	54.5%	406	45.5%	
Cascade	16981	71.2%	6866	28.8%	
Chouteau	1766	59.5%	1201	40.5%	
Custer	2998	68.1%	1402	31.9%	
Daniels	814	56.3%	632	43.7%	
Dawson	2639	62.8%	1563	37.2%	
Deer Lodge	4051	74.2%	1408	25.8%	
Fallon	790	52.7%	709	47.3%	
Fergus	2822	51.9%	2614	48.1%	
Flathead	6694	50.5%	6568	49.5%	
Gallatin	5981	56.7%	4564	43.3%	
Garfield	371	47.0%	419	53.0%	
Glacier	2053	61.6%	1279	38.4%	
Golden Valley	270	52.9%	240	47.1%	
Granite	525	51.9%	486	48.1%	
Hill	4099	68.8%	1863	31.2%	
Jefferson	1003	60.0%	669	40.0%	
Judith Basin	889	61.4%	560	38.6%	
Lake	2526	47.9%	2751	52.1%	
Lewis & Clark	8297	64.8%	4500	35.2%	
Liberty	566	54.7%	468	45.3%	
Lincoln	2608	58.3%	1866	41.7%	
Madison	1140	50.4%	1123	49.6%	
McCone	775	59.6%	525	40.4%	
Meagher	356	45.9%	419	54.1%	
Mineral	650	60.0%	433	40.0%	
Missoula	11857	60.2%	7827	39.8%	
Musselshell	1059	58.9%	739	41.1%	
Park	2348	50.5%	2303	49.5%	
Petroleum	161	55.1%	131	44.9%	
Phillips	1524	62.0%	936	38.0%	
Pondera	1713	63.8%	970	36.2%	
Powder River	436	42.3%	595	57.7%	
Powell	1645	63.6%	941	36.4%	
Prairie	490	56.5%	378	43.5%	
Ravalli	2800	49.5%	2859	50.5%	
Richland	2156	62.1%	1314	37.9%	
Roosevelt	2276	65.5%	1200	34.5%	
Rosebud	1166	59.0%	811	41.0%	
Sanders	1506	55.0%	1234	45.0%	
Sheridan	1745	70.4%	735	29.6%	
Silver Bow	12281	72.2%	4734	27.8%	
Stillwater	1066	52.6%	962	47.4%	
Sweet Grass	546	38.7%	864	61.3%	
Teton	1726	58.8%	1207	41.2%	
Toole	1296	52.7%	1163	47.3%	
Treasure	278	51.6%	261	48.4%	
Valley	2784	66.8%	1382	33.2%	
Wheatland	732	57.8%	535	42.2%	
Wibaux	402	64.2%	224	35.8%	
Yellowstone	16427	56.8%	12517	43.2%	
TOTALS	**150060**	**60.5%**	**97809**	**39.5%**	

1970 U.S. House Election, 1st District

COUNTIES	Arnold Olsen (D)		Dick Shoup (R)		Other
Beaverhead	958	35.1%	1772	64.9%	
Big Horn					
Blaine					
Broadwater	487	42.8%	652	57.2%	
Carbon					
Carter					
Cascade					
Chouteau					
Custer					
Daniels					
Dawson					
Deer Lodge	3696	67.7%	1762	32.3%	
Fallon					
Fergus					
Flathead	5928	44.4%	7426	55.6%	
Gallatin	4438	42.2%	6072	57.8%	
Garfield					
Glacier	1728	52.5%	1561	47.5%	
Golden Valley					
Granite	413	40.6%	604	59.4%	
Hill					
Jefferson	874	51.9%	810	48.1%	
Judith Basin					
Lake	2069	39.0%	3234	61.0%	
Lewis & Clark	5996	46.8%	6827	53.2%	
Liberty	440	42.9%	585	57.1%	
Lincoln	2658	59.1%	1839	40.9%	
Madison	956	42.1%	1313	57.9%	
McCone					
Meagher	285	36.4%	497	63.6%	
Mineral	586	53.9%	502	46.1%	
Missoula	9266	47.0%	10467	53.0%	
Musselshell					
Park	2100	45.1%	2558	54.9%	
Petroleum					
Phillips					
Pondera	1397	52.2%	1278	47.8%	
Powder River					
Powell	1338	51.7%	1251	48.3%	
Prairie					
Ravalli	2369	41.8%	3297	58.2%	
Richland					
Roosevelt					
Rosebud					
Sanders	1493	54.2%	1262	45.8%	
Sheridan					
Silver Bow	11108	64.9%	6013	35.1%	
Stillwater					
Sweet Grass					
Teton	1507	51.6%	1414	48.4%	
Toole	1085	43.8%	1392	56.2%	
Treasure					
Valley					
Wheatland					
Wibaux					
Yellowstone					
TOTALS	**63175**	**49.5%**	**64388**	**50.5%**	

1970 U.S. House Election, 2nd District

COUNTIES	John Melcher (D)		Jack Rehberg (R)		Other
Beaverhead					
Big Horn	1956	63.2%	1141	36.8%	
Blaine	1763	70.6%	734	29.4%	
Broadwater					
Carbon	2276	64.6%	1247	35.4%	
Carter	501	56.5%	386	43.5%	
Cascade	16357	68.9%	7381	31.1%	
Chouteau	2009	67.2%	981	32.8%	
Custer	2780	62.6%	1662	37.4%	
Daniels	911	62.6%	544	37.4%	
Dawson	2726	64.9%	1473	35.1%	
Deer Lodge					
Fallon	887	59.0%	616	41.0%	
Fergus	3285	60.1%	2178	39.9%	
Flathead					
Gallatin					
Garfield	495	61.7%	307	38.3%	
Glacier					
Golden Valley	281	54.7%	233	45.3%	
Granite					
Hill	4253	71.1%	1725	28.9%	
Jefferson					
Judith Basin	992	68.3%	461	31.7%	
Lake					
Lewis & Clark					
Liberty					
Lincoln					
Madison					
McCone	883	68.5%	406	31.5%	
Meagher					
Mineral					
Missoula					
Musselshell	1218	67.3%	593	32.7%	
Park					
Petroleum	183	62.2%	111	37.8%	
Phillips	1679	67.8%	797	32.2%	
Pondera					
Powder River	509	48.9%	532	51.1%	
Powell					
Prairie	527	60.7%	341	39.3%	
Ravalli					
Richland	2171	62.2%	1320	37.8%	
Roosevelt	2349	66.9%	1163	33.1%	
Rosebud	1450	72.5%	550	27.5%	
Sanders					
Sheridan	1840	74.6%	628	25.4%	
Silver Bow					
Stillwater	1217	59.5%	828	40.5%	
Sweet Grass	694	48.6%	733	51.4%	
Teton					
Toole					
Treasure	393	71.6%	156	28.4%	
Valley	2724	66.2%	1391	33.8%	
Wheatland	813	64.0%	458	36.0%	
Wibaux	426	67.2%	208	32.8%	
Yellowstone	17534	58.4%	12468	41.6%	
TOTALS	**78082**	**64.1%**	**43752**	**35.9%**	

Call for a Constitutional Convention

COUNTIES	Yes		No		
Beaverhead	1584	66.3%	805	33.7%	
Big Horn	1561	63.5%	896	36.5%	
Blaine	1365	66.3%	695	33.7%	
Broadwater	638	61.5%	400	38.5%	
Carbon	1733	59.4%	1183	40.6%	
Carter	380	56.5%	293	43.5%	
Cascade	13134	67.3%	6393	32.7%	
Chouteau	1466	55.1%	1196	44.9%	
Custer	2555	67.0%	1256	33.0%	
Daniels	707	63.5%	407	36.5%	
Dawson	2018	57.2%	1511	42.8%	
Deer Lodge	2912	67.6%	1395	32.4%	
Fallon	540	46.8%	614	53.2%	
Fergus	3085	64.2%	1723	35.8%	
Flathead	8915	75.2%	2947	24.8%	
Gallatin	6102	69.5%	2674	30.5%	
Garfield	304	49.5%	310	50.5%	
Glacier	1561	59.5%	1061	40.5%	
Golden Valley	239	54.0%	204	46.0%	
Granite	520	60.7%	336	39.3%	
Hill	3409	67.7%	1627	32.3%	
Jefferson	908	65.7%	474	34.3%	
Judith Basin	670	54.6%	556	45.4%	
Lake	2965	66.6%	1490	33.4%	
Lewis & Clark	7996	68.6%	3658	31.4%	
Liberty	491	55.4%	396	44.6%	
Lincoln	2631	68.2%	1225	31.8%	
Madison	1102	59.0%	765	41.0%	
McCone	724	68.0%	341	32.0%	
Meagher	393	59.6%	266	40.4%	
Mineral	599	65.4%	317	34.6%	
Missoula	13482	74.1%	4707	25.9%	
Musselshell	672	47.2%	752	52.8%	
Park	2212	55.3%	1790	44.7%	
Petroleum	130	52.2%	119	47.8%	
Phillips	1193	62.0%	732	38.0%	
Pondera	1375	60.4%	901	39.6%	
Powder River	414	48.4%	442	51.6%	
Powell	1168	53.6%	1013	46.4%	
Prairie	344	55.0%	282	45.0%	
Ravalli	2996	62.1%	1831	37.9%	
Richland	1630	62.7%	970	37.3%	
Roosevelt	1629	61.4%	1023	38.6%	
Rosebud	1090	64.5%	599	35.5%	
Sanders	1389	61.3%	877	38.7%	
Sheridan	1349	69.2%	601	30.8%	
Silver Bow	8237	67.5%	3967	32.5%	
Stillwater	921	53.4%	805	46.6%	
Sweet Grass	571	51.5%	538	48.5%	
Teton	1570	62.7%	933	37.3%	
Toole	775	36.7%	1335	63.3%	
Treasure	249	55.2%	202	44.8%	
Valley	2346	70.1%	1000	29.9%	
Wheatland	647	62.1%	395	37.9%	
Wibaux	250	52.4%	227	47.6%	
Yellowstone	13636	62.5%	8188	37.5%	
TOTALS	**133482**	**65.1%**	**71643**	**34.9%**	

1972 Presidential Election

COUNTIES	George McGovern (D)		Richard Nixon (R)		Other
Beaverhead	775	22.7%	2460	72.0%	182
Big Horn	1552	40.6%	2148	56.2%	124
Blaine	1151	41.4%	1513	54.4%	115
Broadwater	411	29.9%	916	66.6%	49
Carbon	1292	33.6%	2378	61.9%	171
Carter	218	22.2%	726	73.9%	39
Cascade	12899	41.8%	16159	52.4%	1778
Chouteau	1149	33.8%	2027	59.6%	223
Custer	1875	34.1%	3486	63.3%	145
Daniels	570	36.2%	973	61.8%	31
Dawson	1685	33.6%	3207	64.0%	122
Deer Lodge	3979	60.3%	2373	35.9%	252
Fallon	531	33.1%	1034	64.5%	39
Fergus	1652	27.3%	4082	67.5%	315
Flathead	5412	31.5%	10417	60.7%	1327
Gallatin	5096	31.7%	10663	66.3%	329
Garfield	173	19.4%	695	77.8%	25
Glacier	1496	38.9%	2143	55.7%	207
Golden Valley	170	30.7%	359	64.9%	24
Granite	422	32.7%	804	62.3%	65
Hill	3061	43.2%	3759	53.1%	265
Jefferson	904	39.6%	1281	56.1%	100
Judith Basin	557	34.5%	961	59.5%	96
Lake	2260	33.6%	4172	62.1%	287
Lewis & Clark	6081	35.1%	10719	61.9%	516
Liberty	365	29.6%	808	65.4%	62
Lincoln	2402	38.7%	3276	52.8%	530
Madison	562	38.4%	854	58.3%	49
McCone	669	25.9%	1780	68.8%	139
Meagher	230	24.4%	674	71.5%	38
Mineral	659	46.4%	706	49.8%	54
Missoula	13784	45.9%	15557	51.8%	708
Musselshell	689	35.0%	1202	61.1%	76
Park	1923	32.6%	3771	63.9%	208
Petroleum	87	26.8%	232	71.4%	6
Phillips	828	32.4%	1659	64.9%	70
Pondera	1215	36.9%	1890	57.4%	187
Powder River	267	21.9%	844	69.4%	106
Powell	1050	36.4%	1720	59.7%	112
Prairie	303	30.3%	685	68.6%	11
Ravalli	2480	33.3%	4611	61.8%	367
Richland	1438	33.4%	2645	61.5%	217
Roosevelt	1464	37.5%	2304	59.0%	139
Rosebud	777	33.1%	1486	63.2%	87
Sanders	1197	36.8%	1779	54.7%	275
Sheridan	1197	43.1%	1500	54.0%	83
Silver Bow	11704	57.4%	7967	39.0%	733
Stillwater	716	28.7%	1698	67.9%	85
Sweet Grass	350	21.1%	1260	76.0%	48
Teton	1121	33.8%	1991	60.0%	209
Toole	897	31.9%	1679	59.6%	239
Treasure	176	30.7%	377	65.7%	21
Valley	1973	36.9%	3210	60.0%	165
Wheatland	445	33.6%	761	57.4%	120
Wibaux	283	40.3%	390	55.5%	30
Yellowstone	13602	33.8%	25205	62.6%	1430
TOTALS	**120197**	**37.8%**	**183976**	**57.9%**	**13430**

1972 Gubernatorial Election

COUNTIES	Tom Judge (D)		Edward "Big Ed" Smith (R)		Other
Beaverhead	1473	42.4%	2003	57.6%	
Big Horn	2380	61.4%	1497	38.6%	
Blaine	1492	52.4%	1357	47.6%	
Broadwater	474	34.2%	911	65.8%	
Carbon	2036	52.0%	1876	48.0%	
Carter	299	30.1%	696	69.9%	
Cascade	17709	58.1%	12794	41.9%	
Chouteau	1502	43.3%	1965	56.7%	
Custer	3081	54.8%	2544	45.2%	
Daniels	483	30.0%	1126	70.0%	
Dawson	2747	53.5%	2384	46.5%	
Deer Lodge	5320	79.5%	1374	20.5%	
Fallon	709	42.9%	942	57.1%	
Fergus	2718	44.1%	3446	55.9%	
Flathead	9641	55.0%	7876	45.0%	
Gallatin	8296	52.2%	7604	47.8%	
Garfield	224	24.6%	687	75.4%	
Glacier	2183	57.0%	1645	43.0%	
Golden Valley	245	43.0%	325	57.0%	
Granite	676	51.1%	647	48.9%	
Hill	3987	55.1%	3246	44.9%	
Jefferson	1324	57.0%	997	43.0%	
Judith Basin	784	47.7%	858	52.3%	
Lake	3202	46.9%	3625	53.1%	
Lewis & Clark	8061	47.3%	8990	52.7%	
Liberty	500	40.2%	743	59.8%	
Lincoln	3995	64.6%	2188	35.4%	
Madison	642	42.4%	871	57.6%	
McCone	1142	43.5%	1484	56.5%	
Meagher	297	31.1%	659	68.9%	
Mineral	912	63.0%	535	37.0%	
Missoula	18426	62.0%	11302	38.0%	
Musselshell	1081	53.2%	952	46.8%	
Park	3204	53.3%	2802	46.7%	
Petroleum	131	39.6%	200	60.4%	
Phillips	1065	40.7%	1554	59.3%	
Pondera	1701	51.6%	1597	48.4%	
Powder River	436	35.4%	794	64.6%	
Powell	1625	55.1%	1326	44.9%	
Prairie	414	40.5%	609	59.5%	
Ravalli	3517	46.4%	4058	53.6%	
Richland	1584	36.2%	2797	63.8%	
Roosevelt	1408	35.3%	2579	64.7%	
Rosebud	1231	51.1%	1178	48.9%	
Sanders	1652	50.1%	1643	49.9%	
Sheridan	369	13.0%	2473	87.0%	
Silver Bow	15286	76.1%	4789	23.9%	
Stillwater	1160	45.6%	1386	54.4%	
Sweet Grass	568	33.7%	1116	66.3%	
Teton	1485	43.9%	1901	56.1%	
Toole	1260	44.3%	1585	55.7%	
Treasure	299	50.2%	297	49.8%	
Valley	2522	46.9%	2851	53.1%	
Wheatland	708	52.0%	654	48.0%	
Wibaux	367	51.2%	350	48.8%	
Yellowstone	22490	56.2%	17543	43.8%	
TOTALS	**172523**	**54.1%**	**146231**	**45.9%**	

1972 U.S. Senate Election

COUNTIES	Lee Metcalf (D)		Henry Hibbard (R)		Other
Beaverhead	1233	35.5%	2244	64.5%	
Big Horn	2199	56.8%	1672	43.2%	
Blaine	1585	55.3%	1279	44.7%	
Broadwater	521	37.5%	868	62.5%	
Carbon	1940	49.8%	1952	50.2%	
Carter	375	38.3%	604	61.7%	
Cascade	17121	57.5%	12654	42.5%	
Chouteau	1621	46.8%	1841	53.2%	
Custer	2952	52.3%	2691	47.7%	
Daniels	858	54.2%	725	45.8%	
Dawson	2814	54.9%	2311	45.1%	
Deer Lodge	4986	74.7%	1693	25.3%	
Fallon	785	47.5%	866	52.5%	
Fergus	2501	40.8%	3629	59.2%	
Flathead	8012	46.4%	9259	53.6%	
Gallatin	6614	44.5%	8265	55.5%	
Garfield	260	28.7%	647	71.3%	
Glacier	2140	55.9%	1685	44.1%	
Golden Valley	255	44.9%	313	55.1%	
Granite	524	39.7%	796	60.3%	
Hill	4201	58.1%	3026	41.9%	
Jefferson	1240	53.1%	1094	46.9%	
Judith Basin	775	47.3%	865	52.7%	
Lake	2774	40.6%	4065	59.4%	
Lewis & Clark	8294	50.0%	8298	50.0%	
Liberty	563	45.5%	675	54.5%	
Lincoln	3460	55.6%	2758	44.4%	
Madison	788	52.3%	718	47.7%	
McCone	1009	38.3%	1623	61.7%	
Meagher	333	35.0%	618	65.0%	
Mineral	780	54.1%	663	45.9%	
Missoula	17280	57.0%	13046	43.0%	
Musselshell	916	45.4%	1100	54.6%	
Park	3015	50.3%	2984	49.7%	
Petroleum	118	35.8%	212	64.2%	
Phillips	1252	48.0%	1358	52.0%	
Pondera	1674	50.3%	1652	49.7%	
Powder River	474	38.5%	758	61.5%	
Powell	1571	53.3%	1376	46.7%	
Prairie	437	42.6%	589	57.4%	
Ravalli	3091	41.0%	4455	59.0%	
Richland	2192	50.5%	2151	49.5%	
Roosevelt	2122	53.3%	1861	46.7%	
Rosebud	1159	48.2%	1248	51.8%	
Sanders	1490	44.9%	1829	55.1%	
Sheridan	1652	59.6%	1119	40.4%	
Silver Bow	13112	68.1%	6135	31.9%	
Stillwater	1137	44.7%	1409	55.3%	
Sweet Grass	535	31.6%	1157	68.4%	
Teton	1550	46.4%	1790	53.6%	
Toole	1358	48.1%	1464	51.9%	
Treasure	281	47.3%	313	52.7%	
Valley	2956	57.3%	2202	42.7%	
Wheatland	678	49.9%	680	50.1%	
Wibaux	397	56.1%	311	43.9%	
Yellowstone	19649	49.9%	19720	50.1%	
TOTALS	**163609**	**52.0%**	**151316**	**48.0%**	

1972 U.S. House Election, 1st District

COUNTIES	Arnold Olsen (D)		Dick Shoup (R)		Other
Beaverhead	997	28.6%	2489	71.4%	
Big Horn					
Blaine					
Broadwater	524	37.8%	863	62.2%	
Carbon					
Carter					
Cascade					
Chouteau					
Custer					
Daniels					
Dawson					
Deer Lodge	4505	66.9%	2228	33.1%	
Fallon					
Fergus					
Flathead	7270	41.8%	10135	58.2%	
Gallatin	5687	36.6%	9832	63.4%	
Garfield					
Glacier	1863	48.6%	1967	51.4%	
Golden Valley					
Granite	479	36.1%	847	63.9%	
Hill					
Jefferson	1101	47.5%	1218	52.5%	
Judith Basin					
Lake	2520	37.0%	4289	63.0%	
Lewis & Clark	7290	43.0%	9669	57.0%	
Liberty	473	38.0%	772	62.0%	
Lincoln	3219	51.9%	2989	48.1%	
Madison	1112	74.4%	382	25.6%	
McCone					
Meagher	314	33.2%	633	66.8%	
Mineral	746	51.7%	698	48.3%	
Missoula	14507	48.1%	15672	51.9%	
Musselshell					
Park	2420	40.4%	3575	59.6%	
Petroleum					
Phillips					
Pondera	1462	44.2%	1849	55.8%	
Powder River					
Powell	1382	46.8%	1572	53.2%	
Prairie					
Ravalli	2788	36.8%	4785	63.2%	
Richland					
Roosevelt					
Rosebud					
Sanders	1521	46.1%	1778	53.9%	
Sheridan					
Silver Bow	12996	64.8%	7074	35.2%	
Stillwater					
Sweet Grass					
Teton					
Toole	1130	40.2%	1681	59.8%	
Treasure					
Valley					
Wheatland					
Wibaux					
Yellowstone					
TOTALS	**76073**	**46.3%**	**88373**	**53.7%**	

1972 U.S. House Election, 2nd District

COUNTIES	John Melcher (D)		Dick Forester (R)		Other
Beaverhead					
Big Horn	3134	81.4%	718	18.6%	
Blaine	2297	80.9%	542	19.1%	
Broadwater					
Carbon	2950	75.6%	954	24.4%	
Carter	608	63.1%	356	36.9%	
Cascade	22683	79.1%	5984	20.9%	
Chouteau	2728	78.9%	731	21.1%	
Custer	4316	76.9%	1298	23.1%	
Daniels	1121	70.8%	463	29.2%	
Dawson	3804	74.6%	1298	25.4%	
Deer Lodge					
Fallon	1141	69.4%	504	30.6%	
Fergus	4299	70.4%	1805	29.6%	
Flathead					
Gallatin					
Garfield	721	80.0%	180	20.0%	
Glacier					
Golden Valley	415	72.9%	154	27.1%	
Granite					
Hill	5805	80.8%	1375	19.2%	
Jefferson					
Judith Basin	1345	82.0%	295	18.0%	
Lake					
Lewis & Clark					
Liberty					
Lincoln					
Madison					
McCone	879	33.3%	1758	66.7%	
Meagher					
Mineral					
Missoula					
Musselshell	1635	80.6%	394	19.4%	
Park					
Petroleum	243	73.9%	86	26.1%	
Phillips	1984	76.5%	609	23.5%	
Pondera					
Powder River	775	63.6%	443	36.4%	
Powell					
Prairie	704	69.6%	308	30.4%	
Ravalli					
Richland	3075	71.4%	1231	28.6%	
Roosevelt	2928	74.6%	999	25.4%	
Rosebud	2088	86.1%	336	13.9%	
Sanders					
Sheridan	2174	78.8%	584	21.2%	
Silver Bow					
Stillwater	1880	73.8%	669	26.2%	
Sweet Grass	1064	63.5%	611	36.5%	
Teton	2464	73.9%	872	26.1%	
Toole					
Treasure	493	81.6%	111	18.4%	
Valley	3743	74.2%	1302	25.8%	
Wheatland	1018	75.0%	340	25.0%	
Wibaux	551	77.5%	160	22.5%	
Yellowstone	29226	74.6%	9969	25.4%	
TOTALS	**114524**	**76.1%**	**36036**	**23.9%**	

Approval of the new state constitution

COUNTIES	Yes		No	
Beaverhead	996	36.0%	1770	64.0%
Big Horn	1119	42.7%	1501	57.3%
Blaine	817	37.0%	1394	63.0%
Broadwater	308	26.8%	841	73.2%
Carbon	1172	39.2%	1820	60.8%
Carter	145	19.3%	607	80.7%
Cascade	13792	63.0%	8117	37.0%
Chouteau	1063	36.3%	1868	63.7%
Custer	2178	56.7%	1666	43.3%
Daniels	483	42.3%	659	57.7%
Dawson	1826	51.7%	1707	48.3%
Deer Lodge	3880	71.0%	1587	29.0%
Fallon	284	23.8%	910	76.2%
Fergus	1639	34.6%	3101	65.4%
Flathead	6959	59.0%	4840	41.0%
Gallatin	5514	47.9%	5999	52.1%
Garfield	156	20.9%	589	79.1%
Glacier	1079	43.1%	1427	56.9%
Golden Valley	180	36.4%	315	63.6%
Granite	416	38.3%	669	61.7%
Hill	2694	50.0%	2695	50.0%
Jefferson	806	44.8%	995	55.2%
Judith Basin	462	33.5%	918	66.5%
Lake	1842	39.4%	2837	60.6%
Lewis & Clark	7926	59.3%	5444	40.7%
Liberty	402	36.9%	687	63.1%
Lincoln	2462	58.5%	1747	41.5%
Madison	626	29.4%	1500	70.6%
McCone	418	36.1%	741	63.9%
Meagher	185	23.8%	592	76.2%
Mineral	610	55.6%	488	44.4%
Missoula	13271	66.4%	6703	33.6%
Musselshell	724	45.2%	879	54.8%
Park	2033	47.9%	2213	52.1%
Petroleum	61	24.6%	187	75.4%
Phillips	530	26.8%	1448	73.2%
Pondera	1422	55.7%	1133	44.3%
Powder River	195	18.1%	882	81.9%
Powell	808	33.9%	1578	66.1%
Prairie	174	22.5%	600	77.5%
Ravalli	2851	53.7%	2461	46.3%
Richland	1290	41.8%	1794	58.2%
Roosevelt	1067	37.8%	1758	62.2%
Rosebud	497	29.9%	1164	70.1%
Sanders	878	38.9%	1379	61.1%
Sheridan	837	40.7%	1218	59.3%
Silver Bow	7738	46.9%	8774	53.1%
Stillwater	862	43.2%	1134	56.8%
Sweet Grass	411	28.8%	1014	71.2%
Teton	1201	44.1%	1521	55.9%
Toole	961	41.2%	1372	58.8%
Treasure	138	27.8%	358	72.2%
Valley	1730	46.7%	1975	53.3%
Wheatland	410	37.7%	677	62.3%
Wibaux	146	27.3%	389	72.7%
Yellowstone	13741	55.0%	11241	45.0%
TOTALS	**116415**	**50.5%**	**113883**	**49.5%**

1974 U.S. House Election, 1st District

COUNTIES	Max Baucus (D)		Dick Shoup (R)		Other
Beaverhead	1049	38.3%	1689	61.7%	
Big Horn					
Blaine					
Broadwater	555	43.3%	727	56.7%	
Carbon					
Carter					
Cascade					
Chouteau					
Custer					
Daniels					
Dawson					
Deer Lodge	3918	73.1%	1441	26.9%	
Fallon					
Fergus					
Flathead	7802	54.4%	6527	45.6%	
Gallatin	6178	46.3%	7179	53.7%	
Garfield					
Glacier	1570	53.4%	1370	46.6%	
Golden Valley					
Granite	598	48.7%	629	51.3%	
Hill					
Jefferson	1118	53.6%	969	46.4%	
Judith Basin					
Lake	2572	42.0%	3555	58.0%	
Lewis & Clark	7792	54.4%	6525	45.6%	
Liberty	411	38.8%	649	61.2%	
Lincoln	3269	62.6%	1956	37.4%	
Madison	911	40.4%	1346	59.6%	
McCone					
Meagher	329	38.7%	521	61.3%	
Mineral	849	57.5%	628	42.5%	
Missoula	12458	56.1%	9739	43.9%	
Musselshell					
Park	2435	48.8%	2558	51.2%	
Petroleum					
Phillips					
Pondera	1329	48.3%	1424	51.7%	
Powder River					
Powell	1354	53.2%	1191	46.8%	
Prairie					
Ravalli	3441	49.2%	3546	50.8%	
Richland					
Roosevelt					
Rosebud					
Sanders	1516	48.2%	1631	51.8%	
Sheridan					
Silver Bow	11740	72.9%	4362	27.1%	
Stillwater					
Sweet Grass					
Teton					
Toole	1110	49.2%	1147	50.8%	
Treasure					
Valley					
Wheatland					
Wibaux					
Yellowstone					
TOTALS	**74304**	**54.8%**	**61309**	**45.2%**	

1974 U.S. House Election, 2nd District

COUNTIES	John Melcher (D)		Jack McDonald (R)		Other
Beaverhead					
Big Horn	1979	65.7%	1034	34.3%	
Blaine	1550	68.6%	710	31.4%	
Broadwater					
Carbon	2203	65.8%	1147	34.2%	
Carter	502	59.8%	338	40.2%	
Cascade	12531	62.6%	7491	37.4%	
Chouteau	1883	63.9%	1064	36.1%	
Custer	3024	62.9%	1787	37.1%	
Daniels	892	65.3%	473	34.7%	
Dawson	2803	66.0%	1441	34.0%	
Deer Lodge					
Fallon	1132	66.0%	582	34.0%	
Fergus	2992	59.4%	2047	40.6%	
Flathead					
Gallatin					
Garfield	558	62.7%	332	37.3%	
Glacier					
Golden Valley	319	66.3%	162	33.7%	
Granite					
Hill	4358	73.6%	1562	26.4%	
Jefferson					
Judith Basin	851	57.1%	640	42.9%	
Lake					
Lewis & Clark					
Liberty					
Lincoln					
Madison					
McCone	852	65.3%	453	34.7%	
Meagher					
Mineral					
Missoula					
Musselshell	1256	68.9%	566	31.1%	
Park					
Petroleum	142	60.4%	93	39.6%	
Phillips	1500	65.2%	799	34.8%	
Pondera					
Powder River	604	58.0%	438	42.0%	
Powell					
Prairie	577	64.0%	324	36.0%	
Ravalli					
Richland	2202	62.0%	1350	38.0%	
Roosevelt	2047	64.5%	1127	35.5%	
Rosebud	1924	77.8%	550	22.2%	
Sanders					
Sheridan	1681	71.3%	677	28.7%	
Silver Bow					
Stillwater	1424	62.5%	853	37.5%	
Sweet Grass	679	46.6%	777	53.4%	
Teton	1793	59.1%	1239	40.9%	
Toole					
Treasure	350	73.4%	127	26.6%	
Valley	2483	62.2%	1507	37.8%	
Wheatland	763	59.7%	514	40.3%	
Wibaux	472	69.7%	205	30.3%	
Yellowstone	16354	58.8%	11444	41.2%	
TOTALS	**74680**	**63.0%**	**43853**	**37.0%**	

1976 Presidential Election

COUNTIES	Jimmy Carter (D)		Gerald Ford (R)		Other
Beaverhead	1013	28.6%	2461	69.5%	69
Big Horn	1962	54.0%	1615	44.5%	53
Blaine	1356	49.5%	1349	49.3%	34
Broadwater	557	40.1%	820	59.0%	12
Carbon	1853	45.8%	2121	52.4%	71
Carter	344	35.4%	558	57.4%	70
Cascade	14678	48.1%	15289	50.1%	544
Chouteau	1568	45.3%	1814	52.4%	83
Custer	2425	42.9%	3120	55.3%	102
Daniels	797	48.6%	816	49.8%	26
Dawson	2201	44.4%	2639	53.2%	120
Deer Lodge	3859	62.5%	2197	35.6%	120
Fallon	847	47.1%	934	52.0%	16
Fergus	2470	40.1%	3556	57.7%	134
Flathead	7827	41.5%	10494	55.7%	524
Gallatin	6215	35.6%	11062	63.4%	183
Garfield	273	29.6%	625	67.8%	24
Glacier	1755	47.1%	1892	50.8%	77
Golden Valley	255	44.8%	302	53.1%	12
Granite	509	40.0%	746	58.6%	17
Hill	3878	53.4%	3274	45.1%	108
Jefferson	1210	45.6%	1387	52.3%	57
Judith Basin	772	47.8%	809	50.1%	33
Lake	3253	45.1%	3809	52.8%	148
Lewis & Clark	8118	43.8%	10155	54.8%	244
Liberty	506	43.5%	638	54.9%	19
Lincoln	3146	50.1%	3017	48.0%	120
Madison	870	33.3%	1688	64.7%	52
McCone	749	50.0%	730	48.7%	20
Meagher	364	38.8%	565	60.2%	10
Mineral	819	54.1%	679	44.8%	16
Missoula	15099	47.4%	16350	51.4%	388
Musselshell	922	44.6%	1117	54.1%	26
Park	2364	41.2%	3281	57.2%	95
Petroleum	110	33.2%	211	63.7%	10
Phillips	1117	44.9%	1347	54.2%	22
Pondera	1413	44.9%	1666	52.9%	71
Powder River	429	34.7%	683	55.3%	123
Powell	1302	44.1%	1610	54.6%	39
Prairie	415	40.7%	597	58.6%	7
Ravalli	3504	40.3%	4894	56.3%	296
Richland	1961	46.0%	2189	51.3%	113
Roosevelt	2061	52.5%	1822	46.4%	45
Rosebud	1413	46.3%	1583	51.9%	55
Sanders	1725	48.2%	1738	48.6%	113
Sheridan	1560	57.5%	1114	41.0%	40
Silver Bow	11377	59.5%	7506	39.3%	227
Stillwater	1143	43.4%	1446	54.9%	46
Sweet Grass	502	30.3%	1135	68.4%	22
Teton	1506	45.0%	1730	51.7%	109
Toole	1080	41.5%	1469	56.4%	54
Treasure	239	42.4%	315	55.9%	10
Valley	2352	47.4%	2520	50.8%	87
Wheatland	535	40.5%	755	57.2%	30
Wibaux	352	50.9%	308	44.6%	31
Yellowstone	18329	41.5%	25201	57.1%	595
TOTALS	**149259**	**45.4%**	**173703**	**52.8%**	**5772**

1976 Gubernatorial Election

COUNTIES	Tom Judge (D)		Bob Woodahl (R)		Other
Beaverhead	1685	50.0%	1682	50.0%	0
Big Horn	2327	66.0%	1171	33.2%	29
Blaine	1679	61.5%	914	33.5%	137
Broadwater	677	50.0%	565	41.8%	111
Carbon	2436	61.9%	1500	38.1%	0
Carter	472	49.3%	466	48.7%	19
Cascade	19944	69.1%	8596	29.8%	327
Chouteau	1853	54.2%	1097	32.1%	466
Custer	3396	62.0%	1734	31.7%	348
Daniels	917	57.0%	686	42.6%	6
Dawson	3107	63.2%	1704	34.6%	108
Deer Lodge	4045	67.8%	1922	32.2%	0
Fallon	999	56.1%	765	43.0%	17
Fergus	3626	58.7%	2316	37.5%	231
Flathead	11233	60.9%	7209	39.1%	0
Gallatin	9188	57.4%	6809	42.6%	0
Garfield	244	27.9%	147	16.8%	482
Glacier	2299	64.1%	1127	31.4%	163
Golden Valley	331	58.4%	218	38.4%	18
Granite	671	53.6%	581	46.4%	0
Hill	4919	66.3%	2343	31.6%	152
Jefferson	1571	62.7%	936	37.3%	0
Judith Basin	940	60.1%	515	32.9%	108
Lake	3629	50.6%	3392	47.3%	156
Lewis & Clark	11381	63.8%	5871	32.9%	593
Liberty	617	54.4%	368	32.5%	149
Lincoln	4096	67.5%	1968	32.5%	0
Madison	1100	43.0%	1431	55.9%	30
McCone	848	57.2%	543	36.6%	92
Meagher	510	58.4%	363	41.6%	0
Mineral	1032	68.9%	465	31.1%	0
Missoula	18723	61.2%	11334	37.1%	523
Musselshell	1308	63.5%	692	33.6%	61
Park	3499	62.5%	2100	37.5%	0
Petroleum	171	52.8%	112	34.6%	41
Phillips	1460	59.8%	929	38.1%	51
Pondera	1962	67.1%	960	32.9%	0
Powder River	567	46.7%	585	48.1%	63
Powell	1568	54.9%	1201	42.1%	86
Prairie	555	55.6%	429	42.9%	15
Ravalli	4757	56.9%	3597	43.1%	0
Richland	2514	60.7%	1630	39.3%	0
Roosevelt	2580	66.2%	1280	32.8%	37
Rosebud	1850	64.5%	1016	35.5%	0
Sanders	1880	54.1%	1550	44.6%	42
Sheridan	1552	59.0%	1057	40.2%	20
Silver Bow	12252	66.6%	6084	33.0%	73
Stillwater	1514	59.7%	1022	40.3%	0
Sweet Grass	644	41.2%	702	44.9%	217
Teton	1753	53.2%	1375	41.7%	166
Toole	1484	62.1%	907	37.9%	0
Treasure	331	59.4%	197	35.4%	29
Valley	2842	59.4%	1851	38.7%	95
Wheatland	769	62.4%	464	37.6%	0
Wibaux	411	60.9%	264	39.1%	0
Yellowstone	26702	63.6%	15106	36.0%	191
TOTALS	**195420**	**61.7%**	**115848**	**36.6%**	**5452**

1976 U.S. Senate Election

COUNTIES	John Melcher (D)		Stanley Burger (R)		Other
Beaverhead	1563	44.0%	1990	56.0%	
Big Horn	2398	66.6%	1203	33.4%	
Blaine	1871	67.2%	912	32.8%	
Broadwater	730	52.0%	673	48.0%	
Carbon	2690	65.7%	1402	34.3%	
Carter	558	56.8%	425	43.2%	
Cascade	20522	69.9%	8856	30.1%	
Chouteau	2204	62.3%	1335	37.7%	
Custer	3722	65.3%	1982	34.7%	
Daniels	1118	67.5%	539	32.5%	
Dawson	3182	63.4%	1835	36.6%	
Deer Lodge	4332	77.5%	1261	22.5%	
Fallon	1060	58.7%	746	41.3%	
Fergus	3599	57.0%	2713	43.0%	
Flathead	11018	58.8%	7728	41.2%	
Gallatin	8146	51.7%	7596	48.3%	
Garfield	548	58.9%	382	41.1%	
Glacier	2288	61.6%	1429	38.4%	
Golden Valley	355	61.6%	221	38.4%	
Granite	717	54.6%	595	45.4%	
Hill	5282	72.3%	2023	27.7%	
Jefferson	1678	62.2%	1019	37.8%	
Judith Basin	1042	63.6%	596	36.4%	
Lake	3971	54.4%	3323	45.6%	
Lewis & Clark	10288	61.5%	6435	38.5%	
Liberty	641	54.2%	542	45.8%	
Lincoln	4331	70.2%	1841	29.8%	
Madison	1170	43.9%	1493	56.1%	
McCone	964	63.3%	559	36.7%	
Meagher	509	53.6%	441	46.4%	
Mineral	1108	72.8%	413	27.2%	
Missoula	21754	68.1%	10196	31.9%	
Musselshell	1492	71.2%	603	28.8%	
Park	3508	60.4%	2300	39.6%	
Petroleum	188	55.8%	149	44.2%	
Phillips	1597	63.9%	904	36.1%	
Pondera	1892	59.7%	1277	40.3%	
Powder River	670	52.8%	600	47.2%	
Powell	1709	62.9%	1009	37.1%	
Prairie	602	58.7%	423	41.3%	
Ravalli	4632	52.7%	4150	47.3%	
Richland	2603	60.4%	1707	39.6%	
Roosevelt	2547	64.2%	1423	35.8%	
Rosebud	2437	80.2%	602	19.8%	
Sanders	2300	64.5%	1268	35.5%	
Sheridan	1890	69.3%	836	30.7%	
Silver Bow	13194	76.5%	4052	23.5%	
Stillwater	1729	64.6%	948	35.4%	
Sweet Grass	814	49.1%	845	50.9%	
Teton	1987	58.9%	1389	41.1%	
Toole	1494	56.4%	1153	43.6%	
Treasure	431	75.2%	142	24.8%	
Valley	3099	64.0%	1746	36.0%	
Wheatland	842	62.9%	496	37.1%	
Wibaux	487	68.4%	225	31.6%	
Yellowstone	28729	66.8%	14262	33.2%	
TOTALS	**206232**	**64.2%**	**115213**	**35.8%**	

1976 U.S. House Election, 1st District

COUNTIES	Max Baucus (D)		Bill Diehl (R)		Other
Beaverhead	1750	50.1%	1742	49.9%	
Big Horn					
Blaine					
Broadwater	740	52.8%	662	47.2%	
Carbon					
Carter					
Cascade					
Chouteau					
Custer					
Daniels					
Dawson					
Deer Lodge	4888	81.3%	1125	18.7%	
Fallon					
Fergus					
Flathead	11230	59.6%	7624	40.4%	
Gallatin	9468	58.8%	6628	41.2%	
Garfield					
Glacier	2271	61.5%	1424	38.5%	
Golden Valley					
Granite	768	59.7%	519	40.3%	
Hill					
Jefferson	1644	60.8%	1060	39.2%	
Judith Basin					
Lake	4341	59.4%	2964	40.6%	
Lewis & Clark	11370	63.9%	6424	36.1%	
Liberty	655	56.4%	507	43.6%	
Lincoln	4373	71.5%	1743	28.5%	
Madison	1223	46.1%	1431	53.9%	
McCone					
Meagher	504	54.8%	415	45.2%	
Mineral	1111	73.3%	404	26.7%	
Missoula	24014	74.9%	8032	25.1%	
Musselshell					
Park	3644	63.2%	2119	36.8%	
Petroleum					
Phillips					
Pondera	2066	65.3%	1097	34.7%	
Powder River					
Powell	1930	68.0%	910	32.0%	
Prairie					
Ravalli	5330	60.7%	3448	39.3%	
Richland					
Roosevelt					
Rosebud					
Sanders	2254	63.0%	1323	37.0%	
Sheridan					
Silver Bow	14478	80.5%	3518	19.5%	
Stillwater					
Sweet Grass					
Teton					
Toole	1435	54.9%	1178	45.1%	
Treasure					
Valley					
Wheatland					
Wibaux					
Yellowstone					
TOTALS	**111487**	**66.4%**	**56297**	**33.6%**	

1976 U.S. House Election, 2nd District

COUNTIES	Tom Towe (D)		Ron Marlenee (R)		Other
Beaverhead					
Big Horn	1775	51.7%	1661	48.3%	
Blaine	1261	45.7%	1496	54.3%	
Broadwater					
Carbon	1730	42.9%	2304	57.1%	
Carter	298	33.0%	604	67.0%	
Cascade	14706	50.9%	14194	49.1%	
Chouteau	1316	38.1%	2139	61.9%	
Custer	2212	39.6%	3372	60.4%	
Daniels	490	29.9%	1150	70.1%	
Dawson	2201	44.7%	2728	55.3%	
Deer Lodge					
Fallon	693	39.1%	1080	60.9%	
Fergus	2354	38.0%	3847	62.0%	
Flathead					
Gallatin					
Garfield	159	17.5%	750	82.5%	
Glacier					
Golden Valley	188	33.6%	372	66.4%	
Granite					
Hill	4082	56.5%	3141	43.5%	
Jefferson					
Judith Basin	630	39.1%	980	60.9%	
Lake					
Lewis & Clark					
Liberty					
Lincoln					
Madison					
McCone	639	42.7%	858	57.3%	
Meagher					
Mineral					
Missoula					
Musselshell	720	37.3%	1210	62.7%	
Park					
Petroleum	81	24.8%	245	75.2%	
Phillips	989	40.2%	1474	59.8%	
Pondera					
Powder River	372	30.3%	854	69.7%	
Powell					
Prairie	338	33.4%	674	66.6%	
Ravalli					
Richland	1723	40.9%	2492	59.1%	
Roosevelt	1643	42.1%	2261	57.9%	
Rosebud	1380	46.7%	1577	53.3%	
Sanders					
Sheridan	1024	38.2%	1656	61.8%	
Silver Bow					
Stillwater	1069	41.1%	1535	58.9%	
Sweet Grass	448	27.1%	1206	72.9%	
Teton	1380	41.7%	1929	58.3%	
Toole					
Treasure	222	40.4%	328	59.6%	
Valley	2102	43.7%	2706	56.3%	
Wheatland	542	41.3%	770	58.7%	
Wibaux	275	39.9%	414	60.1%	
Yellowstone	19930	47.3%	22169	52.7%	
TOTALS	**68972**	**45.0%**	**84149**	**55.0%**	

1978 U.S. Senate Election

COUNTIES	Max Baucus (D)		Larry Williams (R)		Other
Beaverhead	1213	37.1%	2054	62.9%	
Big Horn	1816	57.0%	1369	43.0%	
Blaine	1506	58.3%	1077	41.7%	
Broadwater	641	47.2%	718	52.8%	
Carbon	2033	56.9%	1539	43.1%	
Carter	431	44.9%	528	55.1%	
Cascade	13861	57.2%	10356	42.8%	
Chouteau	1715	52.3%	1563	47.7%	
Custer	2624	54.0%	2234	46.0%	
Daniels	713	52.3%	651	47.7%	
Dawson	2381	53.2%	2093	46.8%	
Deer Lodge	3928	75.3%	1289	24.7%	
Fallon	851	51.4%	804	48.6%	
Fergus	2451	47.5%	2710	52.5%	
Flathead	8705	51.5%	8211	48.5%	
Gallatin	7944	52.9%	7068	47.1%	
Garfield	451	46.5%	518	53.5%	
Glacier	1705	53.7%	1470	46.3%	
Golden Valley	269	48.7%	283	51.3%	
Granite	610	50.3%	603	49.7%	
Hill	3841	62.3%	2327	37.7%	
Jefferson	1376	54.5%	1149	45.5%	
Judith Basin	784	50.9%	755	49.1%	
Lake	3411	48.1%	3674	51.9%	
Lewis & Clark	9913	59.5%	6743	40.5%	
Liberty	549	48.0%	594	52.0%	
Lincoln	3698	65.4%	1953	34.6%	
Madison	978	39.5%	1501	60.5%	
McCone	708	54.4%	593	45.6%	
Meagher	358	41.1%	513	58.9%	
Mineral	998	62.9%	588	37.1%	
Missoula	17745	65.0%	9574	35.0%	
Musselshell	969	52.2%	889	47.8%	
Park	2888	54.3%	2431	45.7%	
Petroleum	147	47.3%	164	52.7%	
Phillips	1109	49.1%	1148	50.9%	
Pondera	1568	52.3%	1429	47.7%	
Powder River	603	45.0%	738	55.0%	
Powell	1548	60.8%	998	39.2%	
Prairie	437	46.7%	498	53.3%	
Ravalli	4227	48.9%	4421	51.1%	
Richland	1689	44.9%	2075	55.1%	
Roosevelt	1858	51.4%	1760	48.6%	
Rosebud	1577	55.7%	1252	44.3%	
Sanders	1892	56.3%	1470	43.7%	
Sheridan	1346	58.8%	944	41.2%	
Silver Bow	11367	69.0%	5109	31.0%	
Stillwater	1517	56.6%	1161	43.4%	
Sweet Grass	631	41.1%	905	58.9%	
Teton	1498	48.8%	1571	51.2%	
Toole	1057	44.0%	1344	56.0%	
Treasure	336	56.0%	264	44.0%	
Valley	2317	53.8%	1993	46.2%	
Wheatland	597	49.3%	615	50.7%	
Wibaux	380	55.7%	302	44.3%	
Yellowstone	18588	51.9%	17206	48.1%	
TOTALS	**160353**	**55.7%**	**127589**	**44.3%**	

1978 U.S. House Election, 1st District

COUNTIES	Pat Williams (D)		Jim Waltermire (R)		Other
Beaverhead	1293	39.6%	1971	60.4%	
Big Horn					
Blaine					
Broadwater	675	50.0%	676	50.0%	
Carbon					
Carter					
Cascade					
Chouteau					
Custer					
Daniels					
Dawson					
Deer Lodge	3857	75.7%	1236	24.3%	
Fallon					
Fergus					
Flathead	8183	48.9%	8546	51.1%	
Gallatin	6721	46.4%	7768	53.6%	
Garfield					
Glacier	1807	58.4%	1286	41.6%	
Golden Valley					
Granite	640	53.2%	564	46.8%	
Hill					
Jefferson	1438	57.1%	1081	42.9%	
Judith Basin					
Lake	3589	51.1%	3429	48.9%	
Lewis & Clark	8953	56.0%	7047	44.0%	
Liberty	528	47.8%	576	52.2%	
Lincoln	3602	64.9%	1946	35.1%	
Madison	999	40.9%	1446	59.1%	
McCone					
Meagher	350	41.3%	497	58.7%	
Mineral	1045	66.1%	536	33.9%	
Missoula	17141	63.8%	9720	36.2%	
Musselshell					
Park	2663	51.1%	2552	48.9%	
Petroleum					
Phillips					
Pondera	1497	50.8%	1449	49.2%	
Powder River					
Powell	1421	57.1%	1068	42.9%	
Prairie					
Ravalli	4493	53.6%	3887	46.4%	
Richland					
Roosevelt					
Rosebud					
Sanders	1912	57.9%	1393	42.1%	
Sheridan					
Silver Bow	12070	74.2%	4196	25.8%	
Stillwater					
Sweet Grass					
Teton					
Toole	1139	48.2%	1223	51.8%	
Treasure					
Valley					
Wheatland					
Wibaux					
Yellowstone					
TOTALS	**86016**	**57.3%**	**64093**	**42.7%**	

1978 U.S. House Election, 2nd District

COUNTIES	Tom Monahan (D)		Ron Marlenee (R)		Other
Beaverhead					
Big Horn	1589	50.6%	1553	49.4%	
Blaine	1125	43.8%	1446	56.2%	
Broadwater					
Carbon	1635	45.7%	1942	54.3%	
Carter	326	33.6%	645	66.4%	
Cascade	11700	50.3%	11571	49.7%	
Chouteau	1134	35.0%	2106	65.0%	
Custer	2149	44.2%	2709	55.8%	
Daniels	314	22.8%	1063	77.2%	
Dawson	1734	38.8%	2737	61.2%	
Deer Lodge					
Fallon	640	38.6%	1019	61.4%	
Fergus	1895	36.8%	3250	63.2%	
Flathead					
Gallatin					
Garfield	198	20.5%	766	79.5%	
Glacier					
Golden Valley	198	35.6%	358	64.4%	
Granite					
Hill	2928	47.6%	3219	52.4%	
Jefferson					
Judith Basin	588	38.3%	948	61.7%	
Lake					
Lewis & Clark					
Liberty					
Lincoln					
Madison					
McCone	397	30.5%	906	69.5%	
Meagher					
Mineral					
Missoula					
Musselshell	747	40.1%	1115	59.9%	
Park					
Petroleum	74	23.5%	241	76.5%	
Phillips	696	31.2%	1536	68.8%	
Pondera					
Powder River	429	31.6%	927	68.4%	
Powell					
Prairie	304	32.9%	619	67.1%	
Ravalli					
Richland	1324	35.1%	2448	64.9%	
Roosevelt	1286	35.6%	2325	64.4%	
Rosebud	1246	44.0%	1588	56.0%	
Sanders					
Sheridan	688	29.7%	1626	70.3%	
Silver Bow					
Stillwater	1096	40.8%	1593	59.2%	
Sweet Grass	426	27.4%	1127	72.6%	
Teton	1214	40.0%	1821	60.0%	
Toole					
Treasure	219	36.6%	379	63.4%	
Valley	1468	35.5%	2671	64.5%	
Wheatland	532	44.0%	678	56.0%	
Wibaux	243	35.4%	444	64.6%	
Yellowstone	16929	47.9%	18390	52.1%	
TOTALS	**57480**	**43.1%**	**75766**	**56.9%**	

1980 Presidential Election

COUNTIES	Jimmy Carter (D)		Ronald Reagan (R)		Other
Beaverhead	842	20.5%	2955	72.0%	306
Big Horn	1644	44.0%	1730	46.3%	361
Blaine	1107	37.0%	1686	56.3%	202
Broadwater	401	25.6%	1052	67.3%	111
Carbon	1468	33.6%	2471	56.6%	424
Carter	237	22.4%	766	72.4%	55
Cascade	11105	34.5%	17664	54.8%	3465
Chouteau	853	23.8%	2448	68.3%	282
Custer	1822	31.3%	3533	60.7%	461
Daniels	483	29.0%	1086	65.2%	97
Dawson	1543	30.1%	3045	59.5%	530
Deer Lodge	3077	54.6%	1905	33.8%	656
Fallon	512	26.7%	1286	67.0%	122
Fergus	1840	26.9%	4455	65.0%	557
Flathead	6349	26.7%	15102	63.5%	2316
Gallatin	5747	26.5%	12738	58.6%	3241
Garfield	169	17.4%	760	78.0%	45
Glacier	1394	34.1%	2283	55.8%	416
Golden Valley	155	27.9%	362	65.1%	39
Granite	439	31.9%	811	58.9%	126
Hill	2875	35.5%	4448	55.0%	766
Jefferson	1055	32.7%	1841	57.1%	327
Judith Basin	480	29.5%	1030	63.3%	117
Lake	2615	30.6%	5083	59.6%	834
Lewis & Clark	6815	32.1%	12128	57.2%	2269
Liberty	283	22.5%	872	69.4%	101
Lincoln	2422	33.0%	4202	57.2%	724
Madison	676	21.5%	2220	70.6%	249
McCone	349	23.7%	1000	68.0%	122
Meagher	247	24.9%	689	69.6%	54
Mineral	660	40.0%	800	48.5%	188
Missoula	13115	37.9%	16161	46.7%	5318
Musselshell	784	35.6%	1279	58.0%	141
Park	1663	26.8%	3929	63.4%	603
Petroleum	90	26.4%	225	66.0%	26
Phillips	745	28.1%	1723	64.9%	185
Pondera	897	26.1%	2270	66.1%	265
Powder River	336	23.3%	985	68.2%	124
Powell	883	29.5%	1770	59.1%	340
Prairie	283	30.5%	580	62.6%	64
Ravalli	3036	26.7%	7268	63.9%	1073
Richland	1252	24.9%	3348	66.5%	438
Roosevelt	1504	36.2%	2298	55.2%	358
Rosebud	1167	33.9%	1875	54.5%	401
Sanders	1395	34.9%	2194	54.9%	410
Sheridan	955	32.8%	1658	56.9%	299
Silver Bow	9721	50.2%	7301	37.7%	2355
Stillwater	919	30.8%	1828	61.3%	237
Sweet Grass	440	25.4%	1169	67.6%	120
Teton	902	25.3%	2415	67.8%	247
Toole	634	22.2%	2000	70.2%	216
Treasure	181	32.7%	321	57.9%	52
Valley	1567	30.2%	3242	62.5%	381
Wheatland	381	31.0%	742	60.3%	107
Wibaux	219	30.4%	450	62.4%	52
Yellowstone	15272	31.6%	27332	56.6%	5709
TOTALS	**118032**	**32.4%**	**206814**	**56.8%**	**39106**

1980 Gubernatorial Election

COUNTIES	Ted Schwinden (D)		Jack Ramirez(R)		Other
Beaverhead	1764	43.5%	2288	56.5%	
Big Horn	2145	59.5%	1462	40.5%	
Blaine	1702	57.3%	1267	42.7%	
Broadwater	785	49.5%	802	50.5%	
Carbon	2462	56.3%	1909	43.7%	
Carter	413	40.3%	613	59.7%	
Cascade	18099	57.2%	13532	42.8%	
Chouteau	1939	54.0%	1650	46.0%	
Custer	3422	58.4%	2433	41.6%	
Daniels	1168	70.4%	492	29.6%	
Dawson	2879	56.0%	2261	44.0%	
Deer Lodge	3802	70.5%	1592	29.5%	
Fallon	1008	53.7%	868	46.3%	
Fergus	3563	52.0%	3291	48.0%	
Flathead	12329	52.1%	11335	47.9%	
Gallatin	11292	52.2%	10358	47.8%	
Garfield	489	50.3%	484	49.7%	
Glacier	2270	56.0%	1782	44.0%	
Golden Valley	309	54.0%	263	46.0%	
Granite	609	44.3%	765	55.7%	
Hill	4878	60.2%	3221	39.8%	
Jefferson	1848	56.9%	1398	43.1%	
Judith Basin	844	51.4%	798	48.6%	
Lake	4205	49.3%	4333	50.7%	
Lewis & Clark	13334	64.1%	7478	35.9%	
Liberty	632	50.2%	628	49.8%	
Lincoln	4027	55.7%	3209	44.3%	
Madison	1242	39.5%	1900	60.5%	
McCone	932	62.3%	565	37.7%	
Meagher	446	45.1%	544	54.9%	
Mineral	952	57.3%	708	42.7%	
Missoula	20100	58.7%	14166	41.3%	
Musselshell	1133	51.3%	1074	48.7%	
Park	3446	54.9%	2835	45.1%	
Petroleum	191	56.7%	146	43.3%	
Phillips	1350	51.0%	1298	49.0%	
Pondera	1820	53.0%	1614	47.0%	
Powder River	635	45.3%	767	54.7%	
Powell	1508	50.8%	1459	49.2%	
Prairie	528	52.1%	486	47.9%	
Ravalli	4814	42.4%	6545	57.6%	
Richland	2718	54.2%	2297	45.8%	
Roosevelt	3115	75.0%	1036	25.0%	
Rosebud	1743	50.8%	1686	49.2%	
Sanders	1856	46.8%	2114	53.2%	
Sheridan	1917	66.4%	970	33.6%	
Silver Bow	12365	65.0%	6644	35.0%	
Stillwater	1644	55.3%	1331	44.7%	
Sweet Grass	757	43.4%	988	56.6%	
Teton	1819	51.4%	1723	48.6%	
Toole	1451	51.1%	1388	48.9%	
Treasure	347	62.5%	208	37.5%	
Valley	2988	59.6%	2023	40.4%	
Wheatland	671	54.8%	553	45.2%	
Wibaux	390	54.1%	331	45.9%	
Yellowstone	24479	51.6%	22981	48.4%	
TOTALS	**199574**	**55.4%**	**160892**	**44.6%**	

1980 U.S. House Election, 1st District

COUNTIES	Pat Williams (D)		Jack McDonald (R)		Other
Beaverhead	1289	32.4%	2692	67.6%	
Big Horn					
Blaine					
Broadwater	840	55.2%	682	44.8%	
Carbon					
Carter					
Cascade					
Chouteau					
Custer					
Daniels					
Dawson					
Deer Lodge	3946	78.6%	1073	21.4%	
Fallon					
Fergus					
Flathead	13258	56.9%	10061	43.1%	
Gallatin	11733	60.0%	7817	40.0%	
Garfield					
Glacier	2424	61.9%	1492	38.1%	
Golden Valley					
Granite	746	54.8%	615	45.2%	
Hill					
Jefferson	2016	63.6%	1156	36.4%	
Judith Basin					
Lake	4833	57.4%	3582	42.6%	
Lewis & Clark	11864	65.7%	6204	34.3%	
Liberty	480	49.3%	493	50.7%	
Lincoln	4143	57.8%	3031	42.2%	
Madison	1485	48.2%	1594	51.8%	
McCone					
Meagher	426	45.7%	506	54.3%	
Mineral	1117	67.9%	527	32.1%	
Missoula	22440	65.5%	11809	34.5%	
Musselshell					
Park	3433	58.7%	2416	41.3%	
Petroleum					
Phillips					
Pondera	1870	55.8%	1482	44.2%	
Powder River					
Powell	1634	56.2%	1271	43.8%	
Prairie					
Ravalli	5751	51.4%	5448	48.6%	
Richland					
Roosevelt					
Rosebud					
Sanders	2231	57.3%	1665	42.7%	
Sheridan					
Silver Bow	13422	77.2%	3958	22.8%	
Stillwater					
Sweet Grass					
Teton					
Toole	1485	53.3%	1300	46.7%	
Treasure					
Valley					
Wheatland					
Wibaux					
Yellowstone					
TOTALS	**112866**	**61.4%**	**70874**	**38.6%**	

1980 U.S. House Election, 2nd District

COUNTIES	Tom Monahan (D)		Ron Marlenee (R)		Other
Beaverhead					
Big Horn	1733	49.8%	1746	50.2%	
Blaine	1323	45.3%	1596	54.7%	
Broadwater					
Carbon	1900	43.8%	2434	56.2%	
Carter	304	30.1%	707	69.9%	
Cascade	11628	47.9%	12660	52.1%	
Chouteau	1211	34.1%	2342	65.9%	
Custer	2127	39.4%	3270	60.6%	
Daniels	324	19.4%	1344	80.6%	
Dawson	1777	36.2%	3136	63.8%	
Deer Lodge					
Fallon	770	41.3%	1094	58.7%	
Fergus	2473	36.6%	4278	63.4%	
Flathead					
Gallatin					
Garfield	173	18.1%	784	81.9%	
Glacier					
Golden Valley	211	37.7%	348	62.3%	
Granite					
Hill	3663	47.4%	4070	52.6%	
Jefferson					
Judith Basin	648	39.8%	981	60.2%	
Lake					
Lewis & Clark					
Liberty					
Lincoln					
Madison					
McCone	407	27.7%	1062	72.3%	
Meagher					
Mineral					
Missoula					
Musselshell	802	36.9%	1371	63.1%	
Park					
Petroleum	94	28.1%	240	71.9%	
Phillips	780	29.8%	1840	70.2%	
Pondera					
Powder River	450	32.7%	927	67.3%	
Powell					
Prairie	345	34.5%	656	65.5%	
Ravalli					
Richland	1771	35.4%	3225	64.6%	
Roosevelt	1484	36.5%	2587	63.5%	
Rosebud	1284	38.0%	2098	62.0%	
Sanders					
Sheridan	1006	34.8%	1883	65.2%	
Silver Bow					
Stillwater	1144	39.2%	1773	60.8%	
Sweet Grass	472	27.3%	1255	72.7%	
Teton	1310	37.9%	2150	62.1%	
Toole					
Treasure	175	32.0%	372	68.0%	
Valley	1592	35.1%	2938	64.9%	
Wheatland	472	39.3%	730	60.7%	
Wibaux	282	38.6%	448	61.4%	
Yellowstone	19235	43.4%	25086	56.6%	
TOTALS	**63370**	**40.9%**	**91431**	**59.1%**	

228

1982 U.S. Senate Election

COUNTIES	John Melcher (D)		Larry Williams (R)		Other
Beaverhead	1518	42.2%	1929	53.7%	146
Big Horn	3347	68.2%	1454	29.6%	106
Blaine	1740	63.6%	919	33.6%	78
Broadwater	841	52.5%	698	43.6%	62
Carbon	2498	57.0%	1766	40.3%	118
Carter	507	53.7%	428	45.3%	10
Cascade	15929	57.5%	10893	39.4%	857
Chouteau	1778	56.1%	1289	40.6%	105
Custer	2897	55.1%	2170	41.3%	191
Daniels	920	64.4%	490	34.3%	19
Dawson	2393	51.0%	2183	46.5%	120
Deer Lodge	3673	74.5%	1040	21.1%	219
Fallon	979	55.7%	742	42.2%	38
Fergus	3067	50.9%	2785	46.3%	168
Flathead	8596	40.9%	11361	54.1%	1046
Gallatin	8029	44.4%	9178	50.8%	873
Garfield	560	58.2%	389	40.4%	13
Glacier	1946	54.8%	1465	41.3%	137
Golden Valley	340	58.4%	226	38.8%	16
Granite	637	48.4%	594	45.1%	85
Hill	4671	62.0%	2649	35.2%	208
Jefferson	1610	53.2%	1276	42.1%	142
Judith Basin	866	58.8%	571	38.7%	37
Lake	3645	47.0%	3718	48.0%	390
Lewis & Clark	9805	53.0%	7970	43.1%	717
Liberty	585	50.2%	541	46.4%	40
Lincoln	3499	57.8%	2311	38.2%	243
Madison	1121	40.5%	1528	55.2%	118
McCone	835	58.5%	581	40.7%	12
Meagher	475	45.8%	536	51.6%	27
Mineral	881	58.0%	548	36.1%	90
Missoula	15477	53.3%	11499	39.6%	2076
Musselshell	1469	60.0%	909	37.1%	69
Park	2979	50.7%	2691	45.8%	211
Petroleum	159	55.8%	116	40.7%	10
Phillips	1365	55.9%	999	40.9%	76
Pondera	1673	53.8%	1320	42.5%	116
Powder River	710	51.6%	635	46.1%	31
Powell	1498	53.4%	1147	40.9%	162
Prairie	518	52.1%	445	44.7%	32
Ravalli	4158	42.3%	5228	53.2%	446
Richland	2467	58.1%	1726	40.6%	54
Roosevelt	2209	63.5%	1194	34.3%	76
Rosebud	2843	69.5%	1112	27.2%	138
Sanders	2157	57.0%	1436	38.0%	188
Sheridan	1816	72.2%	673	26.8%	26
Silver Bow	11714	73.0%	3666	22.8%	672
Stillwater	1617	56.9%	1139	40.1%	85
Sweet Grass	757	45.6%	854	51.4%	49
Teton	1630	50.6%	1503	46.7%	87
Toole	1315	48.8%	1261	46.8%	121
Treasure	424	71.3%	158	26.6%	13
Valley	2761	60.8%	1707	37.6%	70
Wheatland	644	57.9%	434	39.0%	35
Wibaux	427	63.4%	233	34.6%	14
Yellowstone	21886	54.1%	17476	43.2%	1124
TOTALS	**174861**	**54.5%**	**133789**	**41.7%**	**12412**

1982 U.S. House Election, 1st District

COUNTIES	Pat Williams (D)		Bob Davies (R)		Other
Beaverhead	1308	36.9%	2129	60.0%	109
Big Horn					
Blaine					
Broadwater	813	51.8%	692	44.1%	64
Carbon					
Carter					
Cascade					
Chouteau					
Custer					
Daniels					
Dawson					
Deer Lodge	3714	78.6%	850	18.0%	160
Fallon					
Fergus					
Flathead	11534	55.2%	8793	42.1%	559
Gallatin	8588	47.7%	8834	49.0%	594
Garfield					
Glacier	2272	63.6%	1182	33.1%	121
Golden Valley					
Granite	761	59.1%	487	37.8%	39
Hill					
Jefferson	1830	61.3%	1084	36.3%	70
Judith Basin					
Lake	4354	56.0%	3219	41.4%	201
Lewis & Clark	11868	64.4%	6099	33.1%	469
Liberty	650	58.1%	434	38.8%	34
Lincoln	3631	60.6%	2155	36.0%	207
Madison	1211	45.4%	1385	52.0%	70
McCone					
Meagher	520	51.2%	424	41.7%	72
Mineral	1049	70.5%	386	26.0%	52
Missoula	18064	62.3%	9807	33.8%	1101
Musselshell					
Park	3445	59.3%	2195	37.8%	172
Petroleum					
Phillips					
Pondera	1825	60.0%	1111	36.5%	105
Powder River					
Powell	1700	62.1%	946	34.6%	90
Prairie					
Ravalli	5010	51.2%	4543	46.4%	235
Richland					
Roosevelt					
Rosebud					
Sanders	2154	57.4%	1488	39.7%	109
Sheridan					
Silver Bow	12255	77.6%	3137	19.9%	403
Stillwater					
Sweet Grass					
Teton					
Toole	1531	58.2%	1022	38.9%	77
Treasure					
Valley					
Wheatland					
Wibaux					
Yellowstone					
TOTALS	**100087**	**59.7%**	**62402**	**37.2%**	**5113**

1982 U.S. House Election, 2nd District

COUNTIES	Howard Lyman (D)		Ron Marlenee (R)		Other
Beaverhead					
Big Horn	2740	57.3%	1966	41.1%	72
Blaine	1279	46.8%	1404	51.4%	47
Broadwater					
Carbon	1980	45.9%	2265	52.5%	67
Carter	209	22.7%	701	76.2%	10
Cascade	13331	50.1%	12594	47.3%	704
Chouteau	1196	37.9%	1895	60.0%	66
Custer	2163	41.5%	2923	56.1%	124
Daniels	410	28.8%	1001	70.3%	13
Dawson	1953	44.3%	2388	54.1%	70
Deer Lodge					
Fallon	656	38.3%	1028	60.0%	30
Fergus	2171	36.4%	3695	61.9%	99
Flathead					
Gallatin					
Garfield	207	21.8%	735	77.5%	6
Glacier					
Golden Valley	237	41.1%	335	58.2%	4
Granite					
Hill	3621	48.7%	3678	49.5%	134
Jefferson					
Judith Basin	590	40.1%	854	58.1%	26
Lake					
Lewis & Clark					
Liberty					
Lincoln					
Madison					
McCone	602	42.4%	805	56.7%	13
Meagher					
Mineral					
Missoula					
Musselshell	1027	42.1%	1392	57.1%	18
Park					
Petroleum	88	30.8%	189	66.1%	9
Phillips	826	34.1%	1554	64.2%	40
Pondera					
Powder River	390	29.0%	912	67.7%	45
Powell					
Prairie	415	42.2%	554	56.3%	15
Ravalli					
Richland	1393	33.2%	2744	65.4%	59
Roosevelt	1642	47.8%	1731	50.4%	60
Rosebud	1955	48.3%	1912	47.2%	183
Sanders					
Sheridan	934	37.2%	1549	61.8%	25
Silver Bow					
Stillwater	1171	41.4%	1617	57.1%	43
Sweet Grass	429	26.0%	1191	72.3%	28
Teton	1253	39.4%	1863	58.5%	68
Toole					
Treasure	209	35.1%	374	62.8%	13
Valley	1979	44.5%	2394	53.8%	75
Wheatland	424	38.3%	671	60.7%	11
Wibaux	271	39.8%	395	58.0%	15
Yellowstone	18064	45.5%	20659	52.1%	962
TOTALS	**65815**	**44.2%**	**79968**	**53.7%**	**3154**

1984 Presidential Election

COUNTIES	Walter Mondale (D)		Ronald Reagan (R)		Other
Beaverhead	942	23.3%	3044	75.4%	49
Big Horn	2681	52.5%	2390	46.8%	39
Blaine	1229	41.0%	1736	57.9%	32
Broadwater	458	25.0%	1345	73.5%	27
Carbon	1657	36.1%	2877	62.7%	53
Carter	194	18.9%	823	80.1%	11
Cascade	14252	41.3%	19846	57.5%	407
Chouteau	896	26.7%	2425	72.2%	39
Custer	1982	33.5%	3879	65.5%	58
Daniels	473	32.0%	984	66.6%	20
Dawson	1776	33.4%	3468	65.3%	70
Deer Lodge	3539	64.3%	1901	34.5%	65
Fallon	569	31.1%	1237	67.6%	23
Fergus	1804	27.9%	4585	71.0%	70
Flathead	8310	32.2%	17012	65.9%	481
Gallatin	8163	33.8%	15643	64.8%	334
Garfield	134	14.7%	770	84.5%	7
Glacier	2167	48.9%	2228	50.2%	40
Golden Valley	211	35.2%	384	64.0%	5
Granite	417	31.5%	880	66.6%	25
Hill	3657	43.6%	4635	55.2%	98
Jefferson	1324	36.6%	2226	61.5%	68
Judith Basin	483	31.2%	1050	67.7%	17
Lake	3473	37.2%	5754	61.6%	121
Lewis & Clark	8768	38.8%	13569	60.0%	289
Liberty	323	26.3%	895	72.8%	11
Lincoln	2959	41.2%	4080	56.8%	145
Madison	708	23.1%	2308	75.2%	53
McCone	459	30.7%	1015	67.8%	23
Meagher	283	26.5%	771	72.1%	15
Mineral	718	42.1%	943	55.3%	43
Missoula	16540	44.8%	19777	53.5%	620
Musselshell	781	33.1%	1541	65.3%	37
Park	2387	36.3%	4115	62.5%	79
Petroleum	86	24.8%	258	74.4%	3
Phillips	787	28.6%	1934	70.4%	28
Pondera	1039	31.3%	2239	67.5%	38
Powder River	346	24.2%	1066	74.6%	17
Powell	1066	35.4%	1877	62.3%	69
Prairie	289	29.2%	693	69.9%	9
Ravalli	3825	31.5%	8161	67.1%	168
Richland	1382	26.2%	3847	72.8%	52
Roosevelt	1962	44.0%	2431	54.5%	71
Rosebud	1920	43.6%	2413	54.8%	69
Sanders	1654	39.3%	2467	58.7%	83
Sheridan	1087	37.8%	1774	61.6%	18
Silver Bow	11095	61.6%	6637	36.9%	278
Stillwater	1100	33.8%	2118	65.0%	40
Sweet Grass	378	21.0%	1417	78.6%	8
Teton	1102	32.6%	2257	66.7%	25
Toole	789	28.5%	1949	70.4%	30
Treasure	209	36.3%	353	61.3%	14
Valley	1849	36.6%	3123	61.9%	74
Wheatland	407	34.7%	753	64.2%	13
Wibaux	216	33.2%	423	65.0%	12
Yellowstone	19437	35.9%	34124	63.0%	592
TOTALS	**146742**	**38.2%**	**232450**	**60.5%**	**5185**

1984 Gubernatorial Election

COUNTIES	Ted Schwinden (D)		Pat Goodover (R)		Other
Beaverhead	2262	56.1%	1680	41.7%	88
Big Horn	3932	78.6%	974	19.5%	99
Blaine	2259	75.4%	658	21.9%	81
Broadwater	1257	69.6%	501	27.7%	48
Carbon	3328	72.2%	1198	26.0%	83
Carter	556	56.4%	412	41.8%	17
Cascade	23790	71.0%	8622	25.7%	1106
Chouteau	2224	66.5%	1058	31.6%	64
Custer	4294	72.2%	1464	24.6%	190
Daniels	913	62.9%	518	35.7%	21
Dawson	3628	68.0%	1626	30.5%	84
Deer Lodge	4046	78.4%	831	16.1%	281
Fallon	1208	68.1%	522	29.4%	43
Fergus	4230	65.6%	2065	32.0%	149
Flathead	17910	69.6%	6916	26.9%	917
Gallatin	15823	66.3%	7212	30.2%	829
Garfield	569	63.6%	302	33.7%	24
Glacier	3150	71.6%	1136	25.8%	112
Golden Valley	402	66.2%	195	32.1%	10
Granite	834	63.6%	420	32.0%	58
Hill	6367	76.4%	1802	21.6%	166
Jefferson	2436	67.4%	1015	28.1%	163
Judith Basin	1085	69.7%	430	27.6%	41
Lake	6525	69.7%	2554	27.3%	288
Lewis & Clark	16253	71.0%	5750	25.1%	881
Liberty	774	64.2%	410	34.0%	22
Lincoln	4909	68.7%	1938	27.1%	297
Madison	1789	59.3%	1119	37.1%	111
McCone	1069	70.8%	412	27.3%	28
Meagher	751	70.5%	291	27.3%	24
Mineral	1308	77.1%	304	17.9%	84
Missoula	26422	73.0%	8058	22.3%	1703
Musselshell	1636	70.3%	642	27.6%	50
Park	4800	71.6%	1757	26.2%	150
Petroleum	254	72.4%	90	25.6%	7
Phillips	1909	69.5%	771	28.1%	66
Pondera	2239	68.3%	972	29.6%	69
Powder River	827	59.7%	528	38.1%	30
Powell	1757	58.8%	981	32.8%	249
Prairie	675	68.9%	286	29.2%	18
Ravalli	7926	65.9%	3715	30.9%	382
Richland	2644	50.4%	2516	48.0%	87
Roosevelt	3603	80.1%	799	17.8%	96
Rosebud	3288	75.1%	930	21.2%	160
Sanders	2900	72.6%	957	23.9%	140
Sheridan	2202	78.3%	580	20.6%	31
Silver Bow	14268	80.2%	2934	16.5%	582
Stillwater	2319	72.4%	810	25.3%	74
Sweet Grass	1065	59.4%	699	39.0%	28
Teton	2358	67.7%	1051	30.2%	76
Toole	1702	62.1%	961	35.1%	76
Treasure	443	78.0%	108	19.0%	17
Valley	3554	72.9%	1198	24.6%	121
Wheatland	835	70.8%	314	26.6%	30
Wibaux	462	71.1%	174	26.8%	14
Yellowstone	36609	70.2%	13904	26.7%	1657
TOTALS	**266578**	**70.3%**	**100070**	**26.4%**	**12322**

1984 U.S. Senate Election

COUNTIES	Max Baucus (D)		Chuck Cozzens (R)		Other
Beaverhead	1630	40.4%	2328	57.7%	75
Big Horn	3591	69.4%	1517	29.3%	66
Blaine	1854	61.4%	1122	37.1%	45
Broadwater	887	48.5%	894	48.9%	46
Carbon	2707	58.4%	1826	39.4%	104
Carter	474	47.0%	518	51.3%	17
Cascade	18520	59.9%	11396	36.8%	1017
Chouteau	1743	51.5%	1578	46.6%	66
Custer	3394	57.3%	2449	41.3%	85
Daniels	826	56.8%	609	41.9%	20
Dawson	2847	53.5%	2370	44.5%	103
Deer Lodge	4082	77.4%	1066	20.2%	127
Fallon	1006	55.7%	780	43.2%	20
Fergus	3035	47.2%	3262	50.8%	128
Flathead	13200	50.9%	12116	46.7%	610
Gallatin	13111	54.3%	10497	43.5%	526
Garfield	385	42.3%	511	56.1%	15
Glacier	2766	61.7%	1612	36.0%	105
Golden Valley	319	52.2%	280	45.8%	12
Granite	671	50.5%	630	47.4%	29
Hill	5545	66.2%	2737	32.7%	98
Jefferson	2054	56.6%	1485	40.9%	89
Judith Basin	845	54.1%	689	44.1%	28
Lake	4690	49.4%	4547	47.9%	248
Lewis & Clark	13459	59.1%	8797	38.6%	533
Liberty	563	45.1%	665	53.2%	21
Lincoln	4329	61.4%	2510	35.6%	207
Madison	1303	42.8%	1669	54.9%	69
McCone	863	56.8%	645	42.4%	12
Meagher	557	52.1%	487	45.6%	25
Mineral	1059	62.1%	593	34.8%	52
Missoula	21717	59.0%	13739	37.3%	1364
Musselshell	1317	56.1%	996	42.4%	36
Park	3830	56.1%	2894	42.4%	107
Petroleum	174	49.6%	169	48.1%	8
Phillips	1492	53.7%	1239	44.6%	47
Pondera	1730	52.1%	1529	46.0%	63
Powder River	673	47.7%	721	51.1%	16
Powell	1624	53.9%	1258	41.8%	130
Prairie	523	52.5%	454	45.5%	20
Ravalli	5614	45.9%	6334	51.8%	277
Richland	2515	47.7%	2710	51.4%	52
Roosevelt	3083	68.8%	1313	29.3%	86
Rosebud	2732	62.1%	1568	35.7%	98
Sanders	2396	56.6%	1722	40.7%	117
Sheridan	1907	67.1%	915	32.2%	20
Silver Bow	13862	76.6%	3811	21.1%	425
Stillwater	1873	57.7%	1324	40.8%	47
Sweet Grass	700	38.8%	1079	59.9%	23
Teton	1849	53.1%	1560	44.8%	74
Toole	1359	49.2%	1354	49.0%	51
Treasure	361	62.8%	201	35.0%	13
Valley	2630	58.6%	1760	39.2%	98
Wheatland	631	52.9%	543	45.5%	19
Wibaux	332	50.9%	307	47.1%	13
Yellowstone	28465	54.3%	22623	43.1%	1341
TOTALS	**215704**	**56.9%**	**154308**	**40.7%**	**9143**

1984 U.S. House Election, 1st District

COUNTIES	Pat Williams (D)		Gary Carlson (R)		Other
Beaverhead	1786	45.0%	2097	52.8%	86
Big Horn					
Blaine					
Broadwater	1081	60.2%	671	37.4%	44
Carbon					
Carter					
Cascade					
Chouteau					
Custer					
Daniels					
Dawson					
Deer Lodge	4255	81.2%	881	16.8%	101
Fallon					
Fergus					
Flathead	15944	61.5%	9176	35.4%	797
Gallatin	13942	59.5%	8958	38.2%	549
Garfield					
Glacier	3058	69.1%	1246	28.2%	120
Golden Valley					
Granite	786	60.0%	501	38.2%	23
Hill					
Jefferson	2279	63.3%	1231	34.2%	89
Judith Basin					
Lake	5783	61.9%	3323	35.6%	233
Lewis & Clark	15771	69.3%	6581	28.9%	413
Liberty					
Lincoln	4767	66.4%	2201	30.6%	215
Madison	1539	50.9%	1418	46.9%	69
McCone					
Meagher					
Mineral	1226	72.8%	400	23.8%	58
Missoula	24530	68.0%	10571	29.3%	955
Musselshell					
Park	4345	65.0%	2221	33.2%	123
Petroleum					
Phillips					
Pondera					
Powder River					
Powell	1919	64.6%	941	31.7%	110
Prairie					
Ravalli	6771	56.0%	5074	41.9%	251
Richland					
Roosevelt					
Rosebud					
Sanders	2569	64.4%	1320	33.1%	98
Sheridan					
Silver Bow	14647	81.6%	2983	16.6%	326
Stillwater					
Sweet Grass					
Teton					
Toole					
Treasure					
Valley					
Wheatland					
Wibaux					
Yellowstone					
TOTALS	**126998**	**65.6%**	**61794**	**31.9%**	**4660**

1984 U.S. House Election, 2nd District

COUNTIES	Chet Blaylock (D)		Ron Marlenee (R)		Other
Beaverhead					
Big Horn	2455	47.8%	2684	52.2%	
Blaine	1085	36.2%	1912	63.8%	
Broadwater					
Carbon	1690	36.8%	2902	63.2%	
Carter	137	13.9%	851	86.1%	
Cascade	10850	38.6%	17259	61.4%	
Chouteau	903	27.0%	2443	73.0%	
Custer	1859	31.4%	4068	68.6%	
Daniels	222	15.0%	1257	85.0%	
Dawson	1476	27.7%	3849	72.3%	
Deer Lodge					
Fallon	441	24.2%	1379	75.8%	
Fergus	1696	27.3%	4512	72.7%	
Flathead					
Gallatin					
Garfield	131	14.6%	768	85.4%	
Glacier					
Golden Valley	156	26.1%	442	73.9%	
Granite					
Hill	3123	37.6%	5185	62.4%	
Jefferson					
Judith Basin	439	28.7%	1093	71.3%	
Lake					
Lewis & Clark					
Liberty	317	25.8%	911	74.2%	
Lincoln					
Madison					
McCone	347	22.9%	1166	77.1%	
Meagher	282	27.1%	760	72.9%	
Mineral					
Missoula					
Musselshell	714	30.6%	1621	69.4%	
Park					
Petroleum	70	19.9%	282	80.1%	
Phillips	677	24.7%	2068	75.3%	
Pondera	1017	30.8%	2289	69.2%	
Powder River	331	23.5%	1079	76.5%	
Powell					
Prairie	296	29.9%	694	70.1%	
Ravalli					
Richland	1071	20.2%	4224	79.8%	
Roosevelt	1538	34.3%	2950	65.7%	
Rosebud	1770	40.5%	2596	59.5%	
Sanders					
Sheridan	625	21.8%	2239	78.2%	
Silver Bow					
Stillwater	1095	33.7%	2156	66.3%	
Sweet Grass	378	21.2%	1401	78.8%	
Teton	1039	30.1%	2416	69.9%	
Toole	776	28.4%	1959	71.6%	
Treasure	155	26.9%	422	73.1%	
Valley	1228	28.9%	3023	71.1%	
Wheatland	336	28.5%	841	71.5%	
Wibaux	178	27.0%	481	73.0%	
Yellowstone	19533	38.8%	30750	61.2%	
TOTALS	**60445**	**34.1%**	**116932**	**65.9%**	

1986 U.S. House Election, 1st District

COUNTIES	Pat Williams (D)		Don Allen (R)		Other
Beaverhead	1648	47.1%	1848	52.9%	
Big Horn					
Blaine					
Broadwater	910	55.9%	718	44.1%	
Carbon					
Carter					
Cascade					
Chouteau					
Custer					
Daniels					
Dawson					
Deer Lodge	3594	81.1%	838	18.9%	
Fallon					
Fergus					
Flathead	11972	55.9%	9451	44.1%	
Gallatin	9711	54.7%	8039	45.3%	
Garfield					
Glacier	2062	62.9%	1214	37.1%	
Golden Valley					
Granite	726	55.4%	585	44.6%	
Hill					
Jefferson	1977	57.4%	1465	42.6%	
Judith Basin					
Lake	4409	55.7%	3512	44.3%	
Lewis & Clark	11852	62.1%	7235	37.9%	
Liberty					
Lincoln	4371	68.6%	1998	31.4%	
Madison	1327	46.7%	1512	53.3%	
McCone					
Meagher					
Mineral	1009	73.0%	374	27.0%	
Missoula	18569	64.9%	10027	35.1%	
Musselshell					
Park	3271	61.4%	2054	38.6%	
Petroleum					
Phillips					
Pondera					
Powder River					
Powell	1570	60.4%	1029	39.6%	
Prairie					
Ravalli	5568	53.2%	4898	46.8%	
Richland					
Roosevelt					
Rosebud					
Sanders	2298	65.3%	1221	34.7%	
Sheridan					
Silver Bow	11657	78.4%	3213	21.6%	
Stillwater					
Sweet Grass					
Teton					
Toole					
Treasure					
Valley					
Wheatland					
Wibaux					
Yellowstone					
TOTALS	**98501**	**61.7%**	**61230**	**38.3%**	

1986 U.S. House Election, 2nd District

COUNTIES	Buck O'Brien (D)		Ron Marlenee (R)		Other
Beaverhead					
Big Horn	2168	53.0%	1925	47.0%	
Blaine	1193	44.9%	1464	55.1%	
Broadwater					
Carbon	2000	47.8%	2185	52.2%	
Carter	216	23.4%	706	76.6%	
Cascade	13389	49.9%	13419	50.1%	
Chouteau	1226	40.2%	1821	59.8%	
Custer	2529	49.6%	2573	50.4%	
Daniels	516	39.1%	804	60.9%	
Dawson	2087	44.7%	2583	55.3%	
Deer Lodge					
Fallon	585	33.6%	1158	66.4%	
Fergus	2435	40.7%	3547	59.3%	
Flathead					
Gallatin					
Garfield	320	35.3%	586	64.7%	
Glacier					
Golden Valley	238	43.0%	315	57.0%	
Granite					
Hill	3687	53.1%	3259	46.9%	
Jefferson					
Judith Basin	663	43.2%	871	56.8%	
Lake					
Lewis & Clark					
Liberty	470	41.1%	673	58.9%	
Lincoln					
Madison					
McCone	609	46.1%	713	53.9%	
Meagher	351	36.1%	620	63.9%	
Mineral					
Missoula					
Musselshell	1076	48.7%	1134	51.3%	
Park					
Petroleum	103	37.3%	173	62.7%	
Phillips	849	36.6%	1470	63.4%	
Pondera	1480	46.9%	1674	53.1%	
Powder River	514	38.1%	835	61.9%	
Powell					
Prairie	399	45.2%	483	54.8%	
Ravalli					
Richland	1795	41.2%	2558	58.8%	
Roosevelt	1883	49.7%	1902	50.3%	
Rosebud	1649	48.5%	1751	51.5%	
Sanders					
Sheridan	1167	42.6%	1573	57.4%	
Silver Bow					
Stillwater	1412	44.1%	1793	55.9%	
Sweet Grass	517	31.9%	1106	68.1%	
Teton	1354	43.7%	1742	56.3%	
Toole	1043	42.5%	1414	57.5%	
Treasure	275	47.3%	307	52.7%	
Valley	2042	50.0%	2039	50.0%	
Wheatland	409	40.8%	594	59.2%	
Wibaux	292	37.9%	478	62.1%	
Yellowstone	20642	48.1%	22300	51.9%	
TOTALS	**73583**	**46.5%**	**84548**	**53.5%**	

1988 Presidential Election

COUNTIES	Michael Dukakis (D)		George H. W. Bush (R)		Others
Beaverhead	1274	31.9%	2668	66.7%	56
Big Horn	2233	56.0%	1711	42.9%	40
Blaine	1460	50.1%	1402	48.1%	50
Broadwater	592	35.2%	1054	62.6%	37
Carbon	2039	45.6%	2360	52.8%	71
Carter	242	25.7%	686	72.8%	14
Cascade	15718	48.9%	15946	49.6%	460
Chouteau	1166	36.2%	1980	61.5%	73
Custer	2343	42.9%	3007	55.1%	112
Daniels	571	40.9%	802	57.5%	22
Dawson	2120	43.4%	2658	54.4%	108
Deer Lodge	3185	72.3%	1168	26.5%	53
Fallon	612	37.4%	1002	61.2%	22
Fergus	2052	33.6%	3948	64.6%	116
Flathead	10202	40.4%	14461	57.3%	562
Gallatin	9527	41.1%	13214	56.9%	464
Garfield	196	23.0%	631	74.1%	24
Glacier	2151	53.7%	1728	43.2%	125
Golden Valley	203	37.4%	335	61.7%	5
Granite	511	38.5%	789	59.5%	26
Hill	4219	54.2%	3467	44.5%	105
Jefferson	1746	45.5%	2007	52.3%	84
Judith Basin	590	38.9%	902	59.5%	24
Lake	4109	44.9%	4883	53.4%	158
Lewis & Clark	11932	51.1%	10946	46.9%	456
Liberty	418	34.6%	771	63.8%	19
Lincoln	3601	49.4%	3500	48.0%	193
Madison	878	29.5%	2045	68.6%	57
McCone	567	40.5%	814	58.2%	18
Meagher	337	33.4%	656	65.0%	16
Mineral	789	55.3%	616	43.1%	23
Missoula	19178	53.8%	15965	44.8%	526
Musselshell	898	40.7%	1280	58.1%	26
Park	2526	39.1%	3823	59.1%	116
Petroleum	91	30.1%	204	67.5%	7
Phillips	905	37.3%	1462	60.3%	59
Pondera	1245	40.0%	1795	57.6%	74
Powder River	395	32.1%	815	66.2%	22
Powell	1174	42.0%	1574	56.3%	47
Prairie	343	38.1%	541	60.1%	16
Ravalli	4763	38.1%	7418	59.4%	309
Richland	1824	40.1%	2628	57.8%	94
Roosevelt	2083	50.6%	1957	47.5%	78
Rosebud	1869	49.3%	1822	48.0%	101
Sanders	1959	46.6%	2152	51.2%	89
Sheridan	1354	49.0%	1381	50.0%	28
Silver Bow	11422	68.4%	5043	30.2%	222
Stillwater	1407	41.6%	1920	56.8%	52
Sweet Grass	462	26.7%	1242	71.7%	29
Teton	1303	40.2%	1876	57.8%	65
Toole	1070	40.6%	1505	57.1%	59
Treasure	231	43.1%	291	54.3%	14
Valley	2163	46.0%	2467	52.4%	76
Wheatland	443	39.2%	667	59.0%	20
Wibaux	258	41.0%	358	56.9%	13
Yellowstone	21987	43.4%	28069	55.4%	591
TOTALS	**168936**	**46.3%**	**189412**	**51.9%**	**6326**

1988 Gubernatorial Election

COUNTIES	Tom Judge (D)		Stan Stephens (R)		Other
Beaverhead	1557	38.6%	2414	59.8%	63
Big Horn	2364	57.9%	1636	40.1%	80
Blaine	1541	51.9%	1388	46.7%	41
Broadwater	636	37.5%	1041	61.3%	21
Carbon	2013	45.1%	2379	53.3%	74
Carter	284	30.5%	629	67.6%	17
Cascade	15777	48.6%	16224	50.0%	470
Chouteau	1256	38.3%	1961	59.8%	61
Custer	2704	49.3%	2672	48.7%	109
Daniels	538	39.1%	824	59.9%	13
Dawson	2447	49.8%	2399	48.8%	66
Deer Lodge	3385	73.9%	1117	24.4%	76
Fallon	753	46.9%	817	50.9%	35
Fergus	2504	40.4%	3575	57.7%	116
Flathead	9963	39.3%	14841	58.5%	560
Gallatin	9270	40.5%	13139	57.4%	488
Garfield	304	35.5%	537	62.7%	15
Glacier	2326	57.0%	1607	39.4%	149
Golden Valley	199	36.2%	337	61.4%	13
Granite	499	37.2%	811	60.5%	30
Hill	3936	49.7%	3866	48.8%	114
Jefferson	1807	46.7%	1985	51.3%	77
Judith Basin	735	47.8%	790	51.3%	14
Lake	3864	42.0%	5152	56.0%	186
Lewis & Clark	11869	50.5%	11174	47.5%	470
Liberty	373	30.5%	837	68.5%	12
Lincoln	3885	53.8%	3134	43.4%	202
Madison	974	32.5%	1971	65.7%	54
McCone	672	47.4%	727	51.2%	20
Meagher	390	38.5%	609	60.2%	13
Mineral	805	56.3%	588	41.1%	37
Missoula	17162	47.9%	17731	49.5%	934
Musselshell	935	42.8%	1218	55.7%	32
Park	2575	40.3%	3680	57.6%	135
Petroleum	113	36.6%	186	60.2%	10
Phillips	1034	41.9%	1392	56.4%	44
Pondera	1340	42.6%	1760	56.0%	43
Powder River	457	37.7%	737	60.8%	19
Powell	1358	48.7%	1344	48.2%	85
Prairie	396	43.7%	496	54.7%	14
Ravalli	4500	36.2%	7708	61.9%	240
Richland	1941	42.7%	2540	55.9%	63
Roosevelt	2231	54.2%	1799	43.7%	88
Rosebud	2040	53.6%	1668	43.8%	101
Sanders	2007	48.1%	2060	49.3%	108
Sheridan	1243	44.9%	1508	54.5%	18
Silver Bow	11107	65.9%	5382	31.9%	364
Stillwater	1526	44.9%	1821	53.6%	53
Sweet Grass	451	25.9%	1270	73.1%	17
Teton	1368	42.3%	1837	56.8%	31
Toole	1096	41.3%	1504	56.6%	56
Treasure	222	41.0%	306	56.6%	13
Valley	2263	48.7%	2225	47.9%	155
Wheatland	479	41.7%	652	56.8%	17
Wibaux	329	51.6%	305	47.8%	4
Yellowstone	21513	42.5%	28294	55.9%	764
TOTALS	**169316**	**46.1%**	**190604**	**51.9%**	**7104**

1988 U.S. Senate Election

COUNTIES	John Melcher (D)		Conrad Burns (R)		Other
Beaverhead	1142	28.1%	2918	71.9%	
Big Horn	2250	55.0%	1843	45.0%	
Blaine	1762	59.2%	1212	40.8%	
Broadwater	578	35.0%	1072	65.0%	
Carbon	2217	49.2%	2287	50.8%	
Carter	364	38.0%	594	62.0%	
Cascade	17248	53.1%	15251	46.9%	
Chouteau	1671	50.5%	1637	49.5%	
Custer	2714	49.4%	2782	50.6%	
Daniels	677	48.3%	726	51.7%	
Dawson	2389	51.4%	2256	48.6%	
Deer Lodge	3059	65.7%	1600	34.3%	
Fallon	752	45.1%	917	54.9%	
Fergus	2590	42.0%	3573	58.0%	
Flathead	9844	39.8%	14873	60.2%	
Gallatin	9402	40.5%	13796	59.5%	
Garfield	330	37.8%	543	62.2%	
Glacier	2188	53.7%	1885	46.3%	
Golden Valley	230	41.7%	321	58.3%	
Granite	446	33.2%	896	66.8%	
Hill	4414	56.5%	3401	43.5%	
Jefferson	1652	42.5%	2238	57.5%	
Judith Basin	716	46.3%	830	53.7%	
Lake	4216	46.5%	4850	53.5%	
Lewis & Clark	11375	48.7%	11987	51.3%	
Liberty	524	43.3%	686	56.7%	
Lincoln	2588	44.6%	3216	55.4%	
Madison	840	28.6%	2095	71.4%	
McCone	661	46.0%	777	54.0%	
Meagher	345	34.7%	649	65.3%	
Mineral	800	55.7%	636	44.3%	
Missoula	18873	53.0%	16731	47.0%	
Musselshell	1043	46.9%	1182	53.1%	
Park	2425	38.2%	3927	61.8%	
Petroleum	124	40.4%	183	59.6%	
Phillips	1186	47.8%	1295	52.2%	
Pondera	1488	46.8%	1694	53.2%	
Powder River	501	40.2%	746	59.8%	
Powell	1069	38.0%	1743	62.0%	
Prairie	451	49.3%	463	50.7%	
Ravalli	4644	37.4%	7779	62.6%	
Richland	1865	40.3%	2758	59.7%	
Roosevelt	2401	57.5%	1773	42.5%	
Rosebud	2346	61.1%	1494	38.9%	
Sanders	1967	46.8%	2235	53.2%	
Sheridan	1528	54.1%	1295	45.9%	
Silver Bow	11089	65.7%	5779	34.3%	
Stillwater	1637	47.9%	1779	52.1%	
Sweet Grass	587	33.5%	1167	66.5%	
Teton	1527	46.6%	1749	53.4%	
Toole	1219	46.0%	1429	54.0%	
Treasure	314	57.8%	229	42.2%	
Valley	2157	48.7%	2269	51.3%	
Wheatland	542	46.6%	621	53.4%	
Wibaux	347	52.4%	315	47.6%	
Yellowstone	24495	48.4%	26163	51.6%	
TOTALS	**175809**	**48.3%**	**188144**	**51.7%**	

1988 U.S. House Election, 1st District

COUNTIES	Pat Williams (D)		Jim Fenlason (R)		Other
Beaverhead	1621	40.3%	2400	59.7%	
Big Horn					
Blaine					
Broadwater	853	52.5%	771	47.5%	
Carbon					
Carter					
Cascade					
Chouteau					
Custer					
Daniels					
Dawson					
Deer Lodge	3963	85.3%	682	14.7%	
Fallon					
Fergus					
Flathead	12799	51.2%	12200	48.8%	
Gallatin	11599	51.5%	10906	48.5%	
Garfield					
Glacier	2726	70.1%	1161	29.9%	
Golden Valley					
Granite	610	47.0%	687	53.0%	
Hill					
Jefferson	2342	60.5%	1527	39.5%	
Judith Basin					
Lake	5076	55.4%	4094	44.6%	
Lewis & Clark	15387	66.0%	7915	34.0%	
Liberty					
Lincoln	4150	56.9%	3138	43.1%	
Madison	1351	45.7%	1605	54.3%	
McCone					
Meagher					
Mineral	1005	70.1%	429	29.9%	
Missoula	24040	66.8%	11939	33.2%	
Musselshell					
Park	3270	51.0%	3144	49.0%	
Petroleum					
Phillips					
Pondera					
Powder River					
Powell	1559	56.5%	1201	43.5%	
Prairie					
Ravalli	6310	50.9%	6085	49.1%	
Richland					
Roosevelt					
Rosebud					
Sanders	2530	60.5%	1654	39.5%	
Sheridan					
Silver Bow	14087	83.1%	2867	16.9%	
Stillwater					
Sweet Grass					
Teton					
Toole					
Treasure					
Valley					
Wheatland					
Wibaux					
Yellowstone					
TOTALS	**115278**	**60.8%**	**74405**	**39.2%**	

242

1988 U.S. House Election, 2nd District

COUNTIES	Buck O'Brien (D)		Ron Marlenee (R)		Other
Beaverhead					
Big Horn	2188	54.4%	1832	45.6%	
Blaine	1286	43.7%	1658	56.3%	
Broadwater					
Carbon	2144	48.0%	2326	52.0%	
Carter	166	17.7%	772	82.3%	
Cascade	15685	48.5%	16627	51.5%	
Chouteau	1057	32.2%	2227	67.8%	
Custer	2363	43.0%	3136	57.0%	
Daniels	381	27.2%	1022	72.8%	
Dawson	2014	41.0%	2899	59.0%	
Deer Lodge					
Fallon	458	27.7%	1194	72.3%	
Fergus	2327	38.0%	3795	62.0%	
Flathead					
Gallatin					
Garfield	190	21.8%	683	78.2%	
Glacier					
Golden Valley	196	35.8%	351	64.2%	
Granite					
Hill	3915	50.5%	3835	49.5%	
Jefferson					
Judith Basin	591	38.9%	928	61.1%	
Lake					
Lewis & Clark					
Liberty	417	33.9%	812	66.1%	
Lincoln					
Madison					
McCone	481	33.9%	936	66.1%	
Meagher	326	33.2%	656	66.8%	
Mineral					
Missoula					
Musselshell	930	42.7%	1249	57.3%	
Park					
Petroleum	85	27.6%	223	72.4%	
Phillips	841	34.1%	1625	65.9%	
Pondera	1320	41.8%	1837	58.2%	
Powder River	412	33.8%	807	66.2%	
Powell					
Prairie	318	34.9%	594	65.1%	
Ravalli					
Richland	1607	35.0%	2990	65.0%	
Roosevelt	1808	43.7%	2329	56.3%	
Rosebud	1927	50.6%	1885	49.4%	
Sanders					
Sheridan	1018	36.4%	1778	63.6%	
Silver Bow					
Stillwater	1502	44.0%	1908	56.0%	
Sweet Grass	485	27.8%	1262	72.2%	
Teton	1189	37.0%	2021	63.0%	
Toole	1096	41.6%	1537	58.4%	
Treasure	230	42.6%	310	57.4%	
Valley	1781	43.9%	2273	56.1%	
Wheatland	421	36.5%	734	63.5%	
Wibaux	211	32.1%	446	67.9%	
Yellowstone	24697	48.7%	25968	51.3%	
TOTALS	**78063**	**44.5%**	**97465**	**55.5%**	

1990 U.S. Senate Election

COUNTIES	Max Baucus (D)		Allen Kolstad (R)		Other
Beaverhead	1607	48.4%	1620	48.8%	91
Big Horn	2886	77.9%	746	20.1%	73
Blaine	1894	74.7%	596	23.5%	45
Broadwater	877	54.6%	678	42.2%	52
Carbon	2900	72.8%	1002	25.2%	82
Carter	430	50.5%	408	47.9%	14
Cascade	21113	74.8%	6507	23.0%	616
Chouteau	1905	63.5%	1029	34.3%	68
Custer	3459	73.6%	1148	24.4%	91
Daniels	875	68.2%	394	30.7%	14
Dawson	3038	70.1%	1235	28.5%	59
Deer Lodge	3658	85.0%	582	13.5%	61
Fallon	938	60.3%	596	38.3%	21
Fergus	3642	64.0%	1938	34.0%	115
Flathead	13505	60.9%	7845	35.4%	833
Gallatin	11574	59.9%	7282	37.7%	471
Garfield	491	58.9%	318	38.2%	24
Glacier	2000	64.2%	963	30.9%	151
Golden Valley	316	59.5%	207	39.0%	8
Granite	653	52.4%	549	44.0%	45
Hill	4624	70.0%	1857	28.1%	122
Jefferson	2204	64.7%	1097	32.2%	106
Judith Basin	896	70.6%	346	27.3%	27
Lake	4648	59.6%	2937	37.7%	215
Lewis & Clark	14605	72.6%	4999	24.8%	520
Liberty	554	48.4%	565	49.3%	26
Lincoln	3716	55.7%	2717	40.8%	233
Madison	1342	50.9%	1223	46.4%	70
McCone	895	66.1%	441	32.6%	17
Meagher	553	63.1%	301	34.3%	23
Mineral	1071	72.8%	364	24.7%	36
Missoula	20310	71.2%	7393	25.9%	829
Musselshell	1399	70.0%	554	27.7%	46
Park	3761	61.0%	2292	37.2%	112
Petroleum	164	62.8%	84	32.2%	13
Phillips	1662	68.3%	731	30.0%	40
Pondera	1732	60.8%	1066	37.4%	51
Powder River	571	58.9%	377	38.9%	22
Powell	1591	62.8%	891	35.2%	51
Prairie	497	67.4%	225	30.5%	15
Ravalli	5979	54.5%	4602	42.0%	380
Richland	2865	67.0%	1345	31.4%	69
Roosevelt	2508	71.3%	878	25.0%	130
Rosebud	2362	74.3%	684	21.5%	132
Sanders	2454	62.8%	1318	33.8%	133
Sheridan	1902	75.3%	598	23.7%	26
Silver Bow	12695	82.0%	2472	16.0%	306
Stillwater	2215	72.9%	751	24.7%	73
Sweet Grass	939	58.8%	622	38.9%	36
Teton	1963	66.5%	937	31.7%	53
Toole	1603	62.2%	905	35.1%	68
Treasure	383	75.7%	116	22.9%	7
Valley	2696	69.4%	1093	28.1%	94
Wheatland	712	67.6%	329	31.2%	13
Wibaux	454	66.9%	209	30.8%	16
Yellowstone	31331	72.7%	10874	25.2%	893
TOTALS	**217563**	**68.1%**	**93836**	**29.4%**	**7937**

1990 U.S. House Election, 1st District

COUNTIES	Pat Williams (D)		Brad Johnson (R)		Other
Beaverhead	1414	42.6%	1902	57.4%	
Big Horn					
Blaine					
Broadwater	779	48.9%	813	51.1%	
Carbon					
Carter					
Cascade					
Chouteau					
Custer					
Daniels					
Dawson					
Deer Lodge	3592	83.9%	689	16.1%	
Fallon					
Fergus					
Flathead	11891	53.9%	10181	46.1%	
Gallatin	10263	53.6%	8900	46.4%	
Garfield					
Glacier	2062	67.1%	1013	32.9%	
Golden Valley					
Granite	586	47.5%	647	52.5%	
Hill					
Jefferson	2007	59.2%	1383	40.8%	
Judith Basin					
Lake	4300	55.1%	3504	44.9%	
Lewis & Clark	13520	67.1%	6631	32.9%	
Liberty					
Lincoln	3581	54.1%	3034	45.9%	
Madison	1237	47.1%	1392	52.9%	
McCone					
Meagher					
Mineral	1023	72.3%	392	27.7%	
Missoula	19146	67.0%	9435	33.0%	
Musselshell					
Park	3294	54.4%	2757	45.6%	
Petroleum					
Phillips					
Pondera					
Powder River					
Powell	1491	58.6%	1053	41.4%	
Prairie					
Ravalli	5476	49.9%	5503	50.1%	
Richland					
Roosevelt					
Rosebud					
Sanders	2413	62.0%	1477	38.0%	
Sheridan					
Silver Bow	12334	79.8%	3122	20.2%	
Stillwater					
Sweet Grass					
Teton					
Toole					
Treasure					
Valley					
Wheatland					
Wibaux					
Yellowstone					
TOTALS	**100409**	**61.1%**	**63837**	**38.9%**	

1990 U.S. House Election, 2nd District

COUNTIES	Don Burris (D)		Ron Marlenee (R)		Other
Beaverhead					
Big Horn	1819	49.9%	1826	50.1%	
Blaine	893	35.3%	1638	64.7%	
Broadwater					
Carbon	1487	37.9%	2436	62.1%	
Carter	158	18.8%	682	81.2%	
Cascade	10988	39.3%	17003	60.7%	
Chouteau	723	24.2%	2259	75.8%	
Custer	1587	34.1%	3065	65.9%	
Daniels	372	29.1%	906	70.9%	
Dawson	1616	37.4%	2704	62.6%	
Deer Lodge					
Fallon	380	24.8%	1155	75.2%	
Fergus	1648	29.1%	4012	70.9%	
Flathead					
Gallatin					
Garfield	160	19.3%	670	80.7%	
Glacier					
Golden Valley	143	26.8%	390	73.2%	
Granite					
Hill	2950	45.1%	3590	54.9%	
Jefferson					
Judith Basin	369	27.8%	956	72.2%	
Lake					
Lewis & Clark					
Liberty	299	26.1%	846	73.9%	
Lincoln					
Madison					
McCone	410	30.3%	945	69.7%	
Meagher	255	29.2%	618	70.8%	
Mineral					
Missoula					
Musselshell	743	38.0%	1212	62.0%	
Park					
Petroleum	75	28.6%	187	71.4%	
Phillips	601	24.9%	1811	75.1%	
Pondera	903	32.0%	1923	68.0%	
Powder River	266	27.6%	697	72.4%	
Powell					
Prairie	245	33.7%	482	66.3%	
Ravalli					
Richland	1310	30.8%	2938	69.2%	
Roosevelt	1467	42.3%	2001	57.7%	
Rosebud	1355	42.9%	1807	57.1%	
Sanders					
Sheridan	793	31.6%	1717	68.4%	
Silver Bow					
Stillwater	1083	36.0%	1928	64.0%	
Sweet Grass	397	25.1%	1182	74.9%	
Teton	858	29.3%	2066	70.7%	
Toole	774	30.4%	1776	69.6%	
Treasure	140	27.9%	361	72.1%	
Valley	1385	37.0%	2361	63.0%	
Wheatland	317	30.1%	736	69.9%	
Wibaux	167	24.7%	508	75.3%	
Yellowstone	17603	41.3%	25055	58.7%	
TOTALS	**56739**	**37.0%**	**96449**	**63.0%**	

1992 Presidential Election

COUNTIES	Bill Clinton (D)		George H. W. Bush (R)		Ross Perot (I)		Other
Beaverhead	1098	27.1%	1746	43.2%	1202	29.7%	114
Big Horn	2154	49.3%	1377	31.5%	840	19.2%	23
Blaine	1355	44.8%	971	32.1%	699	23.1%	21
Broadwater	491	26.9%	830	45.5%	505	27.7%	16
Carbon	1549	33.7%	1562	34.0%	1482	32.3%	27
Carter	154	17.7%	497	57.1%	220	25.3%	3
Cascade	14719	40.5%	12494	34.4%	9151	25.2%	214
Chouteau	959	29.9%	1380	43.0%	870	27.1%	27
Custer	1968	35.3%	2105	37.7%	1505	27.0%	33
Daniels	457	33.7%	496	36.6%	402	29.7%	8
Dawson	1785	36.9%	1679	34.7%	1370	28.3%	16
Deer Lodge	3174	60.9%	832	16.0%	1207	23.2%	56
Fallon	446	27.8%	731	45.6%	427	26.6%	4
Fergus	1615	25.7%	2736	43.5%	1934	30.8%	205
Flathead	9746	31.9%	11699	38.3%	9109	29.8%	862
Gallatin	9535	33.6%	11109	39.2%	7711	27.2%	424
Garfield	125	15.5%	403	49.8%	281	34.7%	10
Glacier	2076	48.3%	1222	28.5%	997	23.2%	28
Golden Valley	142	28.9%	192	39.1%	157	32.0%	5
Granite	358	27.5%	556	42.8%	386	29.7%	22
Hill	3618	45.0%	2408	29.9%	2017	25.1%	39
Jefferson	1415	34.3%	1541	37.3%	1172	28.4%	97
Judith Basin	409	28.5%	610	42.5%	415	28.9%	13
Lake	3938	37.8%	3596	34.5%	2878	27.6%	140
Lewis & Clark	11117	42.7%	9351	35.9%	5560	21.4%	151
Liberty	321	26.8%	512	42.8%	363	30.4%	15
Lincoln	2765	33.7%	2799	34.1%	2637	32.2%	177
Madison	779	24.1%	1415	43.7%	1043	32.2%	62
McCone	424	31.5%	528	39.2%	395	29.3%	7
Meagher	260	26.2%	422	42.5%	310	31.3%	10
Mineral	664	41.2%	403	25.0%	543	33.7%	25
Missoula	20347	47.3%	12898	30.0%	9735	22.7%	329
Musselshell	648	29.3%	876	39.5%	691	31.2%	13
Park	2258	31.0%	2846	39.1%	2182	29.9%	196
Petroleum	61	21.0%	135	46.4%	95	32.6%	5
Phillips	634	24.3%	1026	39.3%	949	36.4%	16
Pondera	1046	33.2%	1252	39.7%	855	27.1%	12
Powder River	258	22.5%	547	47.8%	340	29.7%	11
Powell	989	33.9%	1058	36.2%	872	29.9%	19
Prairie	260	30.6%	412	48.4%	179	21.0%	5
Ravalli	4644	31.8%	5392	36.9%	4573	31.3%	410
Richland	1440	30.5%	1760	37.2%	1525	32.3%	23
Roosevelt	1827	44.3%	1212	29.4%	1089	26.4%	65
Rosebud	1669	42.8%	1130	29.0%	1099	28.2%	20
Sanders	1689	38.1%	1361	30.7%	1378	31.1%	78
Sheridan	1077	40.6%	795	30.0%	782	29.5%	9
Silver Bow	9960	55.3%	3491	19.4%	4570	25.4%	125
Stillwater	1178	32.5%	1390	38.4%	1056	29.1%	16
Sweet Grass	395	22.2%	880	49.4%	507	28.5%	19
Teton	1043	30.9%	1364	40.4%	969	28.7%	29
Toole	854	31.6%	943	34.9%	903	33.4%	17
Treasure	157	29.0%	206	38.1%	178	32.9%	6
Valley	1715	37.8%	1497	33.0%	1320	29.1%	36
Wheatland	384	33.5%	478	41.7%	284	24.8%	4
Wibaux	195	32.4%	234	38.9%	173	28.7%	5
Yellowstone	20163	35.9%	22822	40.7%	13133	23.4%	332
TOTALS	**154507**	**37.6%**	**144207**	**35.1%**	**107225**	**26.1%**	**4644**

1992 Gubernatorial Election

COUNTIES	Dorothy Bradley (D)		Marc Racicot (R)		Other
Beaverhead	1569	38.1%	2553	61.9%	
Big Horn	2531	58.1%	1827	41.9%	
Blaine	1682	56.0%	1319	44.0%	
Broadwater	657	36.3%	1155	63.7%	
Carbon	2115	45.2%	2566	54.8%	
Carter	215	25.2%	637	74.8%	
Cascade	19405	53.6%	16819	46.4%	
Chouteau	1376	43.1%	1818	56.9%	
Custer	2658	47.5%	2936	52.5%	
Daniels	531	39.3%	820	60.7%	
Dawson	2238	46.2%	2607	53.8%	
Deer Lodge	3677	70.9%	1510	29.1%	
Fallon	592	37.7%	980	62.3%	
Fergus	2512	38.7%	3973	61.3%	
Flathead	13652	43.8%	17538	56.2%	
Gallatin	12969	45.3%	15654	54.7%	
Garfield	199	24.7%	607	75.3%	
Glacier	2642	60.8%	1701	39.2%	
Golden Valley	182	37.1%	308	62.9%	
Granite	488	37.3%	821	62.7%	
Hill	4582	57.1%	3447	42.9%	
Jefferson	1990	47.1%	2231	52.9%	
Judith Basin	536	37.4%	896	62.6%	
Lake	4998	47.7%	5475	52.3%	
Lewis & Clark	12988	49.8%	13115	50.2%	
Liberty	457	37.7%	755	62.3%	
Lincoln	3648	44.3%	4588	55.7%	
Madison	1111	34.1%	2148	65.9%	
McCone	539	40.0%	808	60.0%	
Meagher	406	41.2%	579	58.8%	
Mineral	933	57.8%	682	42.2%	
Missoula	24453	56.9%	18531	43.1%	
Musselshell	721	32.7%	1483	67.3%	
Park	3156	42.4%	4288	57.6%	
Petroleum	92	31.1%	204	68.9%	
Phillips	884	33.9%	1720	66.1%	
Pondera	1283	40.4%	1892	59.6%	
Powder River	382	37.2%	646	62.8%	
Powell	1386	47.0%	1562	53.0%	
Prairie	305	36.1%	539	63.9%	
Ravalli	6040	40.7%	8814	59.3%	
Richland	2008	42.5%	2722	57.5%	
Roosevelt	2391	57.5%	1765	42.5%	
Rosebud	2224	56.4%	1716	43.6%	
Sanders	2080	46.9%	2352	53.1%	
Sheridan	1462	55.7%	1161	44.3%	
Silver Bow	11470	63.7%	6528	36.3%	
Stillwater	1513	41.7%	2113	58.3%	
Sweet Grass	541	30.5%	1233	69.5%	
Teton	1341	39.9%	2018	60.1%	
Toole	1160	43.0%	1539	57.0%	
Treasure	200	36.8%	344	63.2%	
Valley	2057	47.5%	2278	52.5%	
Wheatland	466	40.9%	672	59.1%	
Wibaux	215	36.0%	383	64.0%	
Yellowstone	26513	46.9%	30025	53.1%	
TOTALS	**198421**	**48.7%**	**209401**	**51.3%**	

1992 U.S. House Election

COUNTIES	Pat Williams (D)		Ron Marlenee (R)		Other
Beaverhead	1531	37.0%	2509	60.7%	95
Big Horn	2542	57.7%	1783	40.5%	78
Blaine	1518	50.3%	1442	47.8%	57
Broadwater	706	38.6%	1068	58.3%	57
Carbon	2279	47.9%	2376	50.0%	99
Carter	160	18.8%	677	79.4%	16
Cascade	18031	49.5%	17413	47.8%	953
Chouteau	1050	32.7%	2098	65.4%	59
Custer	2350	41.7%	3163	56.1%	123
Daniels	359	26.4%	986	72.6%	14
Dawson	2239	45.4%	2593	52.6%	97
Deer Lodge	4151	79.1%	989	18.8%	107
Fallon	448	30.9%	975	67.2%	27
Fergus	2026	33.2%	3871	63.5%	198
Flathead	12327	42.8%	15232	52.8%	1263
Gallatin	14628	50.9%	13441	46.8%	647
Garfield	129	15.8%	678	83.2%	8
Glacier	2401	58.3%	1611	39.1%	106
Golden Valley	156	31.6%	323	65.4%	15
Granite	507	38.5%	768	58.4%	41
Hill	4267	52.8%	3594	44.5%	215
Jefferson	2178	50.9%	1984	46.3%	119
Judith Basin	472	32.3%	944	64.6%	46
Lake	5046	48.5%	5077	48.8%	278
Lewis & Clark	15904	61.0%	9473	36.3%	692
Liberty	397	32.6%	787	64.7%	32
Lincoln	3531	43.1%	4304	52.6%	352
Madison	1212	37.0%	1969	60.1%	95
McCone	458	34.3%	858	64.3%	18
Meagher	305	32.4%	609	64.8%	26
Mineral	925	59.8%	570	36.8%	53
Missoula	27783	64.6%	14206	33.0%	1007
Musselshell	787	35.3%	1404	63.0%	36
Park	3418	45.8%	3843	51.5%	196
Petroleum	69	23.2%	219	73.5%	10
Phillips	663	25.5%	1892	72.7%	47
Pondera	1171	38.7%	1769	58.5%	85
Powder River	310	27.1%	809	70.7%	26
Powell	1390	46.8%	1498	50.5%	81
Prairie	278	32.6%	566	66.4%	9
Ravalli	7098	47.6%	7378	49.5%	426
Richland	1641	36.9%	2716	61.0%	95
Roosevelt	2069	52.0%	1780	44.7%	129
Rosebud	2145	53.5%	1764	44.0%	98
Sanders	2317	52.4%	1954	44.2%	148
Sheridan	1035	39.1%	1580	59.8%	29
Silver Bow	12643	74.2%	3988	23.4%	400
Stillwater	1567	42.7%	2039	55.6%	64
Sweet Grass	522	29.3%	1223	68.7%	35
Teton	1193	35.3%	2125	62.9%	63
Toole	1043	40.8%	1425	55.8%	88
Treasure	195	35.7%	335	61.4%	16
Valley	1710	40.9%	2361	56.5%	107
Wheatland	413	36.1%	714	62.5%	16
Wibaux	215	35.3%	385	63.2%	9
Yellowstone	27803	49.2%	27432	48.6%	1248
TOTALS	**203711**	**50.5%**	**189570**	**47.0%**	**10454**

1994 U.S. Senate Election

COUNTIES	Jack Mudd (D)		Conrad Burns (R)		Other
Beaverhead	795	22.7%	2700	77.3%	
Big Horn	1679	43.3%	2196	56.7%	
Blaine	946	36.3%	1662	63.7%	
Broadwater	460	26.7%	1264	73.3%	
Carbon	1327	31.1%	2939	68.9%	
Carter	87	10.8%	717	89.2%	
Cascade	12952	42.8%	17288	57.2%	
Chouteau	724	25.1%	2165	74.9%	
Custer	1480	31.5%	3219	68.5%	
Daniels	311	27.9%	803	72.1%	
Dawson	1441	33.2%	2900	66.8%	
Deer Lodge	2575	59.7%	1738	40.3%	
Fallon	347	22.2%	1213	77.8%	
Fergus	1386	23.6%	4476	76.4%	
Flathead	8492	31.0%	18892	69.0%	
Gallatin	7819	34.4%	14918	65.6%	
Garfield	61	8.6%	652	91.4%	
Glacier	2090	49.7%	2113	50.3%	
Golden Valley	97	21.0%	364	79.0%	
Granite	361	27.7%	941	72.3%	
Hill	3034	45.6%	3619	54.4%	
Jefferson	1370	33.7%	2693	66.3%	
Judith Basin	299	21.2%	1112	78.8%	
Lake	3460	36.6%	5999	63.4%	
Lewis & Clark	10196	45.1%	12413	54.9%	
Liberty	231	21.1%	866	78.9%	
Lincoln	2517	34.2%	4839	65.8%	
Madison	601	20.0%	2409	80.0%	
McCone	314	25.5%	918	74.5%	
Meagher	184	22.4%	638	77.6%	
Mineral	558	39.9%	842	60.1%	
Missoula	18523	52.7%	16643	47.3%	
Musselshell	461	24.1%	1448	75.9%	
Park	2028	30.8%	4546	69.2%	
Petroleum	48	16.3%	247	83.7%	
Phillips	396	17.2%	1909	82.8%	
Pondera	822	28.5%	2064	71.5%	
Powder River	161	17.1%	779	82.9%	
Powell	750	27.5%	1978	72.5%	
Prairie	169	22.4%	586	77.6%	
Ravalli	4151	32.2%	8746	67.8%	
Richland	987	24.4%	3055	75.6%	
Roosevelt	1392	39.5%	2128	60.5%	
Rosebud	1405	40.7%	2043	59.3%	
Sanders	1597	37.5%	2656	62.5%	
Sheridan	765	30.7%	1726	69.3%	
Silver Bow	8369	55.8%	6633	44.2%	
Stillwater	924	27.4%	2449	72.6%	
Sweet Grass	323	20.3%	1266	79.7%	
Teton	808	26.1%	2285	73.9%	
Toole	707	28.9%	1740	71.1%	
Treasure	114	21.7%	412	78.3%	
Valley	1330	32.8%	2727	67.2%	
Wheatland	248	24.3%	773	75.7%	
Wibaux	133	24.5%	409	75.5%	
Yellowstone	17031	36.4%	29786	63.6%	
TOTALS	**131845**	**37.6%**	**218542**	**62.4%**	

1994 U.S. House Election, At Large

COUNTIES	Pat Williams (D)		Cy Jamison (R)		Other
Beaverhead	1397	40.2%	1729	49.8%	345
Big Horn	2290	59.1%	1278	33.0%	307
Blaine	1551	60.1%	831	32.2%	200
Broadwater	717	41.9%	838	48.9%	158
Carbon	1931	44.9%	1892	44.0%	475
Carter	235	30.1%	508	65.0%	39
Cascade	15369	50.4%	12082	39.6%	3064
Chouteau	1274	44.2%	1358	47.2%	248
Custer	2316	49.0%	2010	42.5%	398
Daniels	490	44.0%	572	51.4%	51
Dawson	2154	50.0%	1882	43.7%	272
Deer Lodge	3413	77.2%	645	14.6%	362
Fallon	589	38.8%	846	55.7%	83
Fergus	2399	41.0%	2896	49.5%	555
Flathead	10438	38.1%	14408	52.5%	2580
Gallatin	9874	43.1%	10723	46.8%	2325
Garfield	178	25.6%	454	65.4%	62
Glacier	2696	64.2%	1235	29.4%	266
Golden Valley	133	27.9%	324	68.1%	19
Granite	517	39.5%	700	53.5%	91
Hill	3853	57.8%	2178	32.7%	639
Jefferson	1969	48.0%	1722	42.0%	413
Judith Basin	624	44.1%	680	48.1%	111
Lake	4129	43.5%	4471	47.1%	902
Lewis & Clark	12689	55.4%	8478	37.0%	1736
Liberty	510	46.6%	500	45.7%	84
Lincoln	3061	41.7%	3635	49.6%	638
Madison	1204	40.1%	1520	50.6%	277
McCone	535	43.9%	627	51.4%	57
Meagher	277	33.9%	464	56.9%	75
Mineral	744	52.8%	485	34.4%	180
Missoula	20097	56.6%	12082	34.1%	3300
Musselshell	715	37.5%	1021	53.5%	173
Park	2995	45.3%	3086	46.7%	527
Petroleum	92	31.3%	169	57.5%	33
Phillips	790	34.6%	1285	56.3%	209
Pondera	1311	45.5%	1324	45.9%	247
Powder River	305	33.5%	520	57.1%	85
Powell	1342	49.1%	1112	40.7%	280
Prairie	281	37.8%	406	54.6%	56
Ravalli	5150	39.7%	6535	50.4%	1286
Richland	1578	39.8%	2140	54.0%	248
Roosevelt	2156	61.6%	1188	33.9%	157
Rosebud	1962	56.5%	1210	34.9%	298
Sanders	2158	51.4%	1646	39.2%	393
Sheridan	1458	60.2%	854	35.3%	108
Silver Bow	11470	74.1%	2678	17.3%	1332
Stillwater	1360	40.5%	1649	49.1%	352
Sweet Grass	492	31.0%	979	61.8%	114
Teton	1337	43.2%	1490	48.2%	265
Toole	1224	50.1%	982	40.2%	236
Treasure	250	47.7%	207	39.5%	67
Valley	2144	53.0%	1624	40.1%	281
Wheatland	350	33.9%	601	58.3%	80
Wibaux	235	45.0%	256	49.0%	31
Yellowstone	20564	43.6%	21700	46.0%	4876
TOTALS	**171372**	**48.7%**	**148715**	**42.2%**	**32046**

1996 Presidential Election

COUNTIES	Bill Clinton (D)		Bob Dole (R)		Ross Perot (I)		Other
Beaverhead	1164	29.2%	2414	60.5%	412	10.3%	29
Big Horn	2453	58.2%	1336	31.7%	424	10.1%	26
Blaine	1316	45.7%	1127	39.2%	435	15.1%	15
Broadwater	603	30.9%	1029	52.8%	318	16.3%	16
Carbon	1854	39.3%	2147	45.5%	713	15.1%	48
Carter	150	19.7%	522	68.6%	89	11.7%	4
Cascade	15707	45.2%	14291	41.1%	4749	13.7%	259
Chouteau	1039	33.2%	1660	53.0%	434	13.9%	24
Custer	2115	40.1%	2467	46.8%	695	13.2%	52
Daniels	510	39.0%	558	42.7%	240	18.3%	4
Dawson	1903	41.1%	1890	40.8%	842	18.2%	38
Deer Lodge	3331	66.8%	883	17.7%	772	15.5%	24
Fallon	452	30.0%	778	51.7%	276	18.3%	10
Fergus	1866	30.4%	3671	59.8%	605	9.9%	52
Flathead	10452	32.9%	16542	52.1%	4786	15.1%	445
Gallatin	10972	38.3%	14559	50.8%	3146	11.0%	402
Garfield	107	14.5%	562	76.2%	69	9.3%	8
Glacier	2292	56.6%	1270	31.3%	491	12.1%	42
Golden Valley	128	26.4%	284	58.6%	73	15.1%	3
Granite	429	30.9%	733	52.7%	228	16.4%	17
Hill	3517	49.8%	2601	36.8%	950	13.4%	43
Jefferson	1775	37.4%	2248	47.3%	729	15.3%	49
Judith Basin	452	34.0%	753	56.6%	126	9.5%	7
Lake	4195	39.1%	4723	44.0%	1804	16.8%	118
Lewis & Clark	11535	43.8%	11665	44.3%	3140	11.9%	207
Liberty	379	32.8%	634	54.8%	144	12.4%	5
Lincoln	2705	35.2%	3552	46.2%	1425	18.5%	184
Madison	955	27.6%	1984	57.4%	516	14.9%	40
McCone	390	31.2%	615	49.2%	244	19.5%	7
Meagher	281	30.3%	505	54.4%	142	15.3%	8
Mineral	658	41.4%	549	34.5%	383	24.1%	25
Missoula	21874	50.3%	16034	36.9%	5586	12.8%	888
Musselshell	652	31.6%	1121	54.3%	291	14.1%	12
Park	2564	34.8%	3837	52.1%	959	13.0%	88
Petroleum	62	21.8%	186	65.5%	36	12.7%	6
Phillips	705	28.2%	1392	55.7%	401	16.1%	13
Pondera	1123	38.1%	1438	48.8%	383	13.0%	19
Powder River	236	22.8%	663	64.0%	137	13.2%	9
Powell	952	34.5%	1274	46.2%	531	19.3%	45
Prairie	259	33.4%	417	53.8%	99	12.8%	5
Ravalli	5200	32.4%	8138	50.6%	2731	17.0%	171
Richland	1614	35.5%	2021	44.5%	906	20.0%	27
Roosevelt	2118	53.3%	1209	30.4%	645	16.2%	25
Rosebud	1681	46.2%	1413	38.8%	547	15.0%	42
Sanders	1573	34.2%	2043	44.4%	990	21.5%	55
Sheridan	1187	48.9%	832	34.3%	408	16.8%	8
Silver Bow	11199	63.8%	3909	22.3%	2447	13.9%	122
Stillwater	1282	34.0%	1871	49.6%	618	16.4%	19
Sweet Grass	469	26.6%	1109	62.9%	186	10.5%	18
Teton	1188	35.9%	1701	51.5%	416	12.6%	22
Toole	874	35.5%	1203	48.8%	386	15.7%	19
Treasure	171	34.5%	237	47.9%	87	17.6%	3
Valley	1674	40.3%	1838	44.2%	645	15.5%	50
Wheatland	391	36.2%	563	52.1%	127	11.7%	7
Wibaux	197	32.3%	284	46.6%	128	21.0%	4
Yellowstone	22992	41.4%	26367	47.5%	6139	11.1%	384
TOTALS	**167922**	**41.3%**	**179652**	**44.1%**	**55229**	**13.6%**	**4280**

1996 Gubernatorial Election

COUNTIES	Judy Jacobson (D)		Marc Racicot (R)		Other
Beaverhead	432	10.8%	3553	89.2%	
Big Horn	1887	45.3%	2281	54.7%	
Blaine	885	31.4%	1930	68.6%	
Broadwater	276	14.2%	1665	85.8%	
Carbon	852	18.3%	3815	81.7%	
Carter	75	10.1%	665	89.9%	
Cascade	6150	17.7%	28511	82.3%	
Chouteau	430	13.7%	2713	86.3%	
Custer	968	18.3%	4315	81.7%	
Daniels	236	18.5%	1037	81.5%	
Dawson	835	18.1%	3781	81.9%	
Deer Lodge	1248	26.5%	3458	73.5%	
Fallon	164	11.7%	1240	88.3%	
Fergus	912	15.3%	5064	84.7%	
Flathead	5152	16.2%	26670	83.8%	
Gallatin	4966	17.5%	23357	82.5%	
Garfield	58	7.8%	682	92.2%	
Glacier	1616	40.0%	2423	60.0%	
Golden Valley	53	11.0%	427	89.0%	
Granite	168	12.3%	1195	87.7%	
Hill	1698	24.5%	5239	75.5%	
Jefferson	775	16.4%	3952	83.6%	
Judith Basin	177	13.2%	1168	86.8%	
Lake	2344	22.3%	8149	77.7%	
Lewis & Clark	4408	16.9%	21668	83.1%	
Liberty	105	9.0%	1058	91.0%	
Lincoln	1186	15.7%	6379	84.3%	
Madison	415	12.1%	3018	87.9%	
McCone	218	18.0%	990	82.0%	
Meagher	105	11.3%	821	88.7%	
Mineral	355	22.6%	1215	77.4%	
Missoula	10453	24.1%	32877	75.9%	
Musselshell	298	14.5%	1755	85.5%	
Park	1199	16.7%	5964	83.3%	
Petroleum	27	9.5%	257	90.5%	
Phillips	275	11.1%	2209	88.9%	
Pondera	435	15.0%	2473	85.0%	
Powder River	120	11.8%	893	88.2%	
Powell	494	17.7%	2293	82.3%	
Prairie	104	13.5%	666	86.5%	
Ravalli	2595	16.5%	13161	83.5%	
Richland	956	21.1%	3576	78.9%	
Roosevelt	1465	37.7%	2416	62.3%	
Rosebud	1037	27.9%	2674	72.1%	
Sanders	937	20.9%	3554	79.1%	
Sheridan	559	23.5%	1820	76.5%	
Silver Bow	5037	29.8%	11876	70.2%	
Stillwater	553	14.6%	3243	85.4%	
Sweet Grass	201	11.4%	1562	88.6%	
Teton	345	10.8%	2858	89.2%	
Toole	390	16.0%	2044	84.0%	
Treasure	69	13.9%	428	86.1%	
Valley	797	19.3%	3326	80.7%	
Wheatland	169	15.6%	915	84.4%	
Wibaux	101	17.3%	484	82.7%	
Yellowstone	8709	16.2%	45005	83.8%	
TOTALS	**76471**	**19.3%**	**320768**	**80.7%**	

1996 U.S. Senate Election

COUNTIES	Max Baucus (D)		Denny Rehberg (R)		Other
Beaverhead	1344	33.6%	2467	61.7%	187
Big Horn	2701	64.3%	1315	31.3%	183
Blaine	1492	52.7%	1215	42.9%	125
Broadwater	811	41.1%	1043	52.9%	118
Carbon	2431	50.4%	2129	44.1%	268
Carter	178	23.1%	567	73.7%	24
Cascade	19357	54.6%	14172	40.0%	1919
Chouteau	1330	41.8%	1722	54.2%	127
Custer	2643	48.9%	2519	46.6%	238
Daniels	591	45.0%	693	52.8%	29
Dawson	2334	49.0%	2268	47.6%	159
Deer Lodge	3739	73.7%	1013	20.0%	323
Fallon	505	33.3%	961	63.3%	52
Fergus	2410	38.8%	3545	57.1%	258
Flathead	11959	38.8%	16890	54.7%	2008
Gallatin	13106	44.9%	14546	49.9%	1507
Garfield	166	22.4%	547	73.9%	27
Glacier	2457	58.9%	1456	34.9%	258
Golden Valley	161	32.9%	298	60.8%	31
Granite	537	38.0%	775	54.8%	102
Hill	3852	53.3%	3046	42.1%	332
Jefferson	2152	44.5%	2293	47.4%	388
Judith Basin	568	42.0%	740	54.7%	44
Lake	4953	45.4%	5210	47.7%	750
Lewis & Clark	14765	55.3%	10368	38.8%	1564
Liberty	460	39.0%	680	57.7%	38
Lincoln	2599	36.1%	4093	56.8%	517
Madison	1216	34.6%	2060	58.6%	237
McCone	500	40.3%	686	55.3%	55
Meagher	310	33.3%	569	61.1%	53
Mineral	794	49.0%	638	39.3%	190
Missoula	25983	57.8%	15860	35.3%	3117
Musselshell	837	40.1%	1142	54.7%	110
Park	3052	40.8%	4057	54.3%	364
Petroleum	90	30.6%	195	66.3%	9
Phillips	869	34.8%	1508	60.5%	117
Pondera	1301	44.1%	1509	51.2%	140
Powder River	299	28.8%	703	67.7%	36
Powell	1222	43.2%	1406	49.7%	202
Prairie	304	37.8%	461	57.3%	40
Ravalli	6649	40.8%	8567	52.5%	1088
Richland	1957	42.8%	2357	51.6%	255
Roosevelt	2528	62.0%	1345	33.0%	203
Rosebud	2130	55.3%	1474	38.3%	248
Sanders	1873	40.0%	2380	50.9%	425
Sheridan	1335	53.5%	1081	43.4%	77
Silver Bow	12666	71.5%	3871	21.8%	1190
Stillwater	1633	44.0%	1961	52.8%	117
Sweet Grass	609	34.2%	1109	62.3%	63
Teton	1389	42.1%	1764	53.5%	147
Toole	1053	42.4%	1291	52.0%	139
Treasure	231	46.6%	239	48.2%	26
Valley	2021	47.0%	2055	47.8%	223
Wheatland	475	43.7%	569	52.4%	42
Wibaux	251	41.2%	325	53.4%	33
Yellowstone	28757	51.4%	24358	43.5%	2833
TOTALS	**201935**	**49.6%**	**182111**	**44.7%**	**23444**

1996 U.S. House Election, At Large

COUNTIES	Bill Yellowtail (D)		Rick Hill (R)		Other
Beaverhead	1147	28.7%	2744	68.7%	102
Big Horn	2662	62.6%	1477	34.7%	115
Blaine	1467	51.3%	1299	45.4%	93
Broadwater	622	32.2%	1227	63.5%	84
Carbon	2008	42.2%	2524	53.1%	224
Carter	164	21.9%	573	76.5%	12
Cascade	16097	46.1%	16940	48.5%	1896
Chouteau	1105	35.2%	1893	60.4%	138
Custer	2043	38.3%	3034	56.9%	252
Daniels	395	31.4%	831	66.1%	32
Dawson	1879	40.3%	2648	56.8%	135
Deer Lodge	3544	70.8%	1238	24.7%	223
Fallon	459	30.8%	986	66.3%	43
Fergus	1905	31.4%	3934	64.9%	219
Flathead	11389	35.4%	19462	60.4%	1361
Gallatin	10763	37.5%	16794	58.5%	1156
Garfield	144	19.8%	574	78.7%	11
Glacier	2451	59.0%	1524	36.7%	176
Golden Valley	149	30.7%	308	63.5%	28
Granite	477	34.3%	850	61.1%	64
Hill	3585	50.3%	3217	45.1%	328
Jefferson	1970	41.1%	2595	54.1%	234
Judith Basin	487	37.8%	767	59.6%	33
Lake	4137	38.5%	6033	56.2%	566
Lewis & Clark	12683	48.0%	12685	48.0%	1038
Liberty	400	34.7%	730	63.3%	24
Lincoln	2961	38.0%	4526	58.1%	299
Madison	1074	30.9%	2287	65.7%	119
McCone	391	32.2%	781	64.3%	43
Meagher	285	31.0%	609	66.3%	25
Mineral	717	45.3%	740	46.7%	127
Missoula	23778	53.4%	18401	41.3%	2325
Musselshell	692	33.6%	1273	61.7%	97
Park	2731	36.8%	4368	58.9%	317
Petroleum	71	24.8%	205	71.7%	10
Phillips	649	26.6%	1693	69.4%	99
Pondera	1121	38.4%	1718	58.8%	84
Powder River	295	28.8%	705	68.8%	24
Powell	1146	41.0%	1520	54.4%	130
Prairie	237	30.5%	499	64.3%	40
Ravalli	6120	37.9%	9209	57.1%	802
Richland	1602	35.9%	2742	61.4%	124
Roosevelt	2202	54.9%	1666	41.5%	143
Rosebud	1947	50.9%	1700	44.4%	180
Sanders	1750	37.7%	2618	56.4%	270
Sheridan	1034	43.3%	1288	53.9%	66
Silver Bow	11321	65.0%	5405	31.1%	678
Stillwater	1317	35.2%	2233	59.7%	188
Sweet Grass	486	27.8%	1216	69.5%	47
Teton	1150	35.3%	1971	60.5%	137
Toole	923	37.8%	1425	58.4%	94
Treasure	192	39.9%	265	55.1%	24
Valley	1721	40.5%	2392	56.3%	132
Wheatland	393	37.1%	637	60.2%	29
Wibaux	218	36.8%	354	59.8%	20
Yellowstone	21860	39.6%	30642	55.5%	2675
TOTALS	**174516**	**43.2%**	**211975**	**52.4%**	**17935**

1998 U.S. House Election, At Large

COUNTIES	Dusty Deschamps (D)		Rick Hill (R)		Other
Beaverhead	1100	30.7%	2417	67.5%	63
Big Horn	2035	59.6%	1271	37.2%	108
Blaine	1197	47.7%	1260	50.3%	50
Broadwater	634	34.3%	1155	62.5%	58
Carbon	1792	42.1%	2354	55.3%	111
Carter	86	13.3%	545	84.4%	15
Cascade	13271	49.8%	12725	47.8%	630
Chouteau	1003	37.5%	1622	60.7%	48
Custer	1890	41.8%	2551	56.4%	83
Daniels	394	37.1%	646	60.8%	22
Dawson	1435	37.7%	2298	60.4%	71
Deer Lodge	2696	67.4%	1160	29.0%	142
Fallon	380	27.8%	965	70.5%	24
Fergus	1678	32.0%	3425	65.4%	137
Flathead	9170	36.1%	15572	61.4%	638
Gallatin	8845	38.3%	13534	58.6%	727
Garfield	136	18.7%	579	79.8%	11
Glacier	2084	56.1%	1514	40.7%	118
Golden Valley	150	33.0%	291	64.1%	13
Granite	523	37.1%	841	59.6%	47
Hill	2992	52.9%	2560	45.2%	106
Jefferson	1809	40.2%	2567	57.0%	126
Judith Basin	500	38.5%	770	59.2%	30
Lake	4061	44.2%	4930	53.6%	199
Lewis & Clark	11072	50.2%	10412	47.2%	562
Liberty	376	36.8%	635	62.1%	11
Lincoln	2348	34.8%	4196	62.2%	204
Madison	847	28.9%	2004	68.3%	84
McCone	319	27.2%	829	70.8%	23
Meagher	277	32.4%	563	65.9%	14
Mineral	699	46.6%	748	49.8%	54
Missoula	19232	55.4%	14505	41.8%	969
Musselshell	686	36.2%	1171	61.8%	37
Park	2336	38.3%	3471	56.9%	289
Petroleum	57	21.9%	194	74.6%	9
Phillips	612	31.4%	1299	66.7%	36
Pondera	1011	38.0%	1591	59.9%	56
Powder River	208	23.7%	657	74.8%	13
Powell	1023	40.9%	1403	56.1%	73
Prairie	189	27.7%	480	70.4%	13
Ravalli	5047	38.8%	7693	59.1%	272
Richland	1327	34.7%	2408	63.1%	84
Roosevelt	1505	48.7%	1476	47.7%	112
Rosebud	1496	46.6%	1607	50.0%	110
Sanders	1560	37.4%	2491	59.7%	119
Sheridan	1037	47.6%	1114	51.1%	29
Silver Bow	8463	61.3%	4838	35.0%	506
Stillwater	1253	39.7%	1827	57.9%	76
Sweet Grass	397	26.0%	1100	72.1%	28
Teton	1127	37.7%	1782	59.6%	80
Toole	839	36.3%	1409	60.9%	66
Treasure	192	38.2%	293	58.4%	17
Valley	1316	36.4%	2211	61.1%	91
Wheatland	380	43.1%	476	54.0%	25
Wibaux	194	30.5%	432	67.9%	10
Yellowstone	19787	45.2%	22881	52.3%	1083
TOTALS	**147073**	**44.4%**	**175748**	**53.0%**	**8730**

2000 Presidential Election

COUNTIES	Al Gore (D)		George W. Bush(R)		Ralph Nader (G)		Other
Beaverhead	799	19.0%	3113	75.4%	218	5.2%	76
Big Horn	2345	57.2%	1651	40.3%	101	2.4%	64
Blaine	1246	45.9%	1410	52.0%	58	2.1%	45
Broadwater	462	23.0%	1488	73.9%	63	3.0%	61
Carbon	1434	30.6%	3008	64.3%	237	4.9%	110
Carter	53	8.3%	573	90.1%	10	1.6%	9
Cascade	13137	40.4%	18164	55.9%	1202	3.6%	814
Chouteau	686	24.4%	2039	72.5%	86	3.0%	64
Custer	1501	31.2%	3156	65.6%	154	3.1%	94
Daniels	303	27.7%	750	68.7%	39	3.5%	18
Dawson	1364	32.5%	2723	64.8%	115	2.7%	69
Deer Lodge	2672	60.8%	1493	34.0%	232	5.1%	137
Fallon	256	19.0%	1061	78.7%	31	2.3%	21
Fergus	1352	23.0%	4353	74.2%	165	2.8%	124
Flathead	8329	25.3%	22519	68.5%	2037	6.0%	954
Gallatin	10009	31.9%	18833	60.0%	2545	7.9%	653
Garfield	61	8.4%	651	89.9%	12	1.6%	20
Glacier	2211	54.5%	1709	42.1%	139	3.4%	65
Golden Valley	88	17.3%	405	79.4%	17	3.2%	21
Granite	295	19.0%	1181	76.1%	75	4.7%	39
Hill	2760	42.9%	3392	52.8%	278	4.2%	128
Jefferson	1513	30.2%	3308	66.0%	189	3.7%	153
Judith Basin	278	20.4%	1057	77.4%	31	2.2%	27
Lake	3884	35.0%	6441	58.1%	762	6.7%	361
Lewis & Clark	9982	37.4%	15091	56.5%	1645	6.0%	551
Liberty	243	23.8%	752	73.8%	24	2.3%	25
Lincoln	1629	21.4%	5578	73.3%	402	5.1%	237
Madison	758	21.2%	2656	74.3%	161	4.5%	81
McCone	267	23.7%	827	73.3%	34	2.9%	14
Meagher	176	19.5%	698	77.5%	27	1.5%	34
Mineral	382	24.1%	1078	67.9%	127	7.7%	52
Missoula	17241	37.7%	21474	47.0%	6999	15.2%	862
Musselshell	512	23.8%	1582	73.7%	53	2.5%	60
Park	2154	30.0%	4523	63.0%	498	6.9%	231
Petroleum	36	12.2%	254	85.8%	6	1.7%	10
Phillips	423	19.3%	1727	78.7%	44	2.0%	34
Pondera	792	27.9%	1948	68.7%	96	3.3%	60
Powder River	115	11.5%	860	86.3%	21	2.1%	12
Powell	638	23.3%	1971	72.0%	129	4.1%	94
Prairie	164	22.5%	541	74.2%	24	3.0%	17
Ravalli	4451	26.5%	11241	66.8%	1128	6.7%	418
Richland	1018	25.7%	2858	72.3%	79	2.0%	78
Roosevelt	2059	54.8%	1605	42.7%	95	2.5%	54
Rosebud	1394	41.6%	1826	54.5%	130	3.9%	73
Sanders	1165	25.2%	3144	68.1%	305	5.9%	107
Sheridan	702	36.2%	1176	60.6%	62	3.1%	25
Silver Bow	8967	55.6%	6299	39.0%	876	5.4%	561
Stillwater	925	24.1%	2765	72.2%	141	3.6%	87
Sweet Grass	305	16.8%	1450	79.9%	59	3.2%	32
Teton	847	26.1%	2294	70.7%	102	3.1%	71
Toole	630	26.9%	1639	69.9%	77	3.2%	32
Treasure	106	22.9%	344	74.5%	12	2.5%	17
Valley	1273	32.8%	2500	64.5%	103	2.6%	87
Wheatland	243	25.0%	708	72.8%	21	1.0%	27
Wibaux	121	23.9%	369	72.9%	16	0.2%	12
Yellowstone	20370	36.1%	33922	60.1%	2145	3.8%	1062
TOTALS	**137126**	**33.4%**	**240178**	**58.4%**	**24437**	**6.1%**	**9244**

2000 Gubernatorial Election

COUNTIES	Mark O'Keefe (D)		Judy Martz (R)		Other
Beaverhead	1246	29.7%	2889	68.8%	62
Big Horn	2699	64.8%	1402	33.6%	66
Blaine	1610	58.5%	1102	40.0%	40
Broadwater	707	34.3%	1316	63.9%	38
Carbon	2019	41.6%	2739	56.4%	101
Carter	106	16.8%	515	81.72%	9
Cascade	18096	54.5%	14479	43.6%	650
Chouteau	1112	38.5%	1722	59.7%	51
Custer	2333	46.9%	2582	51.9%	58
Daniels	377	34.8%	691	63.9%	14
Dawson	1760	41.3%	2433	57.1%	71
Deer Lodge	3297	72.0%	1218	26.6%	61
Fallon	426	32.2%	870	65.7%	29
Fergus	2061	34.3%	3829	63.7%	122
Flathead	12298	36.6%	20593	61.2%	749
Gallatin	14438	45.1%	16909	52.9%	634
Garfield	125	17.1%	597	81.9%	7
Glacier	2700	64.4%	1410	33.6%	82
Golden Valley	137	25.8%	382	71.9%	12
Granite	528	33.3%	1010	63.7%	48
Hill	3858	58.9%	2544	38.9%	145
Jefferson	2086	40.5%	2967	57.6%	94
Judith Basin	459	33.1%	905	65.2%	23
Lake	5179	45.3%	5983	52.3%	268
Lewis & Clark	13704	50.2%	13185	48.3%	424
Liberty	374	35.7%	652	62.3%	21
Lincoln	2833	36.3%	4735	60.6%	241
Madison	1115	30.5%	2468	67.5%	75
McCone	429	37.6%	699	61.3%	12
Meagher	258	27.6%	656	70.2%	21
Mineral	744	45.7%	836	51.3%	49
Missoula	27034	58.4%	18215	39.3%	1052
Musselshell	766	34.9%	1371	62.5%	56
Park	3243	43.8%	4004	54.1%	157
Petroleum	70	22.6%	235	75.8%	5
Phillips	589	26.6%	1598	72.1%	30
Pondera	1300	44.6%	1569	53.9%	43
Powder River	229	23.3%	745	75.8%	9
Powell	1077	37.9%	1688	59.5%	74
Prairie	231	31.2%	498	67.2%	12
Ravalli	6982	40.8%	9772	57.0%	375
Richland	1293	32.1%	2658	66.1%	71
Roosevelt	2417	63.1%	1369	35.7%	46
Rosebud	1955	56.0%	1466	42.0%	71
Sanders	1911	40.9%	2633	56.3%	132
Sheridan	868	44.7%	1052	54.1%	23
Silver Bow	10837	64.5%	5750	34.2%	213
Stillwater	1392	35.8%	2417	62.1%	83
Sweet Grass	422	23.0%	1382	75.4%	30
Teton	1360	41.2%	1892	57.3%	49
Toole	1071	44.7%	1283	53.5%	42
Treasure	163	34.3%	306	64.4%	6
Valley	1750	44.0%	2137	53.8%	86
Wheatland	298	29.9%	688	68.9%	12
Wibaux	187	37.0%	302	59.8%	16
Yellowstone	26572	46.4%	29787	52.0%	956
TOTALS	**193131**	**47.1%**	**209135**	**51.0%**	**7926**

2000 U.S. Senate Election

COUNTIES	Brian Schweitzer (D)		Conrad Burns(R)		Other
Beaverhead	1240	29.7%	2862	68.6%	73
Big Horn	2534	62.8%	1437	35.6%	67
Blaine	1482	53.7%	1238	44.8%	42
Broadwater	724	34.9%	1294	62.5%	54
Carbon	2151	43.8%	2636	53.7%	121
Carter	62	9.7%	571	89.8%	3
Cascade	17288	51.8%	15298	45.9%	777
Chouteau	998	34.5%	1840	63.7%	51
Custer	2158	42.9%	2751	54.7%	116
Daniels	370	33.5%	709	64.3%	24
Dawson	1724	39.8%	2525	58.3%	83
Deer Lodge	3297	72.8%	1154	25.5%	77
Fallon	346	26.9%	914	71.0%	28
Fergus	2067	34.2%	3850	63.7%	125
Flathead	13495	39.7%	19684	57.9%	846
Gallatin	14612	45.5%	16879	52.6%	611
Garfield	135	18.3%	589	79.8%	14
Glacier	2682	63.8%	1415	33.7%	107
Golden Valley	157	30.4%	343	66.3%	17
Granite	552	34.7%	1006	63.2%	34
Hill	3686	56.1%	2757	42.0%	125
Jefferson	2288	44.2%	2762	53.4%	121
Judith Basin	472	34.0%	893	64.3%	23
Lake	5471	47.8%	5632	49.2%	341
Lewis & Clark	14564	53.1%	12373	45.1%	506
Liberty	393	37.2%	648	61.3%	16
Lincoln	2629	33.4%	5010	63.6%	238
Madison	1207	33.0%	2379	65.1%	67
McCone	358	31.2%	777	67.8%	11
Meagher	267	28.7%	625	67.3%	37
Mineral	673	40.6%	926	55.9%	57
Missoula	27494	59.2%	17876	38.5%	1059
Musselshell	732	33.2%	1414	64.1%	60
Park	3229	43.5%	3970	53.4%	229
Petroleum	63	20.3%	240	77.2%	8
Phillips	630	28.3%	1567	70.5%	27
Pondera	1234	43.1%	1563	54.6%	64
Powder River	178	17.8%	806	80.7%	15
Powell	1057	36.8%	1749	61.0%	63
Prairie	227	30.7%	500	67.6%	13
Ravalli	6966	40.5%	9790	56.9%	437
Richland	1220	30.1%	2733	67.5%	95
Roosevelt	2142	55.5%	1629	42.2%	86
Rosebud	1847	52.4%	1582	44.9%	94
Sanders	1819	38.4%	2795	59.1%	117
Sheridan	854	43.7%	1080	55.2%	21
Silver Bow	11298	67.0%	5221	31.0%	347
Stillwater	1487	37.9%	2342	59.7%	97
Sweet Grass	424	23.5%	1346	74.5%	37
Teton	1215	37.7%	1947	60.5%	57
Toole	992	42.1%	1302	55.2%	64
Treasure	182	38.6%	276	58.5%	14
Valley	1746	43.6%	2182	54.4%	81
Wheatland	335	33.6%	642	64.5%	19
Wibaux	187	36.2%	319	61.8%	10
Yellowstone	26790	46.7%	29434	51.3%	1163
TOTALS	**194430**	**47.2%**	**208082**	**50.6%**	**9089**

2000 U.S. House Election, At Large

COUNTIES	Nancy Keenan (D)		Denny Rehberg (R)		Other
Beaverhead	1358	32.7%	2715	65.3%	82
Big Horn	2704	64.9%	1403	33.7%	61
Blaine	1531	55.6%	1170	42.5%	51
Broadwater	710	34.6%	1303	63.4%	41
Carbon	2018	41.3%	2735	56.0%	134
Carter	105	16.5%	527	83.0%	3
Cascade	16751	50.4%	15726	47.3%	785
Chouteau	1090	37.9%	1725	60.0%	59
Custer	2157	43.0%	2760	55.0%	100
Daniels	398	36.1%	686	62.2%	19
Dawson	1860	43.4%	2357	55.0%	69
Deer Lodge	3389	73.9%	1106	24.1%	94
Fallon	372	27.8%	943	70.4%	24
Fergus	2098	35.1%	3742	62.7%	130
Flathead	12894	38.2%	20053	59.4%	810
Gallatin	13595	42.4%	17775	55.4%	712
Garfield	140	19.2%	582	79.9%	6
Glacier	2658	63.7%	1433	34.4%	79
Golden Valley	145	28.2%	351	68.2%	19
Granite	585	36.9%	959	60.5%	40
Hill	3587	54.6%	2864	43.6%	120
Jefferson	2159	42.3%	2795	54.8%	146
Judith Basin	499	35.8%	871	62.5%	23
Lake	5119	44.9%	5984	52.5%	302
Lewis & Clark	13826	50.5%	13035	47.6%	539
Liberty	381	36.1%	661	62.6%	14
Lincoln	3034	38.9%	4576	58.6%	199
Madison	1214	33.2%	2363	64.7%	75
McCone	416	37.0%	703	62.5%	6
Meagher	317	34.2%	585	63.1%	25
Mineral	678	41.8%	899	55.4%	45
Missoula	25685	55.4%	19434	41.9%	1217
Musselshell	690	31.6%	1435	65.8%	56
Park	3045	41.1%	4173	56.4%	183
Petroleum	75	24.1%	230	74.0%	6
Phillips	674	30.4%	1494	67.4%	48
Pondera	1171	40.1%	1698	58.2%	49
Powder River	213	21.9%	748	76.8%	13
Powell	1106	38.7%	1684	58.9%	71
Prairie	258	34.9%	470	63.6%	11
Ravalli	6525	38.0%	10253	59.7%	395
Richland	1680	41.9%	2280	56.8%	51
Roosevelt	2435	63.0%	1379	35.7%	54
Rosebud	1855	52.8%	1569	44.6%	91
Sanders	1857	39.5%	2719	57.8%	126
Sheridan	1029	52.8%	907	46.5%	13
Silver Bow	11465	68.4%	4933	29.4%	372
Stillwater	1489	38.1%	2323	59.4%	99
Sweet Grass	509	27.8%	1292	70.5%	32
Teton	1251	37.7%	2004	60.4%	61
Toole	908	38.0%	1430	59.8%	53
Treasure	173	36.8%	280	59.6%	17
Valley	1766	44.2%	2177	54.4%	56
Wheatland	330	33.3%	641	64.7%	20
Wibaux	195	38.8%	295	58.8%	12
Yellowstone	25799	45.1%	30183	52.8%	1214
TOTALS	**189971**	**46.3%**	**211418**	**51.5%**	**9132**

2002 U.S. Senate Election

COUNTIES	Max Baucus (D)		Mike Taylor (R)		Other
Beaverhead	1587	50.8%	1378	44.1%	162
Big Horn	2970	74.7%	835	21.0%	172
Blaine	1704	71.9%	578	24.4%	88
Broadwater	1028	56.2%	693	37.9%	107
Carbon	2737	63.8%	1306	30.4%	250
Carter	258	41.9%	342	55.5%	16
Cascade	17491	69.1%	6378	25.2%	1451
Chouteau	1697	65.6%	766	29.6%	122
Custer	2679	67.5%	1114	28.1%	174
Daniels	607	58.9%	380	36.9%	44
Dawson	2286	63.6%	1199	33.4%	110
Deer Lodge	3169	83.7%	439	11.6%	176
Fallon	661	52.8%	561	44.8%	29
Fergus	2452	49.4%	2252	45.3%	264
Flathead	13011	50.9%	11069	43.3%	1500
Gallatin	14498	59.7%	8091	33.3%	1677
Garfield	323	57.3%	221	39.2%	20
Glacier	2619	76.7%	656	19.2%	140
Golden Valley	223	51.5%	185	42.7%	25
Granite	604	47.0%	585	45.6%	95
Hill	3819	72.2%	1215	23.0%	259
Jefferson	2593	60.4%	1440	33.5%	260
Judith Basin	716	63.5%	361	32.0%	50
Lake	5145	55.7%	3568	38.6%	529
Lewis & Clark	15543	69.0%	5764	25.6%	1216
Liberty	661	65.2%	295	29.1%	58
Lincoln	3428	50.7%	3026	44.8%	305
Madison	1624	52.7%	1291	41.9%	164
McCone	647	61.0%	388	36.6%	26
Meagher	416	54.9%	310	40.9%	32
Mineral	724	52.7%	569	41.4%	80
Missoula	22111	66.3%	8806	26.4%	2410
Musselshell	1018	55.4%	719	39.1%	100
Park	3657	60.2%	2061	33.9%	360
Petroleum	132	53.9%	91	37.1%	22
Phillips	1024	58.0%	665	37.7%	75
Pondera	1557	63.0%	794	32.1%	122
Powder River	472	50.8%	414	44.5%	44
Powell	1349	57.4%	893	38.0%	110
Prairie	390	58.2%	264	39.4%	16
Ravalli	6640	48.6%	6270	45.9%	746
Richland	2166	60.5%	1341	37.4%	75
Roosevelt	2244	73.8%	722	23.7%	76
Rosebud	2138	71.2%	720	24.0%	146
Sanders	2068	50.9%	1785	43.9%	211
Sheridan	1162	69.5%	465	27.8%	46
Silver Bow	9881	80.8%	1692	13.8%	661
Stillwater	1888	57.8%	1207	37.0%	170
Sweet Grass	699	47.5%	711	48.3%	63
Teton	1754	62.7%	893	31.9%	151
Toole	1225	62.9%	594	30.5%	130
Treasure	266	63.9%	127	30.5%	23
Valley	2520	72.4%	845	24.3%	117
Wheatland	491	60.4%	290	35.7%	32
Wibaux	331	61.5%	191	35.5%	16
Yellowstone	29750	64.5%	13796	29.9%	2561
TOTALS	**204853**	**62.7%**	**103611**	**31.7%**	**18073**

2002 U.S. House Election, At Large

COUNTIES	Steve Kelly (D)		Denny Rehberg (R)		Other
Beaverhead	690	21.6%	2425	76.0%	74
Big Horn	2042	51.7%	1804	45.6%	106
Blaine	978	41.1%	1347	56.5%	57
Broadwater	387	21.2%	1381	75.7%	56
Carbon	1194	27.5%	3018	69.6%	125
Carter	68	10.9%	553	88.8%	2
Cascade	8208	31.9%	16837	65.4%	682
Chouteau	557	21.2%	2034	77.5%	35
Custer	1029	25.3%	2968	72.9%	74
Daniels	244	23.7%	768	74.6%	18
Dawson	1116	30.9%	2427	67.2%	71
Deer Lodge	2165	57.5%	1485	39.4%	117
Fallon	204	16.8%	993	81.9%	16
Fergus	1091	21.5%	3854	76.1%	118
Flathead	7072	27.1%	18198	69.8%	817
Gallatin	8339	33.7%	15545	62.9%	827
Garfield	60	10.3%	517	88.4%	8
Glacier	1734	50.6%	1621	47.3%	75
Golden Valley	69	15.3%	370	82.2%	11
Granite	273	21.0%	976	74.9%	54
Hill	1956	36.6%	3274	61.2%	116
Jefferson	1337	30.4%	2951	67.1%	112
Judith Basin	207	17.9%	926	80.2%	22
Lake	3004	32.1%	6064	64.9%	277
Lewis & Clark	8440	36.7%	13986	60.9%	547
Liberty	172	16.6%	845	81.5%	20
Lincoln	1686	24.9%	4869	72.0%	210
Madison	666	21.2%	2391	76.0%	89
McCone	237	22.1%	820	76.4%	16
Meagher	143	18.3%	612	78.4%	26
Mineral	369	27.3%	932	68.8%	53
Missoula	15083	44.5%	17681	52.1%	1152
Musselshell	354	19.1%	1458	78.6%	42
Park	2072	33.6%	3921	63.6%	173
Petroleum	37	14.6%	207	81.8%	9
Phillips	283	15.6%	1505	82.9%	28
Pondera	567	22.7%	1884	75.3%	52
Powder River	122	13.0%	789	84.3%	25
Powell	571	24.3%	1719	73.1%	61
Prairie	137	20.2%	522	77.0%	19
Ravalli	3539	25.6%	9918	71.8%	350
Richland	993	27.9%	2498	70.2%	68
Roosevelt	1277	42.4%	1681	55.8%	52
Rosebud	1102	36.7%	1814	60.4%	86
Sanders	1150	28.5%	2733	67.7%	151
Sheridan	546	32.9%	1089	65.5%	27
Silver Bow	6700	54.8%	5245	42.9%	278
Stillwater	724	22.1%	2484	75.9%	63
Sweet Grass	263	17.4%	1220	80.8%	26
Teton	658	22.9%	2111	73.5%	102
Toole	444	22.3%	1494	75.1%	52
Treasure	81	19.1%	330	77.8%	13
Valley	1053	30.2%	2359	67.7%	73
Wheatland	174	20.8%	642	76.7%	21
Wibaux	134	25.4%	384	72.7%	10
Yellowstone	14432	30.6%	31627	67.0%	1170
TOTALS	**108233**	**32.7%**	**214100**	**64.6%**	**8988**

Montana Population by County

COUNTIES	1940	1950	1960	1970	1980	1990	2000	% of Total 2000 State Populatin
Beaverhead	6943	6671	7194	8187	8186	8424	9202	1.01%
Big Horn	10419	9824	10007	10057	11096	11337	12671	1.40%
Blaine	9566	8516	8091	6727	6999	6728	7009	0.77%
Broadwater	3451	2922	2804	2526	3267	3318	4385	0.49%
Carbon	11865	10241	8317	7080	8099	8080	9552	1.05%
Carter	3280	2798	2493	1956	1799	1503	1360	0.20%
Cascade	41999	53027	73418	81804	80696	77691	80357	8.90%
Chouteau	7316	6974	7348	6473	6092	5452	5970	0.66%
Custer	10422	12661	13227	12174	13109	11697	11696	1.30%
Daniels	4563	3946	3755	3083	2835	2266	2017	0.22%
Dawson	8618	9092	12314	11269	11805	9505	9059	1.00%
Deer Lodge	13627	16553	18640	15652	12518	10356	9417	1.04%
Fallon	3719	3660	3997	4050	3763	3103	2837	0.30%
Fergus	14040	14015	14018	12611	13076	12083	11893	1.32%
Flathead	24271	31495	32965	39460	51966	59218	74471	8.25%
Gallatin	18269	21902	26045	32505	42865	50463	67831	7.52%
Garfield	2641	2172	1981	1796	1656	1589	1279	0.14%
Glacier	9034	9645	11565	10783	10628	12121	13247	1.47%
Golden Valley	1607	1337	1203	931	1026	912	1042	0.12%
Granite	3401	2773	3014	2737	2700	2548	2830	0.31%
Hill	13304	14285	18653	17358	17985	17654	16673	1.84%
Jefferson	4464	4014	4297	5238	7029	7939	10049	1.11%
Judith Basin	3655	3200	3085	2667	2646	2282	2329	0.26%
Lake	13490	13835	13104	14445	19056	21041	26507	2.94%
Lewis & Clark	22131	24540	28006	33281	43039	47495	55716	6.18%
Liberty	2209	2180	2624	2359	2329	2295	2158	0.24%
Lincoln	7882	8693	12537	18063	17752	17481	18837	2.09%
Madison	3798	3258	3321	2875	2702	2276	1997	0.22%
McCone	7294	5998	5211	5014	5448	5989	6851	0.76%
Meagher	2237	2079	2616	2122	2154	1819	1932	0.21%
Mineral	2135	2081	3037	2958	3675	3315	3884	0.43%
Missoula	29038	35493	44663	58263	75016	78687	95802	10.62%
Musselshell	5717	5408	4888	3734	4428	4106	4497	0.50%
Park	11566	11999	13168	11197	12869	14484	15694	1.73%
Petroleum	1083	1026	894	675	655	519	493	0.05%
Phillips	7892	6334	6027	5386	5367	5163	4601	0.51%
Pondera	6716	6392	7653	6611	6731	6433	6424	0.71%
Powder River	3159	2693	2485	2862	2520	2090	1858	0.20%
Powell	6152	6301	7002	6660	6958	6620	7180	0.80%
Prairie	2410	2377	2318	1752	1836	1383	1199	0.13%
Ravalli	12978	13101	12341	14409	22493	25010	36070	4.00%
Richland	10209	10366	10504	9837	12243	10716	9667	1.07%
Roosevelt	9806	9580	11731	10365	10467	10999	10620	1.18%
Rosebud	6477	6570	6187	6032	9899	10505	9383	1.04%
Sanders	6926	6983	6880	7093	8675	8669	10227	1.13%
Sheridan	7814	6674	6458	5779	5414	4732	4105	0.46%
Silver Bow	53207	48422	46454	41981	38092	33941	34606	3.83%
Stillwater	5694	5416	5526	4632	5598	6536	8195	0.91%
Sweet Grass	3719	3621	3290	2980	3216	3154	3609	0.40%
Teton	6922	7232	7295	6116	6491	6271	6445	0.71%
Toole	6769	6867	7904	5839	5559	5046	5267	0.58%
Treasure	1499	1402	1345	1069	981	874	861	0.09%
Valley	15181	11353	17080	11471	10250	8239	7675	0.85%
Wheatland	3286	3187	3026	2529	2359	2246	2259	0.25%
Wibaux	2161	1907	1698	1465	1476	1191	1068	0.12%
Yellowstone	41182	55875	79016	87367	108035	113419	129352	14.34%
TOTALS	**559456**	**591024**	**674767**	**694409**	**786690**	**799065**	**902195**	

Montana Legislature from 1946 to 2002

| | Montana Senate | | Montana House | |
	Democrats	Republicans	Democrats	Republicans
1946	15	41	31	58
1948	23	31	54	36
1950	26	28	41	49
1952	20	36	28	62
1954	23	33	49	45
1956	31	25	59	35
1958	38	17	61	31
1960	38	17	40	54
1962	29	21	38	58
1964	32	24	56	38
1966	30	25	40	64
1968	30	25	46	58
1970	30	25	49	55
1972	27	23	54	46
1974	30	20	67	33
1976	25	25	57	43
1978	24	25	54	45
1980	22	28	43	57
1982	24	26	55	45
1984	28	22	51	49
1986	28	22	51	49
1988	23	27	52	48
1990	29	21	61	39
1992	30	20	47	53
1994	19	31	33	67
1996	16	34	35	65
1998	18	32	41	59
2000	19	31	41	58
2002	21	29	47	53

Voter Turnout from 1946 through 2002

1946	. . . . .72%	1966	. . . . .80%
1948	. . . . .82%	1968	. . . . .86%
1950	. . . . .77%	1970	. . . . .78%
1952	. . . . .86%	1972	. . . . .85%
1954	. . . . .77%	1974	. . . . .70%
1956	. . . . .83%	1976	. . . . .75%
1958	. . . . .75%	1978	. . . . .72%
1960	. . . . .86%	1980	. . . . .75%
1962	. . . . .78%	1982	. . . . .74%
1964	. . . . .86%	1984	. . . . .75%

1986	. . . . .74%
1988	. . . . .75%
1990	. . . . .75%
1992	. . . . .79%
1994	. . . . .70%
1996	. . . . .71%
1998	. . . . .53%
2000	. . . . .60%
2002	. . . . .54%

Bibliography

Aronson, J. Hugo. *The Galloping Swede.* Missoula: Mountain Press Publishing Co., 1970.

Baldwin, Louis. *Honorable Politician: Mike Mansfield of Montana.* Missoula: Mountain Press Publishing Co., 1979.

Malone, Michael P. *Montana Century: 100 Years in Pictures and Words.* Helena: Falcon Publishing, Inc., 1999.

Malone, Michael P., Richard B. Roeder and William L. Lang. *Montana: A History of Two Centuries.* Seattle: University of Washington Press, 1991.

Merrill, Andrea and Judy Jacobsen. *Montana Almanac.* Helena: Falcon Publishing, Inc., 1997.

Swartout, Robert R. and Harry W. Fritz, eds. *The Montana Heritage.* Helena: Montana Historical Society Press, 1992.

Toole, Kenneth Ross. *Montana: An Uncommon Land.* Norman: University of Oklahoma Press, 1959.

Waldron, Ellis. *An Atlas of Montana Politics Since 1864.* Missoula: The Montana State University Press, 1958.

Waldron, Ellis and Paul Wilson. *Atlas of Montana Elections, 1889-1976.* Missoula: University of Montana, 1978.

Footnotes

1 *The Missoula Sentinel*, July 17, 1946.

2 *The Missoula Sentinel,* October 31, 1946.

3 *The Missoula Sentinel,* October 31, 1946.

4 *The Billings Gazette,* November 3, 1946.

5 *The Missoula Sentinel,* November 1, 1948.

6 *The Missoula Sentinel,* November 1, 1948.

7 *The Missoula Sentinel,* November 1, 1950.

8 *The Billings Gazette,* November 8, 1950.

9 *The Missoula Sentinel,* November 1, 1952.

10 *The Missoula Sentinel,* November 3, 1952.

11 *The Missoula Sentinel,* November 1, 1952.

12 *The Missoula Sentinel,* October 20, 1954.

13 *The Missoula Sentinel,* October 13, 1954.

14 *The Billings Gazette,* October 17, 1954.

15 *The Billings Gazette,* October 31, 1954.

16 *The Missoula Sentinel,* November 1, 1956.

17 *The Missoula Sentinel,* October, 30, 1956.

18 *The Missoula Sentinel,* November 3, 1960.

19 *The Missoula Sentinel,* November 2, 1960.

20 *The Missoula Sentinel,* October 17, 1960.

21 *The Missoulian,* November 5, 1962.

22 *The Great Falls Tribune,* November 2, 1962.

23 *The Great Falls Tribune,* October 18, 1964.

24 *The Great Falls Tribune,* October 18, 1964.

25 *The Great Falls Tribune,* October 5, 1964.

26 *The Great Falls Tribune,* October 29, 1964.

27 *The Great Falls Tribune,* October 16, 1966.

28 *The Great Falls Tribune,* October 8, 1966.

29 *The Great Falls Tribune,* October 25, 1966.

30 *The Great Falls Tribune,* October 13, 1968.

31 *The Great Falls Tribune,* November 1, 1968.

32 *The Great Falls Tribune,* October 22, 1968.

33 *The Great Falls Tribune,* October 5, 1968.

34 *The Great Falls Tribune,* October 6, 1968.

35 *The Great Falls Tribune,* October 3, 1970.

36 *The Great Falls Tribune,* October 17, 1970.

37 *The Great Falls Tribune,* October 26, 1970.

38 *The Billings Gazette,* October 27, 1972.

39 *The Great Falls Tribune,* October 12, 1972.

40 *The Great Falls Tribune,* October 22, 1972.

41 *The Billings Gazette,* October 24, 1972.

42 *The Billings Gazette,* November 6, 1974.

43 *The Great Falls Tribune,* October 19, 1974.

44 *The Billings Gazette,* November 6, 1974.

45 *The Billings Gazette,* November 1, 1974.

46 *The Great Falls Tribune,* October 29, 1976.

47 *The Great Falls Tribune,* October 12, 1976.

48 *The Great Falls Tribune,* October 22, 1976.

49 *The Great Falls Tribune,* October 28, 1976.

50 *The Great Falls Tribune,* October 12, 1976.

51 *The Great Falls Tribune,* October 14, 1978.

52 *The Great Falls Tribune,* October 24, 1978.

53 *The Billings Gazette,* November 1, 1978.

54 *The Great Falls Tribune,* June 1, 1980.

55 *The Great Falls Tribune,* October 17, 1980.

56 *The Great Falls Tribune,* October 24, 1980.

57 *The Billings Gazette,* November 1, 1980.

58 *The Great Falls Tribune,* October 20, 1982.

59 *The Great Falls Tribune,* October 22, 1982.

60 *The Great Falls Tribune,* October 31, 1982.

61 *The Great Falls Tribune,* October 12, 1982.

62 *The Great Falls Tribune,* October 17, 1984.

63 *The Great Falls Tribune,* November 4, 1984.

64 *The Great Falls Tribune,* November 4, 1984.

65 *The Great Falls Tribune,* October 23, 1984.

66 *The Great Falls Tribune,* October 10, 1984.

67 *The Great Falls Tribune,* November 2, 1986.

68 *The Great Falls Tribune,* November 2, 1986.

69 *The Great Falls Tribune,* October 5, 1986.

70 *The Helena Independent Record,* November 7, 1988.

71 *The Billings Gazette*, October 28, 1988.

72 *The Billings Gazette*, November 6, 1988.

73 *The Missoulian,* November 1, 1990.

74 *The Billings Gazette*, October 19, 1990.

75 *The Billings Gazette*, October 16, 1990.

76 *The Billings Gazette*, October 25, 1992.

77 *The Billings Gazette*, October 24, 1992.

78 *The Billings Gazette*, October 21, 1994.

79 *The Billings Gazette*, October 16, 1994.

80 *The Billings Gazette*, October 26, 1996.

81 *The Billings Gazette*, October 22, 1996.

82 *The Billings Gazette*, November 2, 1996.

83 *The Missoulian,* November 1, 1998.

84 *The Missoulian,* November 2, 2000.

85 *The Missoulian,* November 5, 2000.

Index